CONDITION RED
Destroyer Action in the South Pacific

Commander FREDERICK J. BELL, U.S. Navy

TABLE OF CONTENTS

PREFACE

"Condition Red" was an expression that we used to indicate the imminence of any type of engagement. Aboard the G it was a colloquialism that served to express the conviction that the next few hours or days or weeks were going to be packed with action. We first heard it soon after we arrived in the Solomons, where the term was used on Guadalcanal and Tulagi to indicate the approach of the enemy, and when our voice radio blared out the words we went to General Quarters and prepared to greet the Tokyo Express or the Zeros and Mitsubishis when they came within view.

I would like to be able to call the G by her full name, but it is a happy augury that I cannot, inasmuch as I am permitted by the Navy Department to use actual names only in the cases of ships that have been sunk. There are a few exceptions — the Enterprise, Boise, Smith and South Dakota, which have received particular publicity from the Department or the White House, are still very much alive.

Little has been written of the part that our destroyers are playing in the Pacific War, where they are called upon to fulfil such a variety of missions that they have become multi-purpose ships, engaging in any form of combat. Because we lacked suitable escort ships we used destroyers to protect convoys as well as to guard our combatant Task Forces. We used them to bombard enemy shore positions and to carry bombs and aviation gasoline and stores to Guadalcanal during the lean weeks early in our campaign in those far-distant seas.

By nature as well as by name, the purpose of the destroyer is wholly offensive. Bantamweights in comparison with the great battlewagons, they pack a punch out of all proportion to their size. They are triple-threat weapons, built to strike at any enemy on or over or under the sea. In the words of Rear Admiral Tisdale, "They are the fightingest thing afloat."

F.J.B.
Baltimore, Maryland.
October 3, 1943.

HAPPY BIRTHDAY, DEAR ZERO

Thumb to nose, a Japanese face leaned over the edge of the cockpit. He held the pose but an instant, then, hidden in flame, his plane smacked the surface of the Solomons Sea. On his tail another dive bomber roared across the line of fire, caught the blast of our port machine guns, nosed over and died. The 20's swung aft and looked for another target.

Fifteen thousand feet above the carrier, tiny flecks of silver rocketed down through the AA bursts that laid a black mosaic against the sky. Some of them caught a direct hit — disintegrated, became bits of fabric that soared lazily in the afternoon air. Some lost a wing or a tail and spun downward, the pilots aiming their flaming craft at the decks of the nearest ship. Others, coming through unscathed, dropped from the sky, released their bombs and pulled out in a zigzag a few feet above the water — all so fast that it was useless to designate a specific main battery target, for by the time the guns swung around the target was gone.

The sea was filled with geysers; the sky literally black with bursting shells; the ships seemingly on fire as flames tore from their gun muzzles. It was almost too spectacular. Never again would we believe that an "artist's conception" of a naval battle is an exaggerated or distorted picture, for no illustration could catch the sweep of the scene now being enacted.

Two and a half weeks earlier we had taken the marines to Guadalcanal and Tulagi in the original occupation of the Eastern Solomons. Since then we had cruised in a covering position, waiting for the Japanese to counter attack in force. Until today they had contented themselves with sporadic attacks against the marines on shore, air raids on our transports, and one night action in which we came off second best.

Our airmen had action aplenty, but those of us whose job it was to protect the carrier from submarine, air and surface attack had not been given an opportunity for heavy employment. It had been a long, sleepless grind, this six weeks' trek across the South Pacific, eternally on the qui vive, always on watch for the enemy — but we had met no opposition in force — until today.

Early on this August forenoon we received a reconnaissance report that at least one Japanese carrier was within three hundred miles; a stone's throw as distances are measured in the Pacific and as sea battles are waged in their opening phase. With her was the usual guard of destroyers and cruisers. Our own planes took off immediately and for hours they had been hammering the enemy Task Force. From fragments of information during the day we gathered that one Japanese carrier had been sunk, and a second set on fire. It was time, now, for our air group to return. They had exhausted their ammunition and were so nearly out of gas that they would have to follow a direct course in rejoining, thereby showing the way to any Japanese air groups that might still be available to attack. There were too few ships in our screen to spare any of us as a surface striking force. It would be an anti-aircraft engagement. From the carrier our admiral signaled: "Prepare to repel air attack." We gathered close around our Flat Top in readiness for action.

Within the steel walls of the G, three hundred officers and men took a last-minute inventory of their tools of war. In the wardroom the surgeon opened out his equipment on the officers' dining table. On the bulkhead he hung up a square of canvas fitted with pockets and pouches for kits of medical hardware. Along the leather seats of the transoms he laid his bottles, to cushion them against the shattering concussion of gunfire. In destroyers there are no hospital beds or isolation wards. The medical officer dispenses from a cubicle of a sick bay, and in action he uses the wardroom or a crews' compartment for his knotting and splicing. There is duplicate equipment aft, under the charge of a chief pharmacist's mate, and there are bags and boxes of dressings, anti-burn solutions and minor medical aids at all battle stations.

Across from the radio shack, in the cramped spaces of the coding room, the Communication Officer passed a lashing through the grommets of a sea bag and tied it securely. Stuffed with secret books, weighted with fire brick to insure sinking, it would be thrown over the side if the ship had to be abandoned through fire or other cause.

Far below, in the intense heat of their oil-scented, methodical world of steam and light and harnessed power, the engineers cracked their valves wide open and the turbines sang in a higher key.

In all lower deck compartments there were wooden shores and an assortment of plugs and wedges of various sizes that could be used as leak stoppers in a hurry, unless the hole in the side should be so large that the entire compartment would have to be blocked off.

The men of the repair parties buckled on their helmets, strapped tool belts around their waists, inspected the valves of rescue masks and slipped their hands into asbestos mittens. Theirs was a waiting game — until the ship was hit. Then they fought fire and the noxious gases of explosion; struggled against the inrush of water in flooding compartments; worked to keep their ship afloat and on an even keel.

Everyone wore a steel helmet. The men topside were bundled in life jackets. Those belowdecks, in the fierce heat and close confinement of narrow steel passages, kept them ready for use.

Unnecessary electric power and all water systems were closed off to decrease possible sources of fire and flooding. At every gun, on the bridge and in the fire rooms, wherever men were stationed, fresh drinking water was provided, for use during lulls in the action when men have time to notice the intense thirst that battle brings.

These details were checked almost subconsciously, but actually there was little to be attended to when the general alarm sounded — other than closing off systems and doors, for all the preliminaries to action were part of our normal wartime cruising routine. We were ready at any time to open fire with half the battery instantly. Within two and a half minutes from the time the order was given to "go to general quarters," all hands were on station, the entire battery was manned, and the ship was in the prescribed Material Condition that gave maximum internal protection against the spread of damage.

Long before the first attacking planes appeared, the ships of the screen had formed a wall around the carrier, their guns pointed skyward. Aboard the G the events leading up to the action took place hurriedly.

The first group of attackers to get safely clear of the carrier came close aboard the G after leveling off from their dives. The pull out slowed them down in so great a contrast between their plummeting dives and the straightaway recovery that they seemed to drift along our side and only a few feet above us. They did not have retractable landing gear. I remembered our machine-gun officer's instructions to his crews — "If the ducks have feet, they're enemy." These carrier-based dive bomber ducks had feet — wheels with streamlined hoods that projected beneath the dirty slate-gray fuselage.

The first plane cut over our quarter from starboard to port, less than two hundred feet above our decks. The pilot rolled slightly toward us. In the after cockpit the gunner leaned out and thumbed his nose. Braced against the straps of his 20-mm gun, seaman Robert Otto let the fingers of his left hand slide along the trigger. By the time the Jap struck the water Otto was firing on a new target.

At 1713, carrier hit by a bomb on starboard quarter. There was a dense cloud of gray-white smoke, followed almost immediately by flame.

On the bridge of the G a signalman said "Jesus, that's got her." We looked aft and we thought he was right. Forward of the island the carrier was undamaged; her guns firing as rapidly as ever. Abaft the island there was nothing but smoke, and on the quarter, red tongues of flame shot into the air. We knew that her planes had sunk one Japanese carrier earlier today and damaged another. It looked, now, as if we were to pay a price for our victory.

A dive bomber dropped down, overshot the carrier, and loosed his bomb by the side of the G. The ocean soared upward and fell on our deck. Splinters of steel ripped into the hull. The starboard machine guns checked fire. At this moment another plane came out of his dive and droned past us at bare flying speed. It was duck soup for the machine guns. We could have hit him with a rock. But the guns were not on him. The crews, wiping the water from their faces, startled by the bomb, did not see the target. All except one man. Chief Gunner's Mate William C. Hoppers, the fattest man in the crew of the G, was in charge of the after machine-gun battery. His guns already had accounted for two planes. This third one was easy — but there was no activity along the starboard side. Hoppers shouted at the gun crews. His voice was lost in the noise of battle. He reached down, pulled off his shoes and threw them at the back of the nearest gun captain. It was a bull's-eye. The man turned; Hoppers pointed; the gun resumed fire, and the Japanese plane, flames licking its wings, tumbled into the sea.

Forward in the ship, in the lower handling room far below No. 2 gun, someone dropped a shell from a height of several feet. The petty officer in charge beckoned to a seaman. "Run that shell topside and heave it over the side," he ordered. The seaman picked up the hundred-pound projectile and commenced the climb to the upper decks, carefully closing and dogging the doors and hatches behind him. Just as a bomb exploded he arrived on the forecastle. Back down the ladders he went, through compartments, passages and handling room, still remembering to secure the doors and hatches. "Jeez," he said, "Just as I got to the forecastle the damndest biggest bomb you ever saw blew up alongside!" He was eager to tell more, but his shipmates would have none of it, for under his arm he still clutched the defective shell that might explode of itself at any moment. "To hell with the bomb!" shouted the P.O. "Get that shell out of here! So up the seaman climbed again, closing the doors and hatches carefully behind him. And this time he got rid of the shell.

Later the crew talked of how "the Captain saved the ship by putting the rudder hard over so the bomb didn't hit." The truth of the matter was that the Captain put the rudder hard over to avoid collision with something a darned sight bigger than the G, and while he saw the near-miss out of the corner of his eye, it seemed at the time to be by far the lesser of the two evils. If the crew chose to believe that anything other than good luck was responsible for our being able to duck a five-hundred-pound bomb I saw no reason to argue the point.

It was amusing, though, because the incident was a very minor illustration of how facts may be altered and embroidered to make a legend. In Washington there is a painting of Commodore Perry transferring his flag at the Battle of Lake Erie. The artist shows him standing in the bow of his boat amidst a hail of bullets, resplendent in immaculate blue-and-gold full dress. It is one of our cherished bits of naval lore that the Commodore, on that day of victory, wore a red-flannel undershirt and a disreputable pair of pants; that he sweated and swore and became as black in the face from powder marks as any member of a gun crew. "We have met the enemy and they are ours." That laconic report is factual. The gold-laced coat is artist's fancy — but it makes a pretty picture.

Then there is the story of Captain Phillips, of the Texas, after the Battle of Santiago, who called out to his crew "Don't cheer, boys. The poor devils are dying." Perhaps he did say that, but I have it from an old gunner who was there that the quotation was not quite as reported. The gunner told me that the Captain had suffered all that day with a severe headache, which was not helped by the noise of the firing. When the after-battle silence was broken by the triumphant shouts of the crew, it was too much. The Captain stepped to the edge of the bridge, shook his fist toward the crowded forecastle and bellowed "Belay that goddamn racket. This is no madhouse!" I merely repeat what the gunner said, and old navy gunners are not averse to distorting facts in order to make a good story.

Aboard the burning carrier the repair parties were at work. One moment the ship was ablaze for a third of her length. The next the flames had stopped and, as we could spare a glance from our own busy party we saw the smoke decrease, gradually die away. Our carrier was hurt. The miracle was that she still remained afloat. Score another victory for the training of our fleet in damage control.

At about this time the G commenced to receive damage of her own. The main battery guns were laying an umbrella over the carrier. The 20 millimeters were firing, reloading, changing magazines, shifting red-hot barrels as fast as they could. It was not quite fast enough. We needed more guns than one destroyer could handle.

A section of Japanese bombers that had escaped the intense AA fire came out of their dives in the manner to which we were becoming accustomed, and drove past our side and over the after portion of the G. They were not wasting time in idle nose-thumbing gestures. Their machine guns raked our fantail and superstructure.

Chief Torpedoman Phineas Causey was standing alongside No. 2 torpedo mount. There was no possible target for our torpedoes in this vicious air attack. Causey could well have dropped behind the protection of the tubes, but his battle station was at the breech, and there he chose to remain, and there he was when a machine-gun bullet ripped through his chest.

With the exception of Gun Four, all of our 5-inch guns had roofs of steel. Over Gun Four the cover was made of canvas. Over Gun Four the Japanese bombers seemed to hang motionless before they gathered speed from the pull-out. The canvas cover was ripped to ribbons. Beneath it, Gun Captain Garrison caught a bullet in the shoulder, another in the lower arm. In the noise and excitement of working the main-battery gun no one heard the zing of machine-gun bullets. They showed themselves so suddenly, so weirdly; a quick jet of blood, a surprised expression on the face of the shellman, a scarlet stain on the faded blue of dungarees.

The rate of fire from Gun Four did not decrease. On the bridge we didn't know that anyone had been wounded. The talker stepped close to me and said "They're getting a relief crew for Gun Four." In the midst of a turn with hard rudder I glanced aft. Along the catwalk outboard of the torpedo tubes a little procession of wounded men moved forward. Under steel helmets their faces were white. They were going to the Battle Dressing Station, but not until fresh crews had come up from the handling rooms; not until the Gun Captain, unconscious and fast bleeding to death, had been carried from his post. The ship's company were doing only what they had been trained to do; what every other crew in the formation was doing. Not for a moment did they falter. They stuck to their guns regardless of wounds. It wasn't remarkable, but it was mighty satisfying.

At 1800 the Task Force Commander signaled: "Enemy torpedo planes are preparing to attack."

On one side of us a battleship; on the other an anti-aircraft cruiser. Each looked to be on fire. Three times during the action I received reports that the battleship had been struck by a bomb. It was a false alarm — more "artist's conception." A steady stream of flame came from the guns of the two ships. Close ahead of the G they laid a curtain of fire that caught every Japanese bomber to get clear of the carrier and destroyer screen. I thought of all the recent discussions about battleships: their day is done; they are an anachronism in modem warfare. If the battlewagon close on my starboard hand was defunct I should hate to have been near it in the days of its youth.

The torpedo planes started their attack. We could see them on the horizon but they never got within gun range. Our fighters swooped down from the top of the ceiling. No Japanese torpedoes were launched.

There was a lull in the action — the lull that every respectable battle is supposed to have. During this interval you cared for the wounded, checked the ammunition supply to the guns, inspected any damage you may have received, fed the crew and looked after the situation in general. This particular lull was not prolonged. It gave me time, though, to look around and see that all was well on the topside and to receive telephone confirmation that our damage belowdecks was being attended to. It gave us time, too, to count noses around the formation. Everyone was present. The fire on board the carrier was out, and both she and the screen were ready for more Japs.

But they didn't return. As suddenly as they had appeared, the dive bombers were no more. One or two escaped. The others were beneath the sea or floating in fragments upon the surface.

Our own planes commenced to circle, preparatory to landing aboard the carrier. One torpedo plane made an emergency landing on the water. A destroyer swung out of formation and snagged the crew aboard.

In our pilot house the voice radio sounded loud.

Task Force Commander to G: "Proceed to the north. Pick up our plane crews that may be in the water. Give directions to planes that have sufficient fuel to return to the carrier. Rejoin Task Force at noon tomorrow or, if unable to make rendezvous, proceed to advance base."

On the bridge: "Right, standard rudder. All stations stand easy. We are headed toward the enemy fleet to find our aviators. The ship will remain at General Quarters until our duty is completed."

I turned to the Executive Officer. "Frank, take the conn, please. I'll be aft for the next few minutes."

Down two ladders to the superstructure deck, then along the narrow catwalk past the torpedo tubes, to the 20-mm battery. The Assistant Machine Gun Officer, an Ensign from Virginia, stepped forward. His life jacket and khaki trousers were stiff with blood. "What the hell, Ross, are you wounded?" I asked.

"No, suh," he replied. "I just helped some of the boys who got hit. Cap'n," he added, "did you see that guy thumb his nose at us?"

"I heard about it," I told him.

"Yes, suh. I just thought I'd tell you we got him."

Around the searchlight platform and the after battery the decks were red. Gun Four was a shambles — but it had never missed a salvo. From the gaff of the stump mainmast our colors flew in miniature — most of the stripes whipped out by the wind; the remnant of the flag torn and spotted with bullet holes.

I noticed that Chief Gunner's Mate Hoppers was without shoes and I wondered why, for we had been given ample time to prepare for the attack. He saw me looking at his feet and explained "I heaved 'em at a gun captain." It was a puzzling explanation but I later found out the details of Hoppers and the shoes.

Seaman Robert Otto pointed to the bullet holes in the after stack, and the troughs sliced in the face of the machine-gun shields. "Will it be all right if we don't paint over these for a while, sir?" he asked. "We'd like to keep 'em for sort of souvenirs." The gun crews, grinning, crowded around to describe the battle as viewed from the after-deck house.

When I returned to the bridge Dr. Peek was waiting. "I believe we can pull them all through," he said. "Causey has a mean wound in the chest but I think he'll be all right."

The Chief Engineer, in sweat-soaked dungarees, climbed the bridge ladder. "It looked like fine shooting," he said. It was our little joke. Etheridge and his engineers could never see a shot fired. They tended their machinery, gave us steam and answered the calls for speed — listening to the sharp sound of our guns and bracing themselves against the explosion of enemy shells, but their battle stations kept them from witnessing the action.

"Yeah, Chief, it looked pretty good. How did things go below?"

"Not so bad, Cap'n. It got up to a hundred and forty degrees in the engine rooms, but we didn't have any trouble."

The First Lieutenant Joined us. "Nice little bomb hole at frame 30, starboard," he reported, "but we put in a temporary patch and she's not making any water."

Lieutenant Linehan phoned from Gun Control. "All guns unloaded. No casualties to material. Replacement crew in Gun Four."

The talker spoke up. "Sir, Mr. Strong reports all wounded men in the 20-mm battery replaced. All guns ready."

We settled down to a good speed, course north. There remained an hour of daylight as we advanced toward the retiring fleet of the enemy. All in all it had been a highly satisfactory afternoon. I remembered, suddenly, that it was my daughter's tenth birthday, but she would not celebrate it until tomorrow, because of the International Date line that ran through the ten thousand miles that separated us. Our little party north of the Solomons had been somewhat noisier than other birthdays I remembered in California and Virginia, but we had had blind man's buff and tag, and we'd certainly pinned the tail on the donkey. There had been "poppers" — not, it is true, in the usual shades of yellow and pale blue; ours had been in harsh red and black, but, like the birthday souvenirs they told your fortune in a not uncertain manner. So — Happy birthday, dear Zero and Mitsubishi and Kawanishi It was a grand party.

AND FAR AWAY

"— and the only tune that he could play
Was Over the Hills and Far Away."

We were dog tired. The past ninety-six hours had been an around-the-clock grind as we drilled and fired the target practices that are necessary even in war. We stood up Pearl Harbor channel, rounded Ford Island and went alongside our tender where the other ships of the Division already were moored.

Before our lines were, doubled-up the supply services arranged by the staff were in evidence. A fuel lighter came alongside amidships; launches came under the stern with replacements for the ammunition expended in the recent firings; officers of the staff checked with our heads of departments for any repairs that might be necessary. These niceties we still accepted as a matter of course, for we had not yet experienced the difficulties of operating far out of reach of tender or supply facilities.

The four skippers — John Higgins, Roland Smoot, Harry Hubbard and I went on board the Gwin for our usual arrival conference with the Division Commander — the "Commodore," in destroyer language. In the Commodore's cabin we could thrash out our problems and settle perplexities that were inconvenient to discuss at sea. We could blow off the steam raised by small difficulties, and accept with signs of modesty — largely simulated — praise for little personal triumphs or "Well Dones" that occurred during the week. Inasmuch as no one was pulling any punches these days we hoarded all tokens of approbation, to be passed along to our own officers and crew in thinly veiled understatements. "The Commodore said we did pretty well on that last practice — The Captain of the Monssen said it looked like our first salvo was right on." There were, of course, the other kind. "The Commodore says why the hell did we make so much smoke when we went up to flank speed. So-an-So claims we damn near clipped his stern on that Emergency Turn the other night." To this sort of thing we gave extra attention, but considerably more privacy.

The G had just completed a convoy cruise and we were worried that our one "Sheep Dog" Job would be the first of many similar assignments.

Someone had to nurse convoys, but like the Gentleman from Hollywood, we wanted to be included out. The Big Staff agreed, so now we found ourselves back again with a high-speed, double-barreled fighting Task Force, and with the four ships of our Division working together for the first time since the Tokyo Raid. We were the youngest destroyers in the outfit, newcomers to the Pacific, and still wore our mottled North Atlantic camouflage, but at the rate ships were being cranked out at home we would not hold our record for long.

Hubbard had recently brought the Meredith up from the South Pacific. The G was just back from a few weeks in a mainland Navy Yard. The Gwin and Monssen were full of the Battle of Midway in which they had taken part. There was much talk about it in Commodore Holcomb's crowded little cabin. With the help of typical navy coffee (if the spoon sinks the coffee is too weak) we forgot our need of sleep in hearing of the Yorktown's last fight; the wonderful work of our aviators; the battered Jap Fleet thrown back across the Pacific; the sub attacks — all the customary shop talk of a Fleet Problem with the added zest of knowing that, as the sailors say, "This ain't no drill." As we got up to return to our own ships the Commodore said: "There will be a conference of all commanding officers on board the Enterprise at nine o'clock tomorrow morning. The Squadron Commander will pick us up in his barge."

"What's it all about?" we asked. The Commodore shrugged his shoulders. "More drills — maybe."

There was a touch of old times in going aboard the Enterprise the next morning; mounting the endless ladder to the hangar deck, then gathering your breath for another climb to the level below the flight deck where the Admiral had his quarters. I stopped to peer into the dark cubbyhole known as "spare stateroom, gallery deck," that had been my home for many months as Flag Lieutenant, when Admiral Andrews had his flag in the carrier. I wouldn't go so far as to say that ship's spirit is hereditary, but certainly there is an affinity between the "Lucky Little Enterprise" of 1812 and the fine modern carrier that bears her name. The Lucky Little etc. could slip into a forgotten corner of the flight deck on her namesake, but the two ships have an esprit and a "service reputation" that seems to run in the family.

We sat in the Admiral's cabin — battleship, carrier, cruiser and destroyer captains and Unit Commanders, casting quick glances through the orders, photographs and thick mimeographed book that had been handed out as we entered. The pages were full of strange names — Guadalcanal, Tulagi, Falsi, Bougainville, and many more. There was something in the air. This was to be no discussion of future drills. The Admiral spoke quietly. He told us that the Task Force would sortie on the morrow; he assumed that we had taken care of all details of food, provisions, ammunition. We would have to be self-supporting for some time. He discussed our recent drills and firings and expressed his satisfaction with them, on the whole. But there was always room for improvement. He relied on each of us to perfect his ship's company; to perfect ourselves; to be ready for anything. It was not a lengthy meeting. We picked up our papers and returned to our ships, curious, in the privacy of our own cabins, to see what our orders might be.

After I had read them I sent for the Executive Officer and Heads of Departments. "Underway at 0645. There'll be a fuel barge alongside some time tonight to top us off, I want to have double our allowance of spare parts, insofar as possible. We may be away from the tender for a long time, but keep it under your shirt. Let's get busy now, on the spare-part boxes. I'll want to see you again after dinner." When they had gone I turned to Lieutenant Commander Peters, who was Navigator as well as Executive and Second-in-Command. "Frank, break out the chart portfolio for the Solomon Islands." For the remainder of the afternoon he and I pored over unfamiliar islands and waters — comparing the charts with the photographs that the Admiral had given us. We didn't know very much about the Solomon Islands. Our naval budget had not allowed us to stray far from home waters. We had a lot to learn.

At six-thirty next morning we cast off our lines and, backing in to the channel, twisted her around and headed out. The area around Ford Island and the approaches to Merry Point was a mass of sister ships, maneuvering to meet a split-second sortie schedule. Out past Hickham Field — its burned and twisted hangars a reminder of a Sunday morning in December; past the twin fortifications of Weaver and Kamehameha, through the reef channels, now, and into the blue Hawaiian waters we steamed; the destroyers in the van, listening for subs, ready to form our screen about the heavy ships.

They came in view, the cruisers and the rest of them, and, finally, the Task Force Flagship, the Enterprise — our Flat Top. It was July, 1942. Our first real offensive in the Pacific War was underway.

The greatest difficulties in the Pacific War and those least understood at home are the distances involved and the lack of bases. You could drop two

Atlantic Oceans in the Pacific and have almost room left for a third. On our present mission we would be at sea for about three weeks before arriving at our destination, and we were neither steaming slowly nor proceeding by devious routes. The Pacific War is a war of distance. It poses a terrific problem of logistics to keep a fleet supplied with the thousand and one necessities over and beyond food, fuel and ammunition. The old "for want of a nail" sequence is equally applicable to ships of a fleet. They need everything that you have in your home, everything that you have in your office, everything you will find in a large manufacturing plant. We have watchmakers and blacksmiths, boilermakers and laundrymen, and tailors, cooks and bakers and machine-tool operators, draftsmen and dentists, men who repair typewriters and men who repair turbines, metalsmiths and master divers, in addition to the gunners and torpedomen, the yeomen, radiomen, signalmen and quartermasters — the machinists, firemen and seamen. And each of them needs the tools of his trade. It is equally important to the signalman that he have needles and thread and a workable sewing machine to repair signal flags soon whipped out by the wind as to the machinist that he has a full allowance of wrenches, gaskets, special tools and spare parts for the main engines, pumps and auxiliary machinery. And there is no handy store around the corner.

With the loss of the Philippines and the Netherlands East Indies, and the capitulation of Singapore, we were brought face to face with an overseas movement of a magnitude never known before. Not that we had ever expected the Pacific War to be a pushover, for in my twenty-three years in the Navy I have never heard an intelligent, experienced officer sell the Japanese short. We knew it would be a bitter war and probably a long war. We hoped it would be a one-ocean war.

Between the west coast of North and South America, and the east coast of Asia, there are no naval bases worthy of the name, Pearl Harbor excepted; no place where a battleship or a large aircraft carrier can be docked for repairs. With the fall of Singapore the little pin used to mark large dry docks on the chart jumped two thousand miles farther west, to Colombo and Bombay. The Japanese did a thorough job in those early days of the war, and they provided a task of gigantic magnitude for the Service Force of the United States Fleet, for it was the problem of the Service Force to back up the fighting units and see that they did not lack for food and clothing, needles and thread, nuts and bolts, and all the imponderable paraphernalia of the sea-borne warfare.

A fleet moves on its fuel tanks rather than on its belly, for we can feed the crew a longer time than we can feed the boilers. Our storeroom and provision holds were crammed; we could cruise for weeks before we began to feel the pinch of hunger, but every turn of the propellers hastened the hour when the destroyers would have to barge up to a heavy ship and ask for the equivalent of five gallons of gas and check the oil and water. Fuelings at sea are always clubby affairs, intimate in that you can chat between the two ships without benefit of megaphone, friendly in that the larger ship — exercising a maternal interest in the destroyer tossing near by — sends over gifts of fresh bread, ice cream, magazines and soft drinks, all the while suffering us to nuzzle greedily at her fount of bunker oil. In the old four-stackers, with no laundry facilities, we could send over soiled clothing during one fueling, and return in a few days for more oil, and clean shirts.

Our first fueling after leaving Pearl Harbor took place on a Sunday morning — the destroyers going up in turn, while the others redoubled their vigilance for subs. We watched them hold Church Services aboard the big fellow from whom we were taking our oil and ice cream, and after Church the band played for our benefit. After a few numbers my chief yeoman, who was wearing our end of the phone that ran between the ships, turned and said: "They want to know if there is anything special you would like to hear." I asked them to play Dixie. It was a bit of a shock to see the band leader send below for the music, for his ship bore a southern name. "It's damyankee propaganda," I assured my Connecticut Gunnery Officer. "They know that piece as well as I do." Besides the ice cream and the music, the Chaplain sent over ten hymnals. That night, while we rolled along ahead of a quartering sea, the officers off watch gathered in the wardroom and vocalized with enthusiasm and commendable volume. To the bridge, three decks above, drifted fragments of the old favorites to mix with the sounds we were beginning to know so well — the ping-ping of our anti-submarine listening device; the "right standard rudder, sir" as the helmsman put the wheel over in our zigzag courses; the interminable and comfortable tones of wind and sea.

Several times each day the Enterprise launched and recovered planes, keeping a patrol around the formation, searching far out toward our van and flanks, then, when they came home, giving exercise to the Task Force in repelling air attacks. Heading as we were for the back door of the Solomons, it would be another week before we would expect to sight enemy aircraft, but not for a moment could we drop our guard for it was by no means improbable that the Japs were trying the same stunt as we, but in reverse. Certainly we could expect subs to be across our track. There were no idle hands, and few idle moments, as we continued on our way.

The crew stood a watch in three; four hours on watch, eight hours off, an arrangement that while apparently giving them only eight hours on watch out of every twenty-four is by no means so simple. A man going off watch at midnight will be free until eight in the morning — except that he must go to his battle station when we go to General Quarters before dawn and remain there for an hour, until after sunrise, which allows him time for a bath and shave before breakfast at seven, and a few moments for a smoke before it is again time to go on watch. Men on the mid-watch (midnight to four a.m.) get no sleep the remainder of the night. During the forenoon they try to crowd in a little rest, but always there are drills, practice firings, or unexpected calls to G.Q. that keep them from their bunks. They welcome the watch ending at eight in the evening, for with any luck they can be turned in by eight-thirty, and sleep until half-past three, when again it is "Rouse the watch. On deck the — section," in the rolling, sleep-penetrating tones possessed by all good boatswain's mates. There is time for a cup of coffee and a cigarette — a face wash if they are inclined — and up to their battle station fifteen minutes before the hour. It is particularly hard on the engineers, especially in the tropics. Our engineers didn't know it at the time — no more did I — but we were to steam for four months before we could secure the plant and let the fires die out under the boilers. The future held many surprises of which we were happily unaware.

Watches for the officers are equally restrictive, except for the Captain and Executive. They have no regular watches, but the Executive Officer, in his capacity of navigator, has little chance for rest, and the Captain is fortunate if he has more than an hour's uninterrupted sleep at any time or if he can spend as many as five hours in his bunk in any twenty-four.

Under the increasing tension of our operating conditions the law of averages was bound to produce someone who could not stand the strain. A machinist's mate went berserk with a knife. He was subdued and put under guard, which meant in addition to our feelings of distress at a shipmate's collapse, the loss of two men's services at a time when we needed everyone. In his more coherent moments he claimed that his mind had been stolen and carried off by another engineer who had been detached from the ship some months before. He had no recurrent spells of violence but it was necessary to continue his confinement. It was a great relief when the Captain of a tanker from which we fueled agreed to take him. We put a life jacket on him, tucked him in a large canvas bag, in which he huddled quite meekly, and sent him across on a trolley line. I was glad to see him arrive safely on the other end, for there was a long ground swell and we were rolling heavily.

We cruised for two weeks when, late one afternoon, we saw the sight for which we had been waiting; the masts and stacks of our transports; the familiar silhouettes of more cruisers, destroyers, carriers — all the components of an amphibious expedition that in point of distance was the vastest ever launched by any navy. By sunset we had joined and the Combined Task Forces headed off together for a small island to conduct the dress rehearsal for our attack on the Solomons.

The rehearsal lasted three days, busy ones for the aviators who came and went continuously between their carriers and the shore objectives. Busy, too, for the marines, who within the week would repeat their maneuvers in the face of enemy fire. I didn't envy them. I had watched them fight off mock foes in beach defense drills during Fleet Problems and I decided at the time that any enemy trying to land against a well-defended beach head was apt to be pretty well cut to pieces before his boats reached the shore.

The carriers, with their guarding ring of destroyers, stayed well off-shore. The transports and their immediate covering force stood close in. These transports were large ships, with names well known in the peacetime American Merchant Marine. They were in the navy for the duration, manned by navy crews, and with tiers of bunks in their luxury cabins. When we thought of those crowded ships and the further discomforts that the marines were so soon to have, we were thankful for our own comparative conveniences. We didn't get much time for sleep, there was no fresh food, we were starting on the "dry stores" that would be our diet for many months, but our bunks were still there, we had unlimited hot and cold water and we were not packed into the ship in a manner that would give claustrophobia to a sardine.

On the fourth day the transports stood out, we again took up that vast cruising formation, and the fleet commenced the final stage of its journey.

For that last fifteen-hundred mile passage the weather was in our favor. They were days of lowering clouds, rain squalls and high winds; the sort of thing that would discourage the Japanese reconnaissance planes from straying too deep in the Coral Sea. But we were approaching their own back yard and we expected momentarily to be sighted. We increased the number of our lookouts, we drilled incessantly at surprise firing, we watched for the slightest indication of a stranger, we had the usual number of false sub-contacts and blasted a few innocent blackfish and porpoises with our depth charges.

In peacetime cruising scarcely a day goes by without a destroyer signaling "Have man with acute appendicitis. Immediate operation required. Request ship be designated to receive patient." Some navy medico should write a brochure about the efficacy of war as a calmative for the vermiform appendix. Throughout all the weeks that we kept the sea I remember no instance of an appendix adding to the complications of our daily routine. When a man is so exhausted that he can flop on a steel deck and sleep without consciousness of rain, spray or broiling sun, he has no time to worry about vague pains in his amidships section.

There were, of course, the other occupational distractions of life at sea. A man tumbled overboard from a cruiser. His ship swung about and recovered him so quickly that he scarcely knew he had been wet. When a boat must be lowered and speed reduced, the knowledge of enemy subs in the vicinity is a great stimulus to prompt ship-handling.

A fighter-plane returning to the carrier gave a mighty zoom that became suddenly a horrifying downward spin. He struck the water and flames and black, oily smoke towered high in the air. The Benham swung in but there was nothing — just gasoline blazing on the surface of the sea.

The last five hundred miles into the Solomons reminded me of a game that we used to play at home when we would "hide" many objects in plain view, then see who could find the most in a given time. A dollar bill, folded twice, lengthwise, and tucked around the back of a book was rarely discovered; a black bow tie on a table leg, a gold ring on top of a lamp, a penny placed in the edge of a picture frame — all were elusive, though none was hidden. Now, within easy air search from Guadalcanal, our Task Force of close to a hundred ships ploughed along in plain view. The moon rose at midnight and shone brightly on the dollar bill, the thimble and the black bow tie. At six-thirty a deep, orange-red sun, so magnified by the mists and scattered squalls that it seemed to fill the whole horizon, laid a faint touch of pink on an ocean turned suddenly chill and grey. We sent below for windproof jackets and hot coffee. We hadn't expected to be cold in the Coral Sea, in Latitude 12, South.

Under the strain of waiting for something to happen the crew showed their tension by forever finding something to keep their hands busy. Outside of the regular drill periods the 20-mm crews practiced by the hour — cocking their guns, timing their speed at re-loading, checking the springs, rubbing oil on steel parts that were flawlessly clean and adequately lubricated.

The torpedomen fussed around their tubes like housewives preparing for week-end guests. One of the shipfitters used this final lull to fashion a fine, keen-edged commando knife for me. A boatswain's mate made a neat leather scabbard with a becket, so I could wear the blade on my hip. When we went to General Quarters we wore and carried such an amazing collection of knives, pistols, canteens, first-aid packets and flashlights that we felt like top-heavy Knights of the Round Table. The First Lieutenant outdid us all. I believe he carried two canteens, pistols, etc., and in addition the special pockets of his life jacket were crammed with a miscellany that would make life comfortable aboard any raft, and enable a group of shipwrecked sailors to set up housekeeping with no trips to a hardware store or corner grocery. Though we poked mild fun at him and called him Panzer Division 808 we agreed that if the occasion ever should arise for an unscheduled swim, the men who found themselves aboard the First Lieutenant's raft could be confident that dry towels and a change of clothing would be waiting.

We were within two hundred miles of the Solomons, and still no contact with the enemy. Our planes were aloft and there was the usual chatter between the carrier and her chickens as she sent them to various heights and distances to seek out the Japanese reconnaissance craft that must be in the area. We heard her call one section and order it to the northwest. The section leader acknowledged. Less than five minutes later we heard his shout: "Bandit 325, Angels eight. Tally-Ho." We sounded the general alarm and swung in to take anti-aircraft stations about the carrier. There was no need. "I got him!" a voice shouted. Then there was a long, thin trail of smoke, a splash, and more heavy, black smoke as a Mitsubishi smacked into the sea. First blood for our side.

During the night the transports moved ahead of us, and in the early morning they swung to the east between Savo Island and Cape Esperance at about the time that our carrier aircraft started pounding the Jap positions. We remained west of the island, to give our carriers plenty of sea room for handling their planes, and to maneuver in the event of enemy counter attack from the air.

A few destroyers went in with the transports and added their gunnery to the aerial bombing. The Monssen accompanied a light cruiser into the tricky, reef-studded passages that form a close barrier around the tiny island of Gavutu and its twin, Tanambogo, to which it is connected by a narrow causeway. These two rocky knolls were the scene of the bitterest fighting on the first day of the Occupation. Like Tulagi they are studded with caves and lack the smooth sandy beaches that facilitate landing on Guadalcanal, twenty miles across the bay. The Monssen slid in with all guns blazing until she was within five hundred yards of Tanambogo. Other destroyers and cruisers crowded around Gavutu and Tulagi, smashing their salvoes into the hillside at point blank range. Our bombers were making round trips between the carriers and their objective as fast as they could. A pall of smoke rose up and hid the nearby shores of Florida Island. In this devastating holocaust it was impossible for any living thing to exist. And yet — when the bombardment stopped and the marines leaped to the shore from their landing boats, Japs poured from the caves, set up machine guns and opened rapid and accurate fire. Each of these three tiny islands was a miniature Gibraltar, a rocky rabbit-warren crowded with soldiers who had never met defeat.

This was warfare reduced to the elemental; kill or be killed; no surrender; if you want us, come in and get us. The Marines went in, and they got 'em. It was a ding-dong fight with many of the characteristics of an eighteenth-century frigate action as the Japs tried to "repel boarders" — firing from the hatches, dropping grenades from the tops, sweeping the gangways with cannister. But there was no stopping the men who swarmed over the "bulwarks" to grapple hand-to-hand on the slippery decks.

The Japs love to play possum, clutching a grenade or knife to use on whoever comes along to investigate the body. They swam over from Florida Island, during darkness, holding a box over their heads as they drifted stealthily with the current. The marines, crouched in shallow fox holes along the beach, enjoyed this nocturnal stalking, a game they had known at home long before anyone handed them a high-powered rifle.

Three Japs came in with hands upstretched. When the marines stepped forward to disarm them the middle one fell to his knees, bringing into position a machine gun that was strapped to his back, and with which the other two killed the marines. Incidents of which these are typical help us to understand why the marines took very few prisoners.

Across the bay our landing on Guadalcanal was proceeding ahead of schedule, in the face of surprisingly little opposition. The bitter fighting was yet to come.

Milling around between the two shores in their job of protecting the transports, the cruisers and destroyers listened for subs and watched the skies for aircraft. They came — torpedo planes from the west in a weaving, low-flying formation. When one was knocked down, another slid in to fill the gap. It was a field day for the anti-aircraft gunners. Not one plane got in close enough to launch his torpedo.

Around the corner we continued to curvet about our carrier. A returning plane reported a periscope. Welcoming a diversion we sounded "submarine attack stations" and went over to investigate. It was a tree trunk with naked upturned branches that looked for all the world like the head of a deer.

Bridge comment: "The damn thing's got horns."

"Yeah. First time I ever saw a sub with antlers on the periscope."

The Plan of the Day of the G for the three opening days of the first Allied Offensive in the South Pacific:

Friday, August 7, 1942

0245 Call duty Master-at-Arms and Mess Cooks.

0315 Call All Hands.

0345 Early breakfast for the 04 to 08 watch.

0415 Relieve the 00 to 04 watch. Breakfast.

0500 General Quarters, Stand by for the Battle of the Solomon Islands.

The 04 to 08 watch will have early breakfast at 0345 and will relieve the mid-watch at about 0415. We will go to General Quarters at 0500 and will be there all day. During any lulls in the battle two or three men at a time may be secured for meals, or coffee and sandwiches may be served at the various battle stations.

Note: I. All hands have been issued life belts in addition to life jackets, and should print their names on the small flap where easily seen. Take care of it, for it may take care of you.

Note: 2. All hands are reminded that a complete change of clean clothes should be left handy to put on prior to entering battle. Clean clothes lessen chances of infection of wounded.

Saturday, August 8, 1942

0245 Call duty Master-at-Arms and Mess Cooks.

0315 Call All Hands.

0345 Early breakfast for the 04 to 08 watch.

0415 Relieve the 00 to 04 watch. Breakfast.

0500 General Quarters. Continue the Battle of the Solomon Islands.

Note: Meals, or coffee and sandwiches, during any lulls in the action. The ship will remain at General Quarters all day.

Sunday, August 9, 1942

0245 Call duty Master-at-Arms and Mess Cooks.

0315 Call All Hands.

0345 Early breakfast for the 04 to 08 watch.

0415 Relieve the 00 to 04 watch. Breakfast.

0500 General Quarters. Continue the Battle of the Solomon Islands.

Note: Same as yesterday.

Note: 3. Projectile hoists are unloaded to prevent excessive wearing of linkage springs. Handling room crews MUST be able to send projectiles to the gun in less than 20 seconds.

After three days of running circles about our carrier, while her planes made mincemeat of the Japs, we were rapidly reaching the bottom of our fuel tanks. The Gwin brought a tanker part way up to meet us and we went off to the southard. This time it was a night job — and one of the blackest nights I have ever seen; no light save the phosphorescent wake that boiled heavily around the G and the tanker. By one in the morning our belly was full but we were required to chase around the outskirts of the formation, and twice through the fleet, on messages of one kind or another, before we could settle down. By then it was time to go to dawn G.Q. so, while we were down to our full-load waterline, there was no letup in the no-sleep cycle. Our Commissary Officer was going about with the sort of expression that denotes intense concentration on cubic content of storerooms versus stores on hand, but the tanker gave us the equivalent of two loaves of bread and a few small fishes so, while no one was going to gain weight, we were reasonably secure from starvation.

As a matter of fact we considered ourselves fortunate by comparison with the aviators and, of course, the marines. The bird men were aloft to the limit of human endurance, and the marines were in the middle of a mud-and-blood regime that made our shower-bath and hot-meal existence a lead-pipe cinch, despite the fact that from eternal watchfulness and no sleep we were commencing to get that drawn-cheek, puffy-eyed look that came to be the trade mark of the destroyer sailor.

The thought behind the old cliché regarding a difference of opinion and horse races was equally applicable in the war we were fighting. We were wholeheartedly sincere in our admiration for the marines and aviators. They, in turn, thought the other fellow was doing a pretty good job, and all agreed that the destroyer sailor was half hero and half demented. With regard to the tin cans they felt that Ben Jonson was guilty of an understatement in expressing the belief that only fools and fish go to sea, and that going to sea is like going to jail, with the added inconvenience of running the risk of being drowned.

On the night of August 8th the Japs came in for the first time with the strong, fast detachment of cruisers and destroyers that we were to learn to call the Tokyo Express. Roaring down the slot between Santa Isabel and Bougainville, sure of their navigation because of excellent charts based on Japanese soundings, they found the cruisers we had stationed on either side of Savo and, in a quick, vicious hit-and-run action sank the fine Australian Canberra and our own Astoria, Quincy and Vincennes. This was a terrific blow from any angle. It cinched our opinion that the Jap was a good night-fighter; it crippled our surface attack force, and it again brought up the question of whether or not the Washington Conference Eight-Inch cruiser was a weak reed in a naval battle. There was no argument that these ships could dish it out; but there was grave doubt as to their ability to take it. More alarming was the knowledge that the three ships lost that night were not tin-clads of the Pensacola-Salt Lake City type, but the best we had been able to build of a type that was admittedly a compromise. The chickens of 1922 were coming home to roost.

No naval officer of any nation came from the sessions of the Washington Conference in a happy state of mind. Our own fleet was tossed into the center of the pond with an anchor about its neck; the British experts felt that they had been "done"; the French were incensed, the Italians angry, and the Japanese, who most certainly got the best of the deal, were pilloried at home. The conditions of the Arms Agreement are available to anyone who cares to read them, and I recommend them to the armchair strategist and the Monday morning quarterback of naval policy.

I recall one morning, as an Ensign in the Texas, when the new and almost completed Washington was towed down from Delaware Bay for us to play with, for she was one of our sacrifices on the altar of disarmament. We whanged away at her for a week with torpedoes, bombs, mines and 14-inch shells. I was told off to carry the flashlights and notebooks for a group of officers who went on board her after each experiment. We crawled and climbed through the eerie darkness of the empty battleship and checked the effects of the punishment to which she was being subjected. We found that she could take it. In fact she was so well constructed that, because I was a very new ensign, my principal concern was that the damn ship wouldn't sink in time for us to get to the Army Game.

Gradually, when she refused to bow her head, I came to have a feeling of admiration and affection for her and a wholehearted respect for the men who built her. When she sank, on a dusty morning with a full northeast gale blowing, some sentimentalist ordered Taps to be sounded and I wept along with the rest of them, admirals and boatswains' mates alike.

There is a story that is told to each class at the Naval Academy about the midshipman who wrote on an examination that the Battle of Salamis — or perhaps it was Tsushima or Trafalgar — was lost because of the lack of three ships; marksmanship, seamanship and leadership. Blame any that you like for the loss of our cruisers off Savo on the night of August 8th. The fact remains that we would not have built those ships had not their characteristics been forced upon us at Washington in 1922.

One afternoon in early 1939, when our Scouting Force was assembled at Culebra, and the President, in the Houston, had just witnessed the completion of our annual Fleet Problem, orders came to designate a cruiser for the purpose of carrying to Japan the body of her late Ambassador, Saito. The Astoria, under the Command of Captain Richmond K. Turner, was assigned this duty. On a black night three years later Rear Admiral Turner, formerly in command of our South Pacific Amphibious Force, saw the destruction of his former ship by the little men who had banzaied her right heartily on another occasion.

The Tokyo Express continued to run, making quick midnight thrusts, lobbing a few shells toward Henderson Field, keeping the Marines from getting any rest. For the most part the physical damage of these attacks was negligible. We expected something bigger to happen; a major effort on the part of the Japs to retake the Eastern Solomons by landing a large army under the protection of their fleet. To meet that threat, and because a carrier had no business in restricted waters, we stayed clear of Guadalcanal while remaining in close covering distance and affording protection to the transports and cargo ships that were engaged in carrying reinforcements and supplies to General Vandegrift's Marines.

Our duty was both monotonous and nerve racking. After almost two straight months at sea you become numb; gradually you cease to think in terms of sea and shore, and all the world is water. It was only by looking at my Night Orders of the previous evening that I knew the day of the week, for the calendar had no significance in our cruising routine. Occasionally a tanker would arrive to give us fuel. Sometimes we obtained it from the larger ships of the Task Force when we went in close for provisions in response to a signaled order or, more rarely, in obedience to some chipper Captain's invitation by voice radio to "come on over and get your groceries." We were on a no-mail, no-sleep cycle. We thought it mightn't be a bad idea to slip a letter in one of the drifting coconuts that bobbed about on the surface of the Solomons Sea. "Special Delivery by Coconut Mail." It seemed a more certain method of posting than to send our mail over by trolley to a tanker that waddled off no one knew where.

There were side excursions and alarums. It became routine to see our aviators shoot down a four-motored Japanese patrol bomber once or twice a day; to hear their familiar "Bandits; Tally-ho!" and a jubilant shout "I got him!" to watch for the splash and the black, curling smoke; then a placid voice from the carrier: "Nice work; return to your patrol station."

Enemy subs were in the area. There was rich hunting for them if they could get in their licks. A destroyer would have a contact and spin toward it with a rush of white water while the large ships turned off to open the range. Then the dull explosions of depth charges and, in a hour or so, a lone destroyer, or a "killer group" of two or three, coming up wide open to rejoin the Force. Check off another Jap pig-boat.

While we consolidated our position on Guadalcanal the next move was up to the Nips. In late August they came down in strength and off we steamed to the northward to meet them. The result was the two-day ding-dong that has been known variously as the Battle of the Carriers, the Battle of Ontong Java, and, officially now, the Battle of the Eastern Solomons. Under any name it carried grief to Tojo. To the G and her sisters it brought an opportunity to shake the salt from our faces and forget the tedium of keeping the sea in the activity of a busy afternoon.

FROM THE BOOK OF JOB

With oil enough for twenty-four more hours sloshing around in her tanks the G slid through the night, her bow riding high on the long swells of the Solomons Sea. A temporary patch covered a Jagged hole on the starboard side a few feet above the waterline. Farther down, a sprung section of plating allowed a steady trickle of water to enter the ordnance storeroom. Every half hour a gunner's mate went in with a bucket and an old lube oil can. He scooped the water into the bucket, then, being very careful to close and dog down the doors and hatches behind him, he carried the bucket to the forecastle and emptied it over the lee side before going to the bridge to report that the leak had not increased and that the storeroom had been bailed out.

On the after superstructure the 20-mm crews of the watch traced with their fingers the furrows ploughed in the face of their guns shields by the Jap bullets. There were other reminders of the strafing attack on the non-skid decking around Gun Four where exhausted men lay sprawled in sleep, unmindful of the dark stains that made a zigzag pattern in the diamond shapes of the treads and formed small sticky pools that clotted slowly.

In the living compartments, dark save for the faint glow of battle lanterns, men in fresh white bandages muttered incoherently in the swirling nightmares of a drugged sleep, or stared, wide-eyed, into nothing.

The Doctor had finished his repair work, though the odor of ether still hung in the air, and the tops of the mess tables smelled of disinfectant and tincture of green soap. Pharmacist's mates felt their way past the tiers of bunks, pausing now and then to inspect the wounded in the beam of a blued flashlight, to see that dressings had not slipped; that ligatures were tight; that no hemorrhage could stealthily undo the effects of blood plasma and medical care.

Empty powder cases, lashed to the rails around the Commodore's deck and stacked on the superstructure clear of the torpedo tubes, gave an occasional brassy clink as the ship heeled in the long, slow rolls that proclaimed the emptiness of her fuel tanks.

Ever since the close of the battle on the preceding afternoon we had been steaming alone to the north, in the direction of the fleeing Japanese Fleet, with orders to look for our aviators who might have crashed or landed in the water, out of fuel, and to give to any friendly planes we might encounter the navigational information they would need to permit them to find their own carrier. We sighted a number of planes; tracking them as they closed, guns loaded and ready to open fire if they failed to answer our challenge, or returned the wrong reply. All of them were friendly. We gave them their sailing directions by signal light. They circled, then straightened out on the course for the carrier.

Now, toward the end of the mid-watch, there had been no contacts for two hours. We had our own rendezvous to make on the morrow; it was time to turn back. We swung to the left and took up a southerly course, away from the Japanese Fleet which we knew to be in the vicinity.

The excitement of the fight, and the rather tense nature of our solitary jaunt to the northward, brought on the hot, dry feeling of flatness that sleep alone will relieve. I regarded with envy the off-watch signalmen, flemished down on top of the flag bags and curled up in a corner of the deck with a life jacket as a pillow, I thought, too, of the sea battles in the days of the wooden ships when the Captain would order the main brace to be spliced, and request his officers to join him in drinking a toast to their recent success. Well, I could request mine to join me in drinking such a toast — in coffee or tea — beverages poorly suited to the occasion, and apt to raise a question in their minds as to just how hard a bump the old man had got on the head. We had a few bottles of toasting material aboard — for medicinal use. It was a temptation to send word to the Doctor and tell him to rush a prescription to the bridge — possibly two; the Commodore looked like he could stand one. But there were nearly three hundred of us on board, many of whom had been working considerably harder than I. With a pleased sensation of mild self-approval I stepped into the charthouse. "Call the wardroom pantry, and tell the watch boy to bring up a cup of coffee."

Though we knew the position of our own Task Force within narrow limits, we were uncertain of the location of other Fleet Units. At about four in the morning we had a report contact on our surface ships. They must have picked us up at the same time, for we could hear mumblings over the voice circuit, reporting a strange ship, followed by orders from the OTC for a destroyer to investigate the contact.

We spoke up promptly to identify ourselves, for strangers in the night are unwelcome in those waters, and there is always a chance that someone might shoot first and ask questions afterward. Then, too, we wanted to save a sister-ship the inconvenience of going to G.Q. on our account.

No one acknowledged the receipt of our message. We repeated "This is —— (our code name); course ——; speed ——; passing near your formation."

Still no answer. We heard the investigating destroyer say that she had the strange ship in sight and was about to challenge. We could see her, coming in on the port bow. We called her by voice but she paid no attention. It was obvious, then, that our voice transmitter was out of order — jarred loose, perhaps, by yesterday's firing. There had been no opportunity to test it after the action.

A pin point of light blinked the challenge and we hastened to signal the reply. The destroyer swung away and informed her OTC in bored tones that the strange ship had answered the challenge correctly. Presumably everyone knew we were a friend but we stayed ready to come up in a hurry if someone else challenged, remembering the sailor's adage that there is always some so-and-so who doesn't get the word.

Once again before daylight we passed through a friendly formation but this time none had cause for alarm. The transmitter had been repaired, and there was a quick "wilco" from the OTC when we announced our name and destination.

The morning was beautiful, the sort of day that you could picture the local Chamber of Commerce snapping photographs of shaded pools and sunny beaches, smiling fondly at the thermometer and rushing off to prepare booklets urging one and all to visit the Sunny Solomons. "Plan to be here for the Cannibal Convention; bring the family — see beautiful Guadalcanal; forget your troubles as you sail the tranquil waters of the Coral Sea."

We were glad for the cool breeze and the pleasant morning. It helped us to keep our eyelids parted. For the rest, we would have settled on the spot for eight hours sleep and a double coke — with lots of ice.

The Doctor came on the bridge with the good news that none of the wounded men had developed complications, and that Causey, the Chief Torpedoman, who had a nasty hole in the chest, and about whom I was most concerned, was resting comfortably. Pretty soon the "walking wounded" came topside to bask alike in the cool morning and the admiration of their shipmates. They wore a jaunty air and narrated their share in the battle with such gestures as bandaged limbs would permit. But they had had a scare — though none showed it. You can't collect a bullet or a jagged fragment of hot steel and fail to think "suppose it had been half an inch to the right; what if I hadn't been picking up a shell just at that instant; suppose —"

Sure, they'd been scared, after it was all over. There's not much time for anything but pulling a trigger and passing the ammunition when dive bombers are dropping in on you.

We got her cleaned up. By mid morning the red stains had disappeared; those after-action fragments of cotton and cork were hosed from corners and washed over the side; the lashings around the empties were set up for a full due. Around Gun Four a group of younger seamen watched the boatswain's mates — Mulno, Davis, Watson and their helpers — turn to with palm and needle, patching the rips and holes in the canvas mount top. It was like trying to make a fish net watertight, but they got the job done. A couple of good boatswain's mates can figure ways to do most anything.

We were to rejoin our carrier at noon, with a second rendezvous farther south if we failed to make contact at the first spot. We wanted to find her soon; she had a tanker along, and we needed oil about as badly as a ship can, and still have enough to turn the wheels. We had kept our peacetime awnings, in a storeroom below the waterline. They could be made into sails, of a sort, but I didn't care particularly for the notion of taking her up to the tanker under jib and jigger. It would be spectacular, but not efficient. We doubled the lookouts and strained our eyes on the horizon for a sight of mastheads or the broad, distinctive stack of the carrier, that looks like a fragment torn loose from the skyline of lower New York.

The weather continued to be strictly Hawaii Tourist Bureau. There was a refreshing nip in the air, and the sea was a pale-blue carpet. Scattered tufts of cumulus in the southeast gave a touch of realism to the stage setting and the sun had reduced its strength to the proper temperature for a slow bake.

"Sail Ho, one point forward of the starboard beam! Looks like a carrier."

"Right, standard rudder. Get a bearing on that ship."

We put our glasses to starboard. Yep, it was a carrier. We could see the flat outline of the flight deck under the island superstructure. Funny we hadn't picked her up while she was still hull down. No one's eyes were much good this morning. You've got to sleep sometime.

I stepped to the pelorus to get a bearing and check our course. "Tell the Commodore we have the carrier in sight and we're headed for her now." I squinted through the vanes and moved the bearing circle to the right, paralleling the horizon, but nothing appeared along the sharp line separating sea and sky. We couldn't be that blind. I reached for binoculars and looked again. Nothing. No carrier; no ship; nothing.

The officer-of-the-deck and the signalmen were looking, too. Realization came to all of us at the same instant.

"Carrier, hell! It's a goddamn submarine!"

"General Quarters. Stations for sub attack."

"Set depth charges."

"All ahead flank."

The General Alarm started honking, the men on the 20's cocked their guns with a metallic clunk and the muzzles of the main battery, pointing at the sky in the ready position for aircraft, swung down and turned their faces toward the surface of the ocean ahead.

There might be a chance later to use the guns, but in the opening round of this cat-and-mouse game the play belonged to the Attack Team. This was where the Soundman came into his own. For hour on hour, day after day, he sat in front of his Sound Machine; listening to the eternal "ping" that was the magnified note of the electrical impulses fired by the projector below our waterline. If these impulses strike the hull of a ship or come upon a submerged submarine they return an echo with a different note. The length of time between the transmission of the outgoing note and the return of the echo is a measure of the distance. The intensity of the note is a gauge of the bearing, for as the submarine draws out of the underwater "beam," the sound in our amplifier changes in volume.

If you know the distance and bearing of the submarine, and you take into account the effect of your own course and speed you should be able to plot the courses of both ships and determine the correct point at which to drop your depth charges. That is the idea, reduced to the simplest terms, but it is not quite so easy as it appears.

Imagine you are leaning over the roof of a twenty-story building with a fistful of grenades in your hand, trying to hit an automobile that is cruising around a large parking lot at twenty-five miles an hour. It's true a submerged submarine cannot make that speed, but neither can your building move along like a destroyer, so we'll combine the speeds of both ships and give the result to the automobile.

You keep a careful watch on the car. It's moving at a steady rate and in a straight line. You estimate the distance that it will advance while your grenade is falling, and when it reaches that point you toss one over. But the driver is watching and, as he spots the grenade, he twists his wheel sharply. When the explosion takes place he is a hundred yards away, waiting to dodge your next one. It's more or less that way with a sub attack, except that sound takes the place of sight. He can't see you; he can't see the depth charges, but his listening devices tell him where you are, and when he thinks you have committed yourself to a firing course he takes advantage of his maneuverability and swings clear. The depth charges may jar him, but they have to be almost direct hits to cripple a modern submarine.

So now the Soundman, the kettle drummer in our orchestra, would have a chance to be heard. As a matter of fact, his was to be virtually a solo number. Behind him in the chart house gathered the other members of the Attack Team; the Executive Officer, poised over a chart, pencil and dividers in hand; the Sound Officer, in the role of the Conductor for our next Selection; another officer crouched over the Asdic; various other gadgets that need not be mentioned here. I stood in the doorway between pilot house and chart house where I could be within arm's reach of the helmsman and the engine telegraphs, and equally close to the Sound Officer.

A talker spoke up: "Fantail reports —— set on the Depth Charges."

Through the chart-house port I could see the eager face of the signalman who was waiting to throw a lever that would let our "ash cans" roll from the racks and carry their TNT to the target.

There was intense quiet on the bridge, broken only by the low-voiced reports of the Soundman:

"Range three-oh —— oh; bearing two seven five."

"Range two eight five —— bearing two six nine."

"Range two six five —— bearing two six eight."

Sound Officer: "He's drawing slightly to the left."

Captain: "Come left a little; steer two six five."

Plotting Officer: "He's making pretty good speed."

"Range one four five — bearing two six-oh."

I wonder what the Jap Captain feels like, fathoms below, listening to the express train roar of our screws.

Plotting Officer: "He's going fast as hell."

Sound Officer: "I think he's still pulling left."

Soundman: "Range one oh —— oh; bearing two five-oh."

Captain: "Left rudder. Steer two four five."

Helmsman: "Steer two four five, sir."

The range is —— closing rapidly.

Captain: "Left standard rudder. Stand by — Drop One!"

The signalman's face in the port disappears as he leans to his levers.

"Drop Two!" "Drop Three!" — watching the second hand on the timer — "Drop Four!"

On each drop a heavy ash can falls over the stem and two smaller ones, fired from "K" guns, soar into the air and smack the surface a hundred yards or so from the ship.

There is a deep rumble from below; the amplifier picks up the sound and magnifies it until it fills the chart house; the ship shudders under the detonation; way astern the ocean bubbles and boils and dark-streaked foam spreads in widening circles.

A Carrier Task Force is coming toward us. We report to the OTC by voice: "Sighted submarine on surface. It submerged as we approached. Have completed first attack and am maneuvering for the second."

The OTC acknowledged, and changed the course of his ships to keep clear of our area. The sub couldn't have been in a better spot if he had been given in advance a copy of our plans. Except that the G happened along, the Japs would have been directly in the path of a Task Force, and within visual range of other ships in about an hour's time. It's true that their destroyers would have found him, but possibly not before he had chanced a browning shot at the formation, and we have never possessed enough carriers to risk them playing tag with torpedoes.

We went into a huddle and decided that the sub had increased speed at the expense of the batteries. He was making radical maneuvers, but he couldn't continue them for long. We picked him up on the sound gear and came in for the second run. This one was better, but he dove deeper in his hole and our charges exploded above him. Bridge talk between runs:

"Damn if he didn't head for the bottom that time."

"Let's see that plot. I don't believe he's zigzagging as much."

"He's going to run down his batteries if he keeps up that speed."

"Yeah, unless he runs us out of depth charges first."

"Sir, Fantail reports both racks reloaded."

"Starting the run; pick him up as soon as you can; all ahead standard."

Soundman: "Contact. Range two four —— oh; bearing three one five."

Captain: "Commence tracking."

The third approach was not good. The sub twisted and dove so radically that our plot did not warrant dropping any charges. We decided to make it a dry run and kicked the engines ahead to raise the underwater noise level and persuade our friend to use up more of the reserve of his batteries.

When we put the rudder over for the fourth attack the ship hung on her side and returned with reluctance to an even keel. We needed oil, and we needed it now.

This one was not a dry run. The plot was good, and we planted ash cans in an even pattern around the sub. There were unmistakable indications that he was trying to come to the surface. We swung quickly for the fifth attack, to help him make up his mind.

The TBS (Voice radio) started speaking to us. The OTC wanted to know if we still had contact.

From G: Affirmative.

From OTC: "I am detaching two destroyers to back you up. When they have made contact proceed with G and proceed to tanker."

We needed oil, right enough, but we'd found this Jap; we'd softened him up, and by golly we were going to finish him ourselves. We had depth charges remaining for two more runs.

"Come on, let's get this guy. Make it good."

He must have been one whale of a submarine — we knew he was a big one, when we mistook him for a carrier! The next attack punished him some more; he was groggy, but he was still in there fighting. We had one more chance — only a handful of ash cans left, and the Monssen and S in sight and coming up fast. We made a quick turn and started in for our last run.

This one turned out to be the kind they give beginners at the Sound School. The Jap was in trouble. He was trying desperately now to come up, and he couldn't quite make it. We sauntered over him and laid a pattern on his deck. That was the end. Our instruments followed him as he went down — and down. On the surface the boiling turbulence of water subsided and the afternoon breeze drew a feathery line of whitecaps over the spot where our late enemy rested — a thousand fathoms below.

The other two destroyers kept clear during our last attack. They made one run, but there was no need to expend any more depth charges. The evidence was there. They very generously sent a signal of corroboration, giving credit to the G for the sinking.

We headed for the tanker. We had nary a depth charge left, but we had gotten ourselves a sub.

From: Task Force Commander.

To: G.

Well Done for your day's operations.

In the sailor's language there is no higher praise. The Attack Team relaxed with coffee and cigarettes and commenced a voluble post mortem. The torpedomen came to the bridge to receive a pat on the back for their speed in hoisting depth charges out of the magazines and mule-hauling them aft for loading in the racks. The Soundman, sitting once more in front of his machine, had lost that bored look. The kettle drummer seldom gets a chance, but when he does you can hear him all over the house. This had been His Day.

At ten p.m., when the fueling was over and we were once more in the cruising formation, when we had secured from evening G.Q. and the Night Orders were written and there was little to do until the next change of course; when I could sit in the emergency cabin and relax for a few brief, peaceful moments, I came across a passage that described the death of the submarine more aptly and in fewer words than the reports and charts and graphs that we would have to submit. I found it in the Book of Job, Chapter 15, 21st. verse: "A dreadful noise is in his ears. In his prosperity the Destroyer has come upon him."

SHEEP DOG

We sat around in the big room at Naval Headquarters, waiting for the conference to begin. One or two of the merchant captains looked like prosperous business men, but for the most part they seemed ill at ease in their shore togs, which were so similar in blue serge, bluff-bowed black shoes and hard hats that they resembled a uniform. Just now the hats were under their chairs as their owners pored through the pages of mimeographed instructions that would govern the conduct and navigation of the convoy on our passage from the west coast to the Hawaiian Islands.

A retired naval captain entered the room and took his place at a table. "Gentlemen, if there is anything in the Convoy Instructions about which you are in doubt, now is the time to mention it."

There was a fumbling of papers and a self-conscious clearing of throats. "My compass isn't so good," a weather-beaten skipper acknowledged. "That will be an inducement for you to stay well closed up in formation," said the navy captain with a smile. "There must be no stragglers."

A tall, blond, red-faced master with a Scandinavian accent rose to his feet. "Captain, vot shall I do iff my ship is torpedoed?" he asked. "I am thinking of my deck cargo."

The captain made a soothing gesture with his hand. "Now, now; don't worry. Just follow the orders of the Convoy Commander."

The Scandinavian master was not convinced. He shook his head stubbornly. "But my deck cargo; what about my deck cargo?"

"All of you have important cargoes," replied the naval officer. "You'll be all right. Just remember to keep station and don't be a straggler."

On the following morning we sortied and before the last of the convoy had cleared the swept channel the senior destroyer officer was recalled to another task and I found myself in nominal command of more than a score of ships. And while few of them would have won a ribbon in a maritime beauty contest, it was so great a change from two weeks before, when I was merely a head of department in a cruiser, that I felt like the commander-in-chief of the combined fleets as I gazed about at the lead-colored merchantmen that were slowly forming in columns.

We were to meet another group of ships that were coming up from the southward to Join us on the following morning. We headed down for them, in the grey mists and fog that I had half forgotten during three years in the tropics.

The rendezvous with the remainder of the convoy was made easy by four tall, straight, shockingly black columns of smoke that rose up from below the horizon; beacons for any Japanese submarine within fifty miles. Lieutenant Etheridge, the G's chief engineer, gazed at this unorthodox wartime spectacle, then glanced with unconcealed satisfaction at our own smokeless stacks. "Well, now how about that?" he asked. In one of our firerooms someone chose this moment to be careless, and a puff of smoke soared from the stack. The Exec grinned. "How about that, Scotty?" Etheridge jammed his oil-soaked cap on his head and slid down the ladder toward his boilers.

The smoke came from four of a group of New Zealand minesweepers, or small corvettes, that had come out from England and were now on their way home. They were coal burners, and champion smokers in any ocean. We felt in duty bound to send them a signal, for a convoy that so boldly heralds its coming is both socially unpopular and economically dangerous.

From: Escort Commander.

To: N.Z. Corvettes.

I appreciate the difficulties under which you arc steaming, but urge that you use every possible means to stop smoke.

Had we known their officers as well then as we did later, as cruising, drinking and fighting companions, we would have sent a more informal message, but by that time, of course, no signal would have been necessary, for it was impossible to keep those ships from smoking.

One of them replied: "I regret the smoke we are making very much. Every effort has been made to stop same, but this Utah coal is beyond control." And another said "We are doing our utmost to minimize the smoke, but your Utah coal has both good steaming and good smoking qualities."

So it was our coal, and we were stuck with it. Two days out of Hawaii a four-stacker joining up with the escort blinked over: "Smoke from convoy was observed forty miles away." But by then we were used to our four pillars of smoke by day and even an occasional pillar of fire by night, when sparks and flame torched from the stacks of our corvettes.

Each day the ships of the escort tried to get in a little shooting. One afternoon, when we were about to launch a small balloon as a target, a corvette signaled us: "Watch me write 'Utah' across the sky." We suggested that he try Mississippi, as we couldn't question his ability to publicize the State of Utah.

They showed us up a few mornings later when one of them required the services of a doctor to patch a crushed hand. "Please close us and we will send our doctor in our boat," we ordered.

We pulled ahead of the convoy, backed the engines and lowered the whaleboat with our medical officer and his repair kit. The boat had barely cleared the side when its engine coughed and sputtered, and stopped. The crew fretted with it, but they were unable to make it run. The boat drifted around in the trough of a moderate sea and began to roil with violence, and we could see the doctor looking at the convoy that was rapidly drawing near. The little corvette stood over, heaved a line to the coxswain, and pulled the boat alongside. By the time the doctor had finished his work the engine had been repaired, the boat returned to us and we hoisted it aboard without further incident.

The next day we received a signal from one of our freighters. "Have man with persecution complex; alcoholic; propose to use sodium amytal; request proper dosage."

Our doctor wrote out a reply and we heard nothing further for two days, except a brief report that the patient had been placed under confinement. We had half forgotten the matter, and when the same ship hoisted a signal "Man Overboard" we didn't connect it with the case for which our doctor had prescribed. We swung around on the flank of the convoy, came around in the wake of the proper column and had no difficulty in locating a man wearing a red life jacket, floating quietly, waiting to be picked up. A PC boat was near at hand and we ordered her to take the man on board. As we snaked past the convoy flagship she called us by light. "Am informed that the man in the water jumped overboard after escaping from confinement."

We remembered, then, the man with the persecution complex. "That being the case," we replied, "will take man on board G and retain him until arrival in port." Our little PC could use an extra hand with the ship's work, but she had no place for an insane merchant seaman. We sent a boat and relieved her of her passenger. Aboard the G we put a mattress in the lucky bag — a little compartment that was intended as a repository for any clothing that was found adrift about the decks, but which we used, during the next year, as provision storeroom and brig for Japanese prisoners. We gave our guest medical treatment and clothing. He was with us for several days and showed his unbalanced state by spending hours making imaginary long-distance telephone calls to friends on the mainland. I don't know what they told him over the phantom phone, but it must have been amusing, for he seemed to derive much enjoyment from listening. His ship was a Matson Line freighter, and remembering the dollars I had contributed to Matson for trips that my family had made in the Lurline and Matsonia it was a temptation to send their office a bill in four figures, representing the cost of their man's telephoning.

JOURNEY FROM JAVA

On our Sheep Dog assignment it was good to see a score or more ships headed west across the Pacific with weapons of war, but there was melancholy in the thought of how these weapons and materials and men could have changed the picture in the Far East three months earlier when we were being pushed back by the southward drive of Japan. Our convoys then were one-ship affairs, and not very big ships.

No one expected our Asiatic Fleet to hold off the entire Japanese navy or even a sizable portion of it. Our fleet — so called — consisted of a few good submarines, some old four-stack destroyers, a handful of patrol planes and two cruisers. They performed miracles, for so long as they were able to fight.

I was in the Boise then, heading into Cebu, in the Southern Philippines, on the morning of December 8th when the war came to us in the Far East. Because the sight of the large convoy recalls those thin-edged days, and because the Boise spent a good deal of time shepherding convoys, as the G was doing at the moment, this seems as good a place as any for a flashback to those early months, and some incidents that have not been told before.

We left Pearl Harbor in mid-November to escort five ships to Manila and then return to the west coast for an overhaul that was long overdue. In Manila the atmosphere on the surface was outwardly placid; the usual dances at the Manila Hotel — but not at the Army-Navy Club; the Service wives had been sent home months before; the Army was in the field, the harbor was empty of naval ships — crowds packing the Hai Alai Club each evening; pleasant dinners at the Polo Club, under a moon that bathed the green turf in mellow light.

At the Headquarters of the Commander-in-Chief it was different. There was a tenseness in the air, much sending of messages, and a sort of feverish haste that showed the strain under which the Admiral and his staff were working. After fifteen minutes in the flag office — where no one mentioned a word about war — I rushed back to the ship and wrote an airmail letter to my wife, telling her to get out of Honolulu and return to the mainland as quickly as she could — we were not allowed to send radios. This letter would leave in the clipper from Hong Kong, in two days.

Of course she never received it — the clipper was sunk at her moorings in Hong Kong. And it would have been too late, in any case. By that time the show had started.

Admiral Hart ordered us to proceed to Cebu, four hundred and eighty miles south of Manila. We were to arrive on Monday, December 8th, but at 0640 that morning the word was passed over the ship's General Announcing System: "The United States is now at war with Japan."

The pages that follow are from my Boise diary, which at that stage of the game we were permitted to keep.

December 8, 1941

I was sleeping on the forecastle as usual. The ship was in Condition Two, with all anti-aircraft guns fully manned; ammunition up in all turrets; turrets partially manned. It was customary, at sunrise, to send the turret ammunition below and keep the AA batteries manned fully during daylight.

At about 0620 I went below to the wardroom for a cup of coffee before dressing and making my usual morning-watch rounds of the ship. (Note: As First Lieutenant I was responsible for the cleanliness and upkeep. The First Lieut. is the "janitor" and "ship's husband." He looks after the anchors when the ship is mooring or getting underway. He also hoists the planes when they are coming in to be recovered. As Damage Control Officer I was charged with repairing battle damage and keeping the ship afloat and on an even keel. At General Quarters I was in a small compartment deep in the ship, called "Central Station," a sort of clearing house for information to and from the repair parties.)

One or two officers who had just been secured from Condition Two dropped in and asked if I had heard the news. I hadn't, and it seemed just another rumor, until I phoned the bridge and talked with Lieut. Lee, the Communication Officer, who said it was the real McCoy.

At about 0700 we were startled to hear, from radio-Manila, news of an attack on Pearl Harbor by units of the Japanese Fleet. At the moment of writing (ten o'clock) the reports are still sketchy and incomplete, but it would appear that there was an attack in force. Radio Manila just reported that there had been 350 casualties in attacks on air bases in the Hawaiian Islands and that there had been air attacks in the Philippines. The steamer Admiral Cole, two hundred miles south of our present position, reports that she is being bombed. Manila further informs that the Japs have assumed control of the International Settlement in Shanghai.

Other bits of intercepted dispatches indicate that Lualualei is being shelled and that strange destroyers are approaching Waialae. It is needless for me to state just how I feel, with Pauline and Barbara still in Honolulu.

The carpenter, the boatswain and I went into a huddle and listed a number of things to be accomplished. We are stowing the oxygen and other gas bottles in the sand locker; leading out hoses; scattering repair equipment at the various substations; issuing gas masks; setting up our After Battle Dressing Station; getting water to the battle stations, etc.

All of these were last-minute things — the final preliminaries to Clearing Ship for Action. Months earlier we had "stripped ship" and landed the pictures, the rugs, curtains and upholstered chairs, retaining only a few for reasonable comfort. Because our furniture is made of metal, there are few inflammables, and there was no need for any wholesale tossing of things over the side. We had been ready for months; we were ready now.

At about 0730 we reversed course and are now heading for a rendezvous with other units of our pathetically small Asiatic Squadron. I overheard a man say: "I don't mind going to war, but I hate like hell to get cheated out of a liberty." (Having in mind getting ashore today at Cebu.) Another man, in one of the repair parties, said that he would like nothing better than to be ordered to escort the King George V and the Prince of Wales. "I'd sure take good care of 'em," he said.

The ship is very quiet. This is the day that we have trained and sweated to prepare for these past few years. Everyone knows that our methods and our training will soon be put to the test. Well, we'll soon see. Meanwhile, there will be more news from radio Manila at 1100. We hope it will bring news of a decisive thrust on our part.

Tuesday, December 9, 1941

The second day of the war finds the Boise heading north in the Sulu Sea in company with the Houston, Barker and Paul Jones. We met the other three this morning, ten miles south of the light on the southwest corner of the island of Panay. This afternoon we expect to fall in with the Langley, Pecos and Trinity. What we will do then we do not know. Our small Task Group is commanded by Rear Admiral Glassford, until recently Commander, Yangtze Patrol. He brought his tiny Gunboats into Manila Bay the same morning that we arrived there.

We continue the same forms of Readiness Watches that we have grown used to these past months. The Captain, Executive and I split the night watches on the bridge.

The action at Pearl Harbor remains the great enigma. What the casualties were is as yet unknown. Why it was allowed to happen is something that I cannot understand. Regardless of the damage incurred, it is the most humiliating thing that has happened to our Navy since the Chesapeake-Leopard affair in 1807.

The Japanese claim four battleships and four cruisers destroyed at Pearl Harbor. Our morning press says that the West Virginia was sunk and the Oklahoma on fire. Later broadcasts state that casualties on Oahu amounted to 3000. We know nothing definite. I know, though, that I wish I had not brought Pauline and Barbara back to the Islands. What will they do now? Presumably they will be evacuated. It would be welcome news to receive a report of some kind about the Boise wives and families. We are completely in the dark.

It is odd how many unforeseen details arise when war actually comes. Little things — like how to relieve the mess cooks so they can prepare the food; how to modify the cleaning details so that the ship will not become dirty and slovenly and yet permit the gun crews to obtain a little rest. In a day or two all of this will be squared away and we will fall naturally into our modified routine.

It cannot be denied that the last few months, with constant "Condition" watches have seasoned the crew. Our war watches do not differ one iota from the peace watches we have been standing for almost a year. The lookouts are (we hope) more alert, but that is the only difference. The men are accustomed to handling ammunition and to seeing "service" shells around them. So far it has been exactly like a Fleet Problem, as far as we are concerned. I doubt if that will hold for much longer.

Shortly after three this afternoon we joined up with the Langley, Pecos, Trinity and two destroyers. The DDs soon left to return to Manila, so now we are en route with two tankers, one seaplane tender, the Houston, Barker and Paul Jones. We sent a signal to Admiral Glassford, in Houston, saying that the Commanding Officer has no information as to present or prospective destination. He replied "Nor I," and added that we would attempt to get through to the Celebes Sea.

This afternoon we commenced to paint our decks. It was a sorrowful sight to the First Lieutenant to see the blue-black mixture being brushed over our beautiful teak, but our glistening planks make too good a target for aircraft. So the deck scrubbers will get a rest, and the holy stones will collect dust.

We launched aircraft for inner air patrol at 0900 and recovered at 1300. It was the first time they have landed with live bombs under their wings, and more beautiful landings you have never seen — gentle is the word. They wouldn't have cracked an egg.

Little in the air tonight. Apparently the Russians have gained a real victory at Rostov and pushed the Germans back. The Germans announce that, in view of the intense cold, they will not attempt to take Moscow this winter.

A hint to the Captain this morning that we are suffering in tight blouses brought prompt action. We may wear white shirts, which are infinitely cooler.

Still no news from Pearl Harbor, save a press paragraph from Washington that the damage was severe. There are many questions that want answering.

U.S.S. BOISE

December 9, 1941

ORDERS FOR THE DAY — WEDNESDAY, DECEMBER 10, 1941

0000 — Execute ship's routine with the following substitutions and additions.

0600 — All idlers.

Sunrise — Light ship. When ordered, secure from Condition Two, set Condition Three in AA battery and sky-forward. Sky-aft remain in Condition Two.

0630 — Scrub down.

0800 — Quarters for muster and physical drill.

0815 — Continue painting weather decks. Set Condition Two.

Sunset — Darken ship.

Duty Section: 2nd.

Duty Division: 6th.

Notes: (1) The following dispatch from Secnav is quoted:

"The enemy has struck a savage, treacherous blow. We are at war, all of us! There is no time now for disputes or delay of any kind. We must have ships and more ships; guns and more guns; men and more men — faster and faster. There is no time to lose. The Navy must lead the way. Speed-up. It is your Navy and your Nation!"

(2) Men having no allotment to dependents, and desiring same, report to pay office to fill out request. These allotments will be forwarded as soon as possible.

(3) Complete censorship of mail is now in effect. All mail in the Post Office will be given back to the originator, who will readdress it, using plain, unsealed envelope, and retain until instructions are issued regarding delivery to censor.

(4) Any man desiring to work in laundry report to head laundryman.

E. J. Moran

Commander, U.S.N.

Executive Officer

As "Note (4)" indicates — the problems of ship's housekeeping continued, unaffected by the war.

Thursday, December 11, 1941

The past twenty-four hours have been hectic. It has been like the "war of attrition" that we have always contemplated in connection with a campaign in the Pacific. Yesterday afternoon there was a submarine scare. The Langley and Pecos fired several rounds, and the Paul Jones dropped a depth charge. Later our aviators said that there was no sub — only refuse and sea weed of some kind.

We went to G.Q. at dusk, and were just securing when the smoke of two ships was sighted on the starboard bow. We went back to G.Q. and remained there from 1725 yesterday until 0625 this morning. Several times during the night we had a contact, but nothing developed. We modified Condition Affirm to provide ventilation but, even so, three men passed out from heat exhaustion — two in the firerooms and one in a repair party. Twice during the night we had sandwiches and coffee. This morning the ship's company all have eyes that look like two holes in a blanket.

At dawn today we commenced passing through the Pangatarang Passage, which separates the Sulu Sea from the Celebes Sea. On Pangatarang Island we saw a number of natives drawn up on the beach, regarding us with curiosity. The low-lying, palm-fringed islands, with their white beaches gleaming, made a lovely picture, but we were too much concerned with watching the skies for enemy aircraft to pay much attention to the beauties of nature.

It is a distinctly unpleasant feeling, this business of being the hare to Japan's hounds. It is humiliating, too, which is a sensation that we of the American Navy have normally been spared.

The 1245 broadcast from Manila announced the loss of the Prince of Wales and Repulse off Malaya; the sinking of a Jap battleship by our bombers north of Luzon; air raids on Manila; continued Jap landing operations in Malaya; Jap reversals in North Borneo (near our present position) but nothing more about the disaster at Pearl Harbor.

Yesterday the President spoke. He said that we were in this to the finish; that we would dictate the peace terms; that the war marked the end of United States isolationism, etc.

Many of us feel that it is senseless to risk two such splendid cruisers as the Boise and Houston for the sake of escorting a 9 ½ knot tanker like the Trinity, and her consort, the Pecos. The Langley can do better, but we are held to the speed of the slowest ship. So far we have been having miraculous luck. We are now heading for the Macassar Straits. This afternoon we are getting rid of all excess paint, varnish, brightwork polish and other inflammables.

We have almost a thousand miles to go before we reach the southern end of the straits, when, if we are so fortunate as to arrive, we may continue on past Bali and along the western coast of Australia — or turn west towards Surabaya or east towards the Torres Straits.

Just sent my personal silver to a storeroom below the waterline. I have had it in the ship since we gave up our Waikiki house last June, when Paul and Barbara went to the coast. I hope the three of us will be able to use it for years to come. Just now I wouldn't give a nickel for the chances, but we may luck it through. Certainly the crew of this ship may be relied upon to do all that is humanly possible both in inflicting damage on the enemy and in repairing our own casualties.

It is hot. It is steaming, stifling and boiling. We stew in our own juices. When an officer gets up after lying for ten minutes on a wardroom transom he leaves a lake of water. My room today is cooler — only loo. It has been up to 109.

Lieut. Smith has the flu. Last night when it looked like things were about to happen, I sent him to sick bay, where at least he would have company.

We have just learned something that changes our views about escorting these slow old ships, and makes us understand why we didn't seek action with the ships we sighted last night. Our convoy carries all the spare torpedoes, war heads and depth charges for the Asiatic Fleet. If they were to be sunk we'd be up against it. A message from Admiral Hart today telling us that last evening we passed through a large Japanese force. The Japs, impressed, apparently, by the number of our ships, and of course not realizing the non-combatant status of most of them, slunk by without starting anything. For our part, it was common sense to avoid action until the tankers and their cargo are in a place of safety.

Everywhere men are sleeping. Think I'll try it again. I've been averaging about four hours a night, but scored only an hour and a half in the past twenty-four.

Later: The sleep idea was no go. Dead tired, but restless, so stretched out in my bunk and read Stendhal's The Red and the Black for a few moments — then Flight Quarters sounded, with "Double Time" tacked on. A sudden violent squall was coming up so we rushed to recover our two aircraft that had been on anti-sub patrol. Snaked them aboard in jig time. Hope this weather holds — low ceiling, heavy clouds, high wind. Perfect for us.

The lower decks very dirty this morning. Hadn't the heart to pass the word to scrub down, so was pleased to note that it was done anyway. Our people can't abide dirt.

Friday, December 12, 1941

Last night was quiet. My watch on the bridge from 2200 to 0200. Black as your hat until 2340 when a faint light to the eastward announced moonrise.

This morning we sent our convoy on its way — the Trinity to Singapore, the Langley and Pecos to Surabaya, the Barker and Paul Jones to Balikpapan. The Houston and Boise have reversed course and are heading back towards Pangatarang Passage to meet some more ships that got out of Manila. Happily free of a 10-knot convoy we are making good speed, ready to meet anything in our weight.

On my watch last night a dispatch came through announcing that Germany and Italy have declared war on us. That makes it unanimous. There's no question about how it will end, but as the British say, "It will take a bit of doing" — especially should Singapore fall, a contingency that appears not unlikely.

The press is already outlining a plan of action for the United States Fleet. What most of us here would be happy to know is where is the fleet, and how badly was it battered at Pearl Harbor? The continuing silence, save Mr. Early's statement to the press that the damage was more extensive than at first realized, is rather alarming. It would give all of us a shot in the arm to know that the fleet is bound west, ready for action.

Saturday, December 13, 1941

Shortly after sundown last evening we picked up our new five-ship convoy. A peaceful night, with the sea like glass and a heavy phosphorescent glow in the wakes that makes it easy to follow astern of the Houston. The moon came up dimly, after midnight, so we zigzagged until daylight.

On my usual 2200 to 0200 watch the gunnery officer tried, with doubtful success, to have the senior men in the turrets use their periscopes — for training, and to serve as additional lookouts. The following conversation took place between control and the turret captain in number five:

Control: Turret Five, what can you see?

Tur 5: I can 't see nothin'.

Control: Well, keep trying.

After 15 min.

Control: Turret Five, what can you see through your periscope?

Tur 5: I can 't see nothin'. I might as well be lookin' up a broom stick.

Control: Keep trying.

Another 15 min.

Tur 5: Control, I can see a couple of stars on the starboard quarter.

Control: Aye, aye.

Another 10 min.

Tur 5: Control, can I train on the port quarter? Tm getting tired of watchin' the same stars.

Control: Can you see the horizon?

Tur 5: I still can 't see nothin'.

Control: Trying desperately: Can you see the wake?

Tur 5: Wake, hell, I can 't even see the airplane crane.

Control: Resignedly: Aye, aye.

Today has been a day of alarms and squalls. We have gone to G.Q. twice, once when a strange plane was sighted, then again, this afternoon, when someone sighted four ships which turned out to be palm trees on a small island. Hence the verse, to the tune of Armored Cruiser Squadron:

We went to G.Q. in the Celebes,

We deployed the fleet on a group of trees —

And ran in circles in various degrees

In the Asiatic Squadron.

And rain — never such rain. It pelts, pounds, drenches, forces its way inside and immerses you with the strength of a hose. Three times we stood by for emergency recovery of aircraft and each time we were drenched to the skin.

Monday, December 15, 1941

Yesterday morning we stood in to Balikpapan, Borneo. The name is pronounced with the accent on the first syllable of each word, and with a broad A in the papan. It is the oil-refining center of the N.E.I. The harbor is splendid — spacious, deep water, ample dock space. After anchoring until the Marblehead cleared the dock we went alongside with the Houston moored ahead of us, and commenced receiving oil in the late afternoon. Set Condition Two at sunset, and darkened ship. The town completely blacked out, of course, so handling aviation gasoline in drums was difficult.

Boatswain O'Neill took a little stroll along the dock but came back pronto when he heard some Dutch challenges to which he was unable to reply. Shorty Gingras came over from the Houston, wearing the white shirt and shorts that is the Asiatic sea uniform. We must try to get some. Also saw Wells Roberts, Navigator of the H, but not much time for social chatter.

Expected to remain moored until this morning but learned that we were to get out at midnight. Everyone dog tired. Many false starts, until finally it was daybreak when we left the dock. Thought we were all bound for Surabaya but only the Houston and a DD will go. The others, under our skipper as Task Group Commander, will go to Macassar.

The Isabel tells us that little is left of Cavite. They said that about sixty bombers, painted white, came over at 20,000 feet. The first they knew the bombs were hitting.

Macassar, Celebes

Thursday, December 18, 1941

Arrived here Tuesday morning and have been at anchor since. Today the Pecos, Trinity, Langley, Marblehead, Wm. B. Freston, Stewart, Barker and Gold Star came in to join us. The Gold Star — station ship at Guam — was bound back for her island when she received the news of war. Joe Lademann, her skipper, calls his ship the "Free Guam Forces."

Last night the German DNB station announced that the major portion of the United States Asiatic Fleet was at Macassar. They're right — for once.

Macassar

December 20, 1941

Still at anchor here. A very fine message to Admiral Hart and his Fleet from the Chief of Naval Operations expressing "admiration and high approval of your skillful and gallant conduct against great odds," etc.

Surabaya, Java

Christmas Day, 1941

After another trip to Balikpapan we sailed for Surabaya, bringing with us two destroyers and two merchantmen. Arrived off the mine fields Christmas Eve afternoon. After dark, and in the pouring, driving rain that we learn is a daily evening occurrence, we went up channel and anchored off the upper reaches of the Navy Yard at about ten o'clock last night.

I had had all the favorite Christmas carols mimeographed and we were to get together in the wardroom and sing them while Ens. Rosseland played the organ. We managed to get in a few, but those of us who had things to do on deck were unable to be there.

Our pilot got too far to the right of the channel with the result that our condensers are filled with mud, rocks and foreign objects which the engineers have worked all night to remove. So here we find ourselves on Christmas morning. "Merry Christmas" is a hollow greeting.

Surabaya

December 26, 1941

One section of the crew and one half the officers may go ashore from 1630 until 2030. This afternoon John Laffan and I went over, going first by the Holland Pier to see the Liaison Officer, Lieut. Comdr. Olivier, whom I have asked to purchase some additional repair equipment for us. The Langley, Marblehead and Holland are alongside the dock. We crowded into a tiny car with Comdr. Stump and the Doctor of the Langley and drove at breakneck speed to the city, and to the Sempang Club, which proved to be a delightful spot, with plenty of the cold beer that we have been thinking of since we left Manila. Later John and Dave Edwards and I had dinner, then Dave and I played a game of pool of an unusual variety, in which we repeatedly hit the wrong ball. The Javanese servants, standing by to chalk up points that we didn't make, would remark "Minus 5" — pronouncing the word with a short "i."

Chatted with a Dutchman who said his wife and daughter each had a pistol and one shell, and would use them on themselves if the Japs land here. When a Hollander starts talking that way, things are serious.

Everywhere along the water front are barbed wire, soldiers, sand bag emplacements, AA guns and searchlights. The Dutch may not have much but they are using their equipment in a realistic manner. Their subs are doing marvelous work. In that connection we expect to hear great things from our own subs when they come in from their first war cruise. Most of them are still on station.

Surabaya

Sunday, December 28, 1941

Alongside the Rotterdamsche Dock, the Barker moored ahead of us. Enjoyed a long talk with Louie McGlone, whom I have not seen since we were in the Concord together in 1929.

The radio announced tonight that Manila, after being declared an open city, was subjected to a two and a half hour bombing today, with attacks concentrated on the Walled City and the business district. The reaction throughout the country is terrific. As the Herald Tribune put it: "The Japanese have sown the wind. Now they shall reap the whirlwind." In simpler words, the Japs are now recognized as barbarians who abide by no rules of international decency.

Our plans have undergone another change. First we were to go on patrol; now it appears that we will operate under Admiral Doorman of the Netherlands Navy.

After dinner this evening Dr. Stelle and I dropped by the Officers Club, in the Navy Yard, with a pleasant veranda overlooking the harbor. Saw Rear Admiral Purnell for a moment — Chief of Staff to Admiral Hart — the first time I have seen him since Scouting Force days. Many of the Dutch officers had their wives and children, and it made us pretty homesick,

January 2, 1942

We sailed from Surabaya on the 31st — presumably for Port Darwin. Very squally going out of port. Also, new mine fields had been planted so at about 1900 we anchored and remained until daylight. Having spent Christmas Eve entering Surabaya in a driving rain we spent New Year's Eve departing from the same port in the same kind of weather. Charlie Stelle, who suffers more than most of us from heat rash, enjoys these daily cloudbursts. He strips down to shorts and roams the forecastle, a pleased expression on his face as the rain pelts his troubled skin.

New Year's morning found us with Bali close aboard to starboard as we headed south through the Lombok Strait.

We were remarking on the bridge a few minutes ago how much geography we have learned during the past few weeks. Twenty miles to port is Soembawa Island, which none of us could have identified a month ago. Sumba is to starboard, while Flores and Timor are over the horizon. Soembawa, the Sailing Directions tell us, has a 10,000 ft. volcano; it is arid, with 5 to 6 months drought each year, and the natives on the west side speak a different language from those on the east. Sumba, or Sandalwood

Island, is very fertile, the breeding place for the huskiest horses in the East Indies. Timor raises the little ponies that pull the carts in Surabaya.

So now we go to Port Darwin which, we gather, is comparable to other bases that we have known at home — Guantanamo, Montauk Point and Menemsha Bight. And what of the future? One of our radiomen went to a fortune teller in Surabaya. He was told that his ship would be sunk within a month, but that he would not be aboard. The next day he was ordered transferred to Admiral Glassford's office ashore. So?

For years most of our Fleet Problems have dealt with a large and complicated movement, presumably against Japan, with some undenoted base as the objective for the Train that we would carry with us. Now there is no base in the Far East except Singapore, which is fast falling, and we are forced to make our own bases before we can commence to move against the enemy. The Japs have played their hand carefully and cleverly, commencing with the Disarmament Conference at Washington when we agreed not to fortify our far-eastern possessions, while allowing the Japs mandates in the Marshalls and Carolines, which they were not to fortify, a provision that unquestionably they have disregarded in keeping with their interpretations of national honor. If ever we are to have peace in Asia we must remove the menace of Japan for the next century. We must guard against false ideas of sentiment, and disregard the cries of the "Japanese People" who, when the war commences to go against them, will, still skillfully led, disavow the acts of their war lords. We believed that sort of thing once, and see where it got us. Perhaps this war will at least have the benefit of molding a uniform foreign policy which will not be in hazard with every change of Administration.

How eagerly we await news from home, and especially from the Fleet. We do not know the extent of damage at Pearl Harbor, nor when we will start an offensive. The longer we delay the longer it will take to drive the Japs out of conquered territory. The Dutch are not panicky, but they expect a move on Borneo and Java unless we act soon.

Tuesday, January 6, 1942

Arrived Port Darwin this afternoon in the blinding rain storm which seems to be our lot on the forecastle these days — it always pours when we are standing by the anchors.

Went ashore with the Captain, Exec and Captain Thomas, R.N., the British Coordinator, to the Darwin Hotel where we wangled a drink from their almost depleted store.

A plane came in from Singapore, loaded with refugees. I understand that as many as six arrive in a day. Women and children — tired, bedraggled, wondering what next. For weeks they have been coming through from Singapore, Borneo and Malaya. Today one of the women had a child in arms and another aged 2 or 3. The little kit bag with their clothes had to be left here, as the plane could carry no additional luggage.

January 9, 1942

Underway for Surabaya with the Marblehead, five destroyers and the Dutch ship Blomfontein. Sixteen knots, for a change.

Still the same routine. G.Q. at dawn and sunset; constant watches; little sleep. Dominoes with the Exec and Clark and Laffan after lunch and dinner. The Exec just received his fourth stripe — so he is Captain Moran now. Jean Clark's engineers turned out a very passable pair of Eagles for Captain M's collar. They look more like barnyard eagles than mountain ditto, but we are not choosy these days.

January 10, 1942

Last night the Marblehead and two destroyers left us. Tomorrow we receive Admiral Glassford, off Surabaya, then, with our destroyers, we will — finally — "Act Offensively." When the Houston joins we will have three cruisers (each with different characteristics) and about eight destroyers. Also, six PBYs that arrive today at Darwin are expected to move to their Patrol stations tomorrow. Hope they have fighter protection, but doubt it.

Friday, January 16, 1942

We are now a flagship. Wednesday evening we had the Admiral and staff for dinner in the wardroom. A very pleasant occasion. As one of the J.O.s said, "The Admiral is someone you can talk to."

Apparently the Japs are concentrating for a push to the southward. The Admiral said, "It looks like we'll have a fight on our hands two days from now."

Later in the morning Froggy Pound's Pillsbury thought they had a sub so we all got underway hurriedly — the Boise receiving a "Well Done" for her speed. Froggy depth-charged the sub, which turned out to be a school of fish, and he was even cheated out of these as the Buhner put her boat in the water and picked them up, Froggy having no fuel for his own boats. So we all returned to the anchorage, and "out gangways and booms" all over again.

Last night the Ford, Pope and Bulmer came up for fuel. The crews in these old tin cans are pretty darned good. Listened to some of the men batting the breeze on the destroyer forecastles. One of their men, to one of ours: "How you feeding?" Our man, who is eating very well indeed: "Not so good. Everything's running out. How're you feeding?" The destroyer man: "We're O.K. Plenty of dogs and crackers."

Tuesday, January 20, 1942

Koepang Bay, Timor, N.E.I.

Arrived here Sunday after a run from Alor Bay where we were in company for a brief period with the Houston, and fueled from the Trinity. The Marblehead attack group, bound north to deliver a torpedo attack on the Japs at Davao, found themselves north of the enemy when the Japs moved earlier than expected and landed on the east coast of Celebes. They — the M and her DDs — got away without injury.

This afternoon I was on the quarter deck talking with Commander Moran when Lee came up with a dispatch to the effect that 12 Jap warships and 30 transports were sighted north of Balikpapan at dawn. A few minutes later we were ordered to take four destroyers and head for Macassar. So now, at 2015, we are three hours on our way; will pass through Sapi Strait at dawn and continue to the northward. Just what we are supposed to do is doubtful. We can't arrive off Macassar until tomorrow afternoon and even then we will be a hundred miles south of Balikpapan. It may be another false alarm — rush up at high speed, then retire. Taking on 12 Jap cruisers and destroyers is akin to playing Notre Dame on the opening game of the season. Anyway, here we go.

The food situation is about to pinch. I inventoried the storerooms yesterday. There's room enough for a hand ball game in most of them. We have a dab of butter once a day in the wardroom. There are 15 cases of eggs remaining in the ship. No fresh foods, of course, and a very limited supply of canned fruits and vegetables.

A busy three or four hours today in which we streamed and recovered paravanes; transferred mail to a destroyer and fueled the Parrott. Nursing a cold and sweating like twenty horses. Have the sheets changed almost hourly and am out of pajamas.

Friday, January 23, 1942

And so we were on our way, with four destroyers, standard speed —— knots, from Timor to the Postilion Islands, where we were to receive further information regarding our attack on the 12 Japanese warships and

30 transports that were enroute to make a landing on Balikpapan or Celebes.

But again something intervened to keep us from fulfilling our appointment with the enemy. At 0807, while passing through the narrow waters of the Sapi Strait, the ship struck an uncharted pinnacle in what should have been 26 fathoms of water. I was standing in my room at the time, reading a dispatch that the Communication Orderly had just brought in. There was a weird rumbling far below and the ship seemed to hesitate, then shudder again, then pass clear. It felt like riding over a corduroy road in a Model T Ford. I ran out in the passage and found the crew pouring up from below to man their battle stations — they thought we had been shaken by a near bomb hit. Passed the word for repair parties to man their stations, and commenced soundings throughout the ship.

The only sign of damage was water pouring onto the second deck from the feed bottom vent under No. 4 fireroom. We checked further, and it was apparent that we would not be able to make the high speeds required by our mission, so we retraced our steps and put in, that evening, at Waworada Bay on the south coast of Soembawa. There we found the Marblehead and a couple of destroyers, so we fueled them during the late afternoon and evening. A Board of Investigation met, headed by Captain Robinson, of the Marblehead. No blame can attach, as the navigation was above reproach. Just a case of poorly charted waters.

Yesterday morning we sent divers down after daybreak. Found that the damage extended over a distance of 116 feet; A-plating torn from the keel plating, and in two places the keel itself bulged upward for a distance of a foot and a half. Took a dive myself to see what she looked like on the bottom.

Yesterday afternoon the flag decided to shift to the Marblehead, so she came alongside again and we moved them, bag and baggage. We hated to see them go, not only because they were thoroughly agreeable and appeared to like the ship, but because we felt that the grounding was an anticlimax that prevented us from going into action. So now where will we go?

Saturday, January 24, 1942

We are proceeding to Tjilatjap, on the south coast of Java. Our war still seems a side show to the people at home. To us, on the spot, it looks again like a question of too little and too late. With 500 fighter aircraft out here we could chase the Japs from the skies. With a compact striking force of carriers, cruisers and destroyers we could harass the very devil out of the Japs and halt their steady advance towards the N.E.I., which is now proceeding without any opposition to speak of. The morning press says that the oil wells at Balikpapan have been destroyed by the Dutch; that the Japs have attacked New Ireland and New Guinea, and that Singapore is having a tough time.

In the Philippines General MacArthur continues to fight, but here is a sad commentary — the war is barely seven weeks old, and already our mighty Corregidor is running out of ammunition, and we are having to take it to them in two submarines. And 3-inch guns are the largest AA armament the army has. The Japanese won their victory in the Philippines at Washington, in 1922, around the table of the Disarmament Conference, when we agreed not to increase the strength of our installations in this area.

Meanwhile our life aboard the Boise continues its way — fairly tranquilly and in an even tenor. We have Precautionary General Quarters during morning and evening twilight, and Condition 2 on the AA battery the rest of the time. At 0815 we have Quarters for muster and physical drill. We try to keep the ship up as best we can, bearing in mind the watches that everyone has to stand, and the consequent lack of sleep.

At about 1130 Commander Moran, John Laffan, Jean Clark and I usually get together for a domino game and continue it after lunch for a few minutes. Then more work, maybe a brief nap, and it is almost time for supper, which is at 1630, because of G.Q. and the watches. By eight or eight-thirty 'most everyone is in bed. My room is so hot, seldom under 102-104, that I sleep on deck, on a cot. In spite of the fact that I park it under the overhang forward of the Captain's cabin the frequent nightly rains pour in, and more often than not, I am chased below, soaking wet, sometime during the night. So we have designed a "Cozy Cruiser Cot Comforter," that fits over the cot like the rounded top of a covered wagon. I tried it out last night. It works perfectly and, despite the jeers of some of my shipmates, I had two requests this morning for more of the same. So maybe I'll have some dry sleeping for a change.

Tuesday, February 3, 1942

Enroute Tjilatjap, Java, to Colombo, Ceylon.

Much has happened during the past few days. We arrived at Tjilatjap on Sunday the 25th of January and, after an expert job on the part of the pilot, and a couple of scares in the narrow channel, moored alongside the dock. The following day Commander Brunner, of Admiral Hart's staff, and Mr.

Convert, a Dutch Naval Architect, came on board to inspect the damage. We showed them the drawings we'd made, based on reports from the divers, and there was much palaver in the Captain's cabin.

A change of command ceremony while we were there. Captain Moran now has the ship. Leon Manees, who had the Bulmer, will come as Exec.

There was little to do in Tjilatjap. The town is small. There is a second-rate hotel and a bare little club where you can get warm beer. Eddie Pearce and I made the rounds of the native market and bought a few trinkets. Later, through the wife of a Dutch officer, I bought a little batik sarong and scarf, and a white waist for Barbara. The crew bought out practically all the canned goods, preserves, Jam and cookies that the town stores had in stock.

The old Asheville was in port — looking strangely ancient with her high stack. She came down from China. Not a great deal that she can do.

On Sunday learned that another fight is forthcoming to the eastward around the south coast of Celebes and in the vicinity of Ambon. The Captain sent a dispatch saying that we were ready for offensive action — —. Forgot to mention that we negotiated for the purchase of about ten tons of rock, and we spent a pleasurable afternoon toting it aboard and passing it by hand to the fireman bilges where it was stacked on the deck over the flooded feed bottoms.

Yesterday the radio carried the news that the American Fleet had attacked the Marshall and Gilbert Islands. It was good news.

The chief mate of a Dutch merchant ship astern of us told of being in a fifty-ship convoy from South Africa to England in the early days of the war and having so many ships torpedoed that the British admiral ordered the convoy to disperse — his ship going to Trinidad then to Halifax and finally to Liverpool where they were subjected to a terrific bombing, in which he apparently did well, as he was awarded the D.S.O.

Saturday, February 7, 1942

Still enroute to Colombo, where we expect to arrive the day after tomorrow. Last night met a British hospital ship bound from Colombo to Batavia. She was lighted from stem to stern, with red crosses, etc., in addition to navigational lights.

A couple of days ago we sighted, in the afternoon, a submarine on the surface, at a range of about 26,000 yards. Went to G.Q. and launched a plane, with Lieut. Marcus, our senior aviator. The sub submerged in a crash dive that threw spray high into the air. Marcus went up-sun and waited. Presently the sub came again to the surface and Marc dove for him with bombs under the wings and an itchy finger on the release. Just in time the sub flashed the proper recognition signal and someone waved a British white ensign. She was the British sub Trion. Yesterday we understood the London news broadcast to say that the Admiralty announced that the submarine Trion was long overdue and must be considered lost. The same one that we sighted? She didn't seem in distress, and she made no request for supplies.

Head of Departments Conference this morning to discuss the work we would like done at the forthcoming Navy Yard period.

The Japs have raided Surabaya. Also, we received word that the Houston was hit by a bomb in the vicinity of No. 3 turret. At about the same time the Marblehead reported planes near her and requested that fighters be sent. Later Red Hourihan, in the Paul Jones, gave an amusing plain English play-by-play description of an attack on his ship. It went something like this: "Being bombed. It missed. Here they come again. Another miss. Here's another. A close one. They look like they're leaving now. No hits; no errors. The attack is over."

So, with the Boise out of the picture for at least four or five weeks; with the Houston badly damaged; with the Marblehead still running around on three engines, the "U.S. Naval Forces, Southwest Pacific" consists of a handful of old destroyers and a few submarines.

Yesterday radio Tokyo announced that in an air attack on a large convoy they sank the deRuyter, sank one Java-class cruiser, damaged another and damaged one Marblehead-class cruiser in addition to sinking many ships of the convoy. Those ships were escorting a large convoy, from Surabaya, but doubtless the Japs exaggerated as usual.

Colombo to Bombay

Friday, 20 February, 1942

We arrived at Colombo without incident. The harbor very crowded — two days later there were —— ships in port, moored bow and stem in parallel lines. Found the drydock obligated for several days ahead. Local officials and the R.N. seemed to feel that our repairs could be done, so we sat down to wait.

Commander Howard Lammers, whom I last saw as Executive Officer of the California, is our Naval Observer at Colombo. The second evening after we arrived he asked the Captain, the Exec and me for dinner at the house that he occupies together with Lord and Lady Mandeville. The former, Lieutenant Commander, Viscount Mandeville, left the navy several years ago, but returned for the war. Most of his classmates are now cruiser captains. Both he and Lady M were most kind to us during our stay. They had the three of us for dinner, and later in the week they drove the Captain and me to Kandy. On the way we passed several elephants going about their business of transporting heavy weights, and saw three wallowing in a little stream. Barbara would have loved it.

Kandy was disappointing. We saw the Temple of the Tooth, where a tooth of Buddha is a most treasured relic which is brought into public annually at a great celebration held each August when there are elephants galore, with fanciful trappings and gaily ornamented tusks. The hotels at Kandy, like those in Colombo, are filled with women and children refugees from Singapore and Malaya — "White Cargo," our sailors call them.

One afternoon while we were still waiting for that dock we went to the zoo. Unique in that you may buy lion or tiger cubs; keep them until they are large enough to devour the living-room rug, then return them, probably at a discount. The zoo elephants do all the hauling, as well as show off their tricks with the mahouts. There was a forty-foot python with a bandage around his amidships section for a distance of about three feet — the first python we had ever seen with the equivalent of a soft patch at frame 91. They feed him a forty-pound pig every four weeks. Magnificent black panthers in a cage. The Indian zoo keepers go quite close to reach out and scratch these jungle pussies behind the ears — then reach out just as far for the tip of a few annas that they expect you to give them.

Other impressions of Colombo — American sailors having their pictures taken at the Cinnamon Gardens, seated in a rickshaw. The "movie set" atmosphere of the Grand Oriental Hotel (which we called the Hotel Conspicuous because it was marked "conspic." on the chart), with hundreds of women and children, Australian soldiers, bluejackets of our own, British and Dutch navies, Tamil women selling lace, barefoot waiters wearing their hair coiled on top of their heads and with round tortoise-shell combs surmounting their coiffure. The Galle Fasse Hotel, out of bounds for enlisted men, with officers of all the various armies and navies. More especially the dapper officers of the —— Hussars and the chain mail epaulets on the shoulders of the khaki tunics that they wore in the evening. The major with the monocle who outranked them all but never so much as loosened the monocle. The stories of how they use their old cavalry orders in their tanks — "Squadron at the gallop, charge!" The amazing whiskers and beards that some of them had. Lieut. Col. Lucas, almost seven feet of Royal Marine, who is here to organize Commando units, as he has been doing at home under Admiral Sir Roger Keyes.

They decided, eventually, that they were unable to do our work at Colombo, and we were ordered to Bombay. It's quite right. They are much too crowded in Ceylon to obligate their dock for a long period. The dockmaster told me they had sent up country for 14,000 square feet of sandalwood from which they intended to construct our docking blocks and shores. We regret that lost opportunity. Docking a cruiser on sandalwood is something new in maritime circles. We would have been a sweet-smelling ship!

Bombay

February 21, 1942

Arrive here this morning shortly after eleven, after an uneventful passage from Colombo.

In the afternoon the Captain, Jean Clark, Squidge Lee and I went ashore to contact the Naval Observer, Lieut. (jg) Phillips Talbot, and, through him, the British Authorities, to see if we can hasten the docking. Apparently not much doing over the week-end, and we hear that the large drydock is in use, so it looks like more delay. Brief drive around the city, then I returned on board to take the duty. Bombay is the first city of any size we have seen since leaving Manila. It looks to be a fascinating and mysterious sort of place — probably not lacking in dirt and smells.

Bombay

Sunday, February 22, 1942

Hope to get started with the work tomorrow.

Monday, February 23

Conference this morning. It was decided that the work could be accomplished here, though the length of time required will not be known until we can dock and have a look at the bottom.

Singapore fell while we were still at Colombo. This place, too, is full of refugees. Tragic little notices in the papers — like "Information desired as to the whereabouts of Forrest Lake, aged 8, last seen on a raft in the Sunda Straits." A young woman refugee from Malaya has been haunting the docks. Today a ship came in and she saw her husband standing at the rail. But their joyous reunion became horribly tragic — each thought the other had their three children.

We met an American and his wife who have several refugees living with them. One is a girl of twenty-two or three. Her ship was bombed and sunk after leaving Singapore. She found a bit of wreckage and drifted up on an island after several hours, with no clothes except her very brief pants. Later two men from the same ship managed to get to the island. The three of them lived there for ten days, then were taken off by a passing ship. Tonight the girl was supposed to dine with her fellow castaways but at the last minute she refused. She said no one had thought about clothes, or the lack of them, on the island, but now that they were back to civilization she was overcome with embarrassment.

24-27 February

Still waiting for the drydock to become available.

Saturday, 28 February

The Captain, Exec and I went to the Bombay Races this afternoon. Bet on seven out of the nine races and lost 5 rupees — about a dollar and a half. Not bad, for me.

The first time I have ever seen a "daily triple." Today it paid 13,000 rupees — $3900 approximately.

A colorful race course, with more color in the stands. Red-coated Sikh guards around the Governor's box; a large enough sprinkling of rajahs and Indian potentates to make us feel that we are seeing the Lives of a Bengal Lancer in technicolor. On the edge of a broad lawn adjacent to the stands the various Bombay clubs have small race course branches — in marquees, with little tables, where you can have tea or drinks between races,

Sunday, March 1, 1942

Unloaded ammunition into lighters. Finished the job in the afternoon, to the great astonishment of the local Ordnance Officer, who expected it to be a two-day affair. We've loaded and unloaded this ammunition so many times that the crew say they've carried it by hand farther than we will ever fire it.

Tuesday, March 3, 1942

This afternoon Chief Carpenter Thomas and I inspected the blocks that have been prepared for our docking. The work was done by the Royal Indian Navy Dockyard — and a nice job. There are no sanitary connections in the dock; the freshwater pressure is low and there are no 440 volt mains, so the chief engineer will have his hands full trying to use his own generators and I will have worries with regard to water pressure for the fire mains.

Rode one of the Governor's horses for an hour or so; the last bit of playing for a while. The Governor's bodyguards are Sikhs. Members of that sect do not cut their hair, but if they are in the army they get it out of the way by winding it under their turbans, and plaiting and combing the beard, then arranging it under the chin in a net.

Wednesday, March 4

Entered drydock this morning. Found the damage to be identical with our divers reports. There is much work to be done. The keel badly distorted; the A-plating ripped and torn.

The four weeks in drydock were the busiest I have ever spent. The repair force of the Boise, under Chief Carpenter (later Lieutenant) Harold Thomas, performed an amazing job in record time. Months earlier we had sent several men to the Fleet Welding School. The experience they gained paid dividends at Bombay. These men voluntarily restricted themselves to the ship until our work was done. During the last three days and nights none of us slept, for it seemed that we would never get the bottom tight. When the outer plating was on, we went inside and welded the intercostals, the ribs, frames and longitudinals. Here we were working against galvanized surfaces, and the resultant fumes were overpowering. We tried to buy milk, as an antidote for the poisoning to which we were exposed. There was no cow's milk to be had, so we ordered buffalo milk — sixteen gallons a day, until the welding was done. It was pretty potent stuff, but the men liked it.

Finally we finished the job — and received orders home, for the Boise hadn't been given the additional anti-aircraft guns that cruisers of her class were supposed to have. Our homemade bottom, to our mild surprise, held up on the long journey across the Pacific. In our home Navy Yard they put us in dock and, feeling like Midshipmen waiting to learn the results of an examination, we went into the dock with the Navy Yard experts. They scrutinized our work rivet by rivet, seam by seam. Finally they said "You can flood the dock and take her out. It's as good as we could do."

Most of the leading shipfitters and carpenter's mates who did the work now hold commissions. Many of them again had an opportunity to show their skill when the Boise was damaged in the night action of October 12-13. Damage Control is unglamorous and frequently unspectacular but twice in the past eighteen months the repair parties of the Boise have been directly responsible for saving their ship when it was in danger of destruction. They are not atypical. The same skill is shown by every

Damage Control organization in the fleet. "Keep 'em floating" is their watchword.

We broke our journey home by visiting two ports in Australia. Here we found a sister ship from whose officers we learned the full effects of the attack on Pearl Harbor. Here we received five months' mail and a supply of American cigarettes. Here, too, we talked with officers we had last seen at Manila and Surabaya, who gave us first-hand accounts of the battles in the Bali Straits and the Java Sea that had taken place during our absence.

On the night of the sea fight off Bali, Lieut. Comdr. Wilford Blinn, commanding the destroyer Pope, was in column astern of the Netherlands destroyer Piet Hein. Just before contact with the enemy Blinn received word that the after whaleboat fall had carried away, and that the boat, hanging by one fall, was beating against the ship's side. There was no time to try and save it. He ordered the other fall to be cut and the boat cast adrift. As his orders were in the process of being carried out the action commenced and the Piet Hein was struck almost at once, and blew up. Aboard the Pope the repair party, acting according to doctrine, tripped a lever as soon as the first salvo was fired, which jettisoned the partially filled drums of diesel oil boat fuel. This was in accordance with doctrine, to reduce the fire hazard aboard the destroyer.

The battling ships drew quickly away, leaving the survivors of the Piet Hein swimming in the Java Sea. They had been in the water only a few minutes when one of them sighted a whaleboat, and all of them clambered aboard. Soon after daybreak they saw several steel drums floating near by. They towed one of them to the boat, opened it and found it about half full of diesel oil. They filled the fuel tank, started the motor and, several hours later, arrived safely at Surabaya, where they could scarcely wait to tell of the American destroyer that had dropped her boat and fuel over the side when they saw the Piet Hein blow up.

Blinn's ship survived the action, but went down later in the Battle of the Java Sea, along with the Houston, Pillsbury and other fine ships. We were fighting a war on a shoestring in those months.

Before we reached the west coast I received orders to command the new destroyer G. It was good news. Every officer wants his own command and, to my mind, there is no more fascinating work in the fleet than duty in destroyers. I hated to leave my shipmates in the Boise, but there is always the knowledge that you will see them again, for every new duty brings meetings with old shipmates from earlier days. Of course we didn't know where the G might be. It was a surprise to find her moored alongside the dock at the navy yard, just a few hundred yards from the berth to which the Boise was assigned. She was a streamlined beauty that had been in commission slightly more than a year; long enough for all the kinks to be ironed out. I flew east for a one-day visit with my family, whom I had not seen, with the exception of ten days seven months earlier, for more than a year, then returned to California and moved my boxes aboard the G. My new shipmates assembled on the forecastle in dungarees and khaki; no fancy change of command ceremonies in war; I read my orders, spoke a few words to the crew, then turned to Lieutenant Peters, the Executive Officer, who had been in temporary command. "I relieve you, sir." For better or worse, the G was now mine. With this ship, and the fighting Task Force that we expected to join, I felt that we would reverse the road that the Asiatic Fleet had been forced to travel. The Journey from Java was over. The Journey to Japan was getting underway.

CANDY CARAVAN

"Candy" was our name for Guadalcanal from the time of our initial attacks on the Eastern Solomons until the day, six months later, when the Japanese High Command on the Island escaped in destroyers during darkness, leaving the remnants of their shattered army to be killed or captured by General Patch's American Forces.

Between the 7th of August and the Jap surrender the G made thirteen trips to Candy, occasionally on a straightforward striking mission with other destroyers or a Major Task Force; sometimes on a solitary search for Jap subs or hidden enemy emplacements along the coast, but generally as a unit of the screen that guarded our transports and supply ships. To use destroyers as escorts for a convoy meant that our combatant Task Forces must be correspondingly weakened, for we had no spare destroyers, and any of us that went with the transports were "on loan" from the carriers, cruisers and battleships. Again it was a case of doing the best we could with what we had. It was fortunate that our destroyers were well built and that our engineers were able to perform minor miracles in the way of upkeep while their ships remained underway. We couldn't afford to break down.

Until we learned the intricacies of the various channels, and until the highways and byways of the sea lanes became as familiar as the garden path at home, the navigational hazards seemed as great a menace as the enemy. The charts abound with such cheering bits of information as "Mariners are warned to navigate this area with great caution." "It has been reported that the coastline lies three miles to the east of its plotted position." "H.M.S. Grampus, in 1873, reported strong currents setting towards the reefs." "These waters have not been fully investigated. Uncharted reefs and shoals abound." It can be understood that this sort of thing does not have a soothing effect on the duodenal condition of captains and navigators.

The enemy did not have these navigational disadvantages. For years Japanese "fishermen" had sounded, plotted, sketched and photographed, until for them there remained no uncharted reefs and shoals. The British Navy, facing the same rigid economies as our own, chose not to use their limited funds for survey work in the Solomons. Any admiral, forced to decide between hydrographic research in an area of remotely possible future combat, or using his money to develop the marksmanship of his fleet, is almost obliged to buy bullets every time. But it was deplorable that we had to learn these waters the hard way. To lose a ship in combat is regrettable. To lose a ship, or to have one so badly damaged that it must leave the fighting area for repairs because of unknown navigational dangers, is not merely tragic, but an event that can bear seriously on the conduct of the campaign, especially when you are operating with limited strength.

When the Boise, going north from the Indian Ocean to the Java Sea, ripped her bottom open on a pinnacle in a spot where the chart showed a least-depth of 26 fathoms, she was immobilized for several months at a time when Admiral Hart needed every gun and every plane that he could possibly obtain. When a destroyer, navigating with habitual caution, ploughed into an uncharted reef in the South Pacific, and had to be sent home for repairs, her Task Force Screen had to cover a proportionately wider arc, and their fighting strength was reduced by the —— torpedoes, five guns and many dozen depth charges that went back to the Yard with the damaged ship. Any reduction in our fleet with no corresponding loss to the enemy is expensive payment for lack of navigational knowledge. In terms of lost services the cost cannot be tallied. In terms of dollars and cents, we could survey and chart every unknown area in the South Pacific for the price of one destroyer.

A few thousand yards to the north of Taivu Point, which marks the eastern entrance to Lengo Channel along the coast of Guadalcanal, there lies a navigational hazard that provided an invariable thrill for each destroyer making its initial visit to the area. Hutchinson Reef looked like a large submarine and in consequence it was so repeatedly attacked that we thought it might be a good idea to anchor a buoy over the shoal, with a placard "This is not a submarine. Save your depth charges."

A mile or so beyond was "the island that looked like a ship." One night early in the campaign when we were moving up Indispensable Strait with our Task Force, two destroyers were detached to proceed ahead as scouts. They stood up the strait at high speed, the remainder of the Task Force following, and all ships at G.Q. as every indication pointed to action. There was silence from our scouts until shortly after midnight, when they began talking to one another about something that one of them had sighted. We heard the senior ship give orders to illuminate, preparatory to opening fire, and we peered ahead for the sight of gun flashes on the horizon. When no flashes came, and there were no amplifying reports by voice radio, our admiral spoke up and asked the scouts what they had found. They replied briefly, and we seemed to detect an embarrassed note in the voice that came over the air. "False alarm," they said. It was, of course, the little island that looked like a ship. It was not until sometime later that the officers of one of the scouts told us that when the order had been given to "illuminate," they were startled to see a faint glow from the searchlight platform, instead of the piercing beam that they expected. An immediate and indignant query from the bridge produced the information that someone had neglected to remove the searchlight cover at sunset. The light was on, but only a pale gleam penetrated the thick folds of the canvas.

A month later the G was standing into Candy in the early morning hours ahead of a convoy when Gun Control reported something to starboard. "The course of the enemy is zero nine zero; speed fifteen knots," said the Gunnery Officer. The navigator and I looked at each other. It was possible for a ship to be on that bearing, but the range put him south of Sealark Channel, in an area of reefs. Control was ordered to check. "He's reduced speed," "Guns" reported. Then — "He's stopped." The navigator grinned, and I ordered Control to "Stand Easy." Once more we had found the island that looked like a ship.

After a few trips "up the line" we swung through the narrow channels between reefs with confidence, and shaved the shoals at any speed without having to rely on information recorded by some ship in the early nineteenth century.

The G learned the ropes soon after we moved into the Solomons when we were ordered, with a sister ship, to inspect the coast line of Guadalcanal and the two neighboring islands, San Cristobal and Malaita, to determine if the Japs were using any of the numerous coves as hideouts for submarines. That five-day experience — while it brought forth no Jap sub bases (the negative information was helpful) — enabled us to qualify as navigators for the Eastern Solomons. It also qualified us as an aviation rescue vessel, as we picked up the crews of three torpedo planes that had been forced to land in Indispensable Strait during darkness when they ran out of fuel after making an attack on a group of Japanese destroyers.

We sighted the crew of one plane — three men in a rubber raft — at ten in the morning. They were uninjured and well supplied with emergency rations and water. There was no wind; the early morning sun had dried their clothes, and they were rowing placidly across the calm Strait to the coast of Guadalcanal. They had not been greatly concerned until they sighted us. They thought we were Japanese and became most unhappy about the whole situation until they made out our bow numbers and caught a glimpse of our colors flying from the short staff abaft the searchlight platform. Our Chief Boatswain's Mate, with the sailor's eye to loot, easily prevailed on the aviators, when they were moved by the initial feeling of relief at being rescued, to give him their parachutes and rubber life raft. The parachutes were made into scarfs; the raft became a punt from which we could paint the water line on the rare occasions when we were at anchor long enough for paint to dry.

Toward midafternoon when we were poking our nose into a broad cove called Kau Kau Bay, near the southeast tip of the island, three red rockets flared up from the jungle near the beach and burst high over the tops of the trees. Undecided whether it meant friends in trouble or Japs luring us into easy range of their shore batteries, as the enemy positions along this section of coast were not well defined, we steamed closer inshore with guns ready. Two more rockets went up, then a score of men burst through the jungle and ran to the water's edge, waving enthusiastically. We sent in an armed boat's crew — following with the ship until the water shoaled. This time our bag was six more aviators.

The Fantail Gazette, quick to lampoon an incident where we loaded for bear and brought home a rabbit, carried the following paragraph:

Solomon Islands:

A daring daylight raid on enemy-infested strongholds was made yesterday by the intrepid crew of the whaleboat. This fearless expedition, led by Lieut. (jg) J. A. Camera, stormed the very throats of the Japanese batteries.

Armed only with twenty sub-machine guns, twelve .45's, several lengths of manila line and an assortment of homemade knives, the group succeeded in terrifying half a dozen ill-fed, ill-housed and ill-clothed natives. The raid was pronounced a triumphing success, and harbinger of greater feats in the future. All hands received an extra measure of forward-fireroom coffee as their reward.

These torpedo-plane crews had pumped their fish into two Jap destroyers before they were forced to land on the water, close in to shore, out of gas. When they sighted us they had just finished a meal of baked bananas, and were being led by the friendly natives to a Catholic Mission from which a trail wound over the mountain range toward our own lines.

These natives are the fiercest-looking people that I have ever seen, not excepting the Fiji Islanders. Strongly built, their skin a brilliant, shiny black; dressed in a short skirt, with bangle charms pulled tightly around the upper arm, they seem to eye you with speculation as to how you will cook up when tossed in the pot. To the Missionaries of all denominations, who have labored for years under conditions that were harrowing, and always difficult, should be given credit for diverting the dietary instincts of the natives; teaching them English of a sort, treating some rather horrible tropical diseases, and implanting some principles of Christianity by precept and example.

There were several destroyers at Guadalcanal and Tulagi, nursing transports and cargo ships; patrolling around them during daylight; taking them clear of the area, or to Tulagi, at night.

For some weeks the Japs had made no effort to reinforce their troops, and since their last shellacking in mid-November they had stopped coming in during darkness to bombard Henderson Field and our shore positions. But now there was no moon, and it was logical that the Tokyo Express, or at least one fast section of it, would resume the nightly dashes into Candy. We organized our destroyers in a Striking Group and made plans to meet the Nips.

Condition Reds and sub alerts kept us on our toes and out of our bunks for three days and nights. We needed match sticks to hold our eyelids open. The wardroom coffee, which someone suggested could be used as low-octane fuel for a jeep, lost its potency and had no more effect than water.

And the heat! On the bridge we sweltered, but in the engine rooms they boiled in temperatures above 130 degrees Fahrenheit. If you tried to take a quick shower between air raids you were covered with sweat before you climbed into your clothes. We lived in a steel box which hugged the heat and wrapped it close around us. Even at dusk, when black clouds tumbled across the mountains and the heavens descended in a mighty deluge there was no relief, for moisture condensed within the ship and dripped down the bulkheads or drifted about in wisps of foggy dampness. We could not get dry. We could not keep cool. And there was no rest.

On the heels of a downpour that closed out all landmarks ahead we ploughed through the narrow channel at an indiscreet speed, trying to beat out another squall that raced up astern. A few yards on either beam the wind-swept surf poured across the reefs and coral heads in a whirl of milky lather. The beads on the Navigator's forehead were not caused entirely by the heat, and on the forecastle the First Lieutenant and his men, standing by to let go the anchor, viewed the situation with mistrust and glanced up at the bridge with an air of hoping that we knew what the hell we were doing.

Just as the rain enveloped us we found our hole, backed down and dropped the hook. The wind hit with a roar and spun us around on the anchor chain in half the time it would take to twist her with the engines. A great spot, Tulagi. I remembered the emphatic sincerity of the Monssen's Captain when he said "I loathe that place!"

The other destroyers had anchored ahead of us, and were at "short stay," ready to heave around and get clear at a second's notice. I wanted to go aboard the R and talk with Roy Hartweg, for he would be in command of the second section if our night action developed. The whaleboat came alongside and I dropped wearily into the puddle of water that covered the seat. Slickers were no good. We were soaked to the skin, but the rain was cool and refreshing. We pulled off our hats and let it beat in our faces.

I had been in Roy's cabin only a few minutes when my Exec burst in. "The Express is on its way. Eight destroyers. Our planes saw 'em coming down the slot late this afternoon. The signal just came through."

We broke out a chart and plotted in the Jap positions. Allowing them maximum speed they couldn't arrive off Esperance before midnight. It was now eight-thirty. There was no great hurry. The welcoming committee had plenty of time to get to its station. I returned to the G and wrote out a brief order to the ships, putting into effect our prearranged plan. Then the Heads of Departments and I brushed the sleep from our eyes; sent for more coffee, and explored again the familiar face of the chart, studying it to see if we had set the trap so that the Nips could not avoid it; prodding our Battle Plan to test it once more for watertightness.

By the time we went to General Quarters the rain had stopped and the tropical night was thick black velvet. The reports came in to the bridge: "Main Battery manned and ready. Torpedo Battery manned and ready." Machine guns. Damage Control. Accompanied by a faint hiss from the safety valves the engineers reported ready, with full boiler power and steam to the throttles. With no wind or current to set us drifting we hove in the chain until the anchor was underfoot, barely touching bottom. We sent a signal that the other destroyers were ready to attack, then turned up the loud speaker in the pilot house so we could listen to the PT boats that were already on station.

The PT's had a language all their own, a jargon that made Double Talk sound like the purest and plainest English.

It has all been changed now, but that evening, when we waited for permission to attack, the air was filled with nostalgic reminders of less hectic times when ships showed lights, when there were movies on deck, and sailors rode through the quiet streets of Panama in a pleasant aroma of frangipani and alcohol, the bells of the carrametas and the clop of the horses' hoofs making soft music in the night.

There was an exchange of pleasantries between a PT and a plane that must have been skimming the waves. "What's the matter?" demanded the PT. Silence from the plane, while the pilot checked to see that he had a full allowance of wings, rudders and engines. "Nothing," he replied: "Why?" The PT skipper, in a bored tone: "We thought for a moment that you were going to come aboard."

As the hour approached for the Tokyo Express to arrive, tension mounted along the air waves.

—— from ——: "Do you see anything?"

—— from ——: "Naw. Is that you riding on my tail?"

—— from ——: "Move over; you're too damned close."

From far out in right field came a plaintive call that we were to hear at intervals all night. "This is ——. Wha-ats the do-ope?" ——'s radio must have been off-frequency. He couldn't hear anything, he couldn't get anyone to answer him. His station kept him from the scene of the action, and he wanted desperately to know what was going on. Every few minutes, for five hours, —— tried to find out the dope. He used simple questioning, polite entreaty, querulous demand, profane invective. But to no avail. That night —— didn't get the dope.

—— from ——: "—— Bearing Two Nine Five distance six miles from ——. Attack! Attack!"

On the bridge of the G we shook off an overpowering weariness and listened to the PT's as they tore in for the enemy to lash out with torpedoes ("pickles," in PT language).

"—— they're headed for you. Cut 'em off — cut 'em off."

"They're headed for the ——. Get in there! What the hell's the matter?"

"O.K. — O.K. I've fired my pickles — we got him — I'm getting out of here."

"All —— Close in — Close in."

Toward Savo there was a red glow — a sudden blinding flash of flame. —— had caught a pickle.

That was swell. The PT's were in there with everything they had. But their pickles were limited in number. Now the destroyers could go after the enemy with our own tin fish and comparatively heavy guns. Scotty Etheridge came up from the engineroom, mopping his sweating face. "'Bout time for us to get in there, isn't it?"

"Looks like they're saving us for the Army Game," said the Exec. All around me, on the bridge, the crew muttered impatiently. This fight was the tonic we needed. Exhaustion was forgotten. It had been seventy-two hours since we slept, but we were wide awake.

"Call radio and ask Brundage if he's sure we haven't missed any messages. Why the hell don't they let us go in?"

Lieutenant Brundage came to the bridge. "Captain, we've got a watch on every possible frequency. We haven't missed a thing."

"Send the SOP another signal to remind him we're ready and waiting."

There was less chatter now from the PT's. Could this mean that the enemy was retiring before we could go after him? There was a roll call and two PT's did not answer. The others formed line and commenced to search. "There's some wreckage over here. I'm picking two men out of the water."

By four a.m. all was quiet. The Tokyo Express, mauled by the PT's, had reversed course and gone home. Angrily we secured from G.Q. and told our destroyers to "stand easy." At dawn we got underway to nurse the transports for another day. As the R came past her signal light began to blink. "MSG from the Captain of the R, sir, 'Regret that your hands were tied and you couldn't take us out last night.'" It was a bitter pill. We had been set to knock the Express right off the tracks, and someone had let us down. Suddenly we were dead tired again, but no one wanted to sleep.

On one visit to Guadalcanal with a cargo ship we began to believe that we would be there for the duration, for each day the officers of the merchant ship would report that they would not be ready on the morrow. This ship was a pain in the neck, but there were compensations, for, not being a naval vessel, her officers could keep a bottle or two for those tired moments. To sink in a soft chair at the end of the day and have someone ask, "What'll you have with yours; soda, or plain water," never failed to cushion the shock of the inevitable announcement that a couple of hundred more tons of cargo had been discovered under the dunnage in Number Two hold, and that the job would not be finished on schedule.

Her voice radio call was "Frank," but we amended it to "Macbeth" when her unloading prediction became a dreary repetition of "tomorrow and tomorrow and tomorrow."

In general the merchant ships are on their toes, keeping as well closed up as their speed will allow; holding their stations smartly and answering signals promptly, considering the meagerness of their personnel. For their masters and mates we have a whole-hearted respect. Without benefit of gyro compasses or fancy navigational gear they take their slow, awkward, single-screw vessels through reef-strewn passages with boldness and confidence. They are good sailormen.

There was one merchantman that added a few grey hairs and scared the wits out of the Galloping G. We brought her out on a broiling morning when the visibility was unlimited; every reef and shallow clearly defined against the dark blue of deep water.

We were feeling pretty chipper as we zigged back and forth across the advance of our sluggish friend, who was giving her all to make a speed of 9.2 knots. Clearing the reef that stretched out past Rua Sura Island we put on right rudder and hoisted a signal for the new course.

Instead of standing on and following us our pal turned with us, and headed for the reef. He hadn't far to go, for we were taking a few short cuts in view of the unusually clear weather.

We waited for him to correct his mistake, but on he ploughed. We had a grandstand seat for a messy bit of maritime hara-kiri that was going to take place in just about five minutes.

I ordered "Hard Right" and "Tell the engineers to give us all they can make." The Exec yanked at the whistle, and with flags spelling the international signal "You are standing into danger," the G swung back and raced toward the acci-dent that was about to happen. We drove up along his port side, thirty feet from his rusty strakes, and sang out through a megaphone: "Come left immediately. There's a reef ahead!"

He came left — fast. Possibly he couldn't read signal flags; maybe he couldn't hear a whistle, but, by jeepers, megaphone talk was something he reacted to in a hurry. A voice on the bridge said: "The son of a bitch is going to ram us."

The G humped her back and slithered across his bow — a rabbit avoiding an elephant. His stem cleared the depth charges on our fantail by ten feet.

All the way south through the Coral Sea that ship was allergic to deep water. She would go a mile out of her way to graze a reef. She had a fondness — almost a mania — for easing up to the beach and sniffing among the palm trees along the shore. It is charitable to assume that her Master was a man with a sense of humor who was having fun at the G's expense. He couldn't have been as leatherheaded as he acted. But he was too much of a sportsman for us. We told him good-bye with no regrets.

WARRIORS FOR THE WORKING DAY

We are but warriors for the working day;
Our gayness and our gilt are all besmirched
With rainy marching in the painful field,
Shakespeare — King Henry V

A YEAR or so before the war, when I was Flag Lieutenant to Vice Admiral Adolphus Andrews, I accompanied the Admiral one morning when he went on board the Pennsylvania to make an official call on the Commander-in-Chief, Admiral Claud C. Bloch.

When the ruffles and flourishes were over and the senior officers had gone aft I lingered for a moment to pass the time of day with Captain Wilbur Brown, who commanded the Marine Detachment on board the Fleet Flagship. "I want to congratulate you," said Wilbur.

The words were cordial enough, but there was something in the way he hissed them, and a certain sinister movement of his naked saber that caused me to keep a weather eye open. "What about?" I asked.

Wilbur, one of the biggest, toughest football players I have ever known, leaned closer. "Because you're the first guy who ever wrote a history of the navy without once mentioning the Marines."

"Oh, no — you're quite wrong," I replied over my shoulder as I hurried aft, hoping that the Admiral had urgent need of my services, "read it again and you'll see plenty about the Marines."

The book he was speaking of, Room to Swing a Cat, did mention the Marines, but not in great detail. In these pages I can make amends — not because the United States Marines have the slightest need of an apologia from me, or anyone else, but because we destroyer sailors have seen a lot of them during the past year and we think they've the most magnificent close-combat fighters the world has ever known. They go about their work with a matter-of-fact confidence; they possess an esprit de corps that is superb. Of all the warriors I have seen — United Nations and Axis, the United States Marines are the ones that I want most to have on my side. They are the shore spearhead of our Pacific Offensive.

A few weeks after the commencement of our Solomons Campaign the G entered Tulagi Harbor and I sent Lieutenant Brundage ashore to check on communications and to invite the Marines to use our showers and washrooms. When he returned he brought the word that Lieutenant Colonel Van Ness was coming out to pay us a visit. This was good news, for Peter Van Ness and I had served together ashore and afloat — in Washington, when he was Aide to the Major General Commandant, and in the cruiser Indianapolis, where he commanded one of the smartest Marine Detachments in the Fleet. In that peacetime state, when the "gayness and the gilt" were unbesmirched, it was somewhat blinding to go on the quarterdeck when the Marine Guard was drawn up for inspection, and the tropical sun threw off dazzling reflections from the polished leather and brass of Peter Van Ness's stalwarts.

It was a startling contrast to see the figure in faded khaki pants and open shirt, standing in the stern of the landing boat that came alongside our sea ladder.

Here was a "warrior for the working day;" a fighting man whom we had brought to the Solomons and who had helped to make the name of "United States Marines" a synonym for defeat among the Sons of Heaven.

We sat in the wardroom while Peter kept my officers enthralled with first-hand accounts of the bitter hand-to-hand fighting in the caves of Tulagi and Gavutu. We were having a second cup of coffee, and admiring the walking stick, intricately carved and decorated with mother-of-pearl, that the Solomon Islanders had presented to Colonel Van Ness, when a radioman dashed down the ladder. "Condition Red, sir," he reported.

"Come on, Peter," I said, as we made a dive for the bridge. "Come and go to sea with us."

"Nothing doing," he replied, heading for his boat that had remained alongside. "Every time there's a Condition Red and a Marine goes out with one of you guys he doesn't get home for a week — if he's lucky enough to get back at all. See you later."

The exhaust from his Landing Boat merged with the clink of our anchor chain as we got clear of the confined little harbor with our transport to gain sea room for the attack. There were twenty-seven Jap bombers overhead, and we had work to do.

Some memories of and for the Marines on Guadalcanal:

The night when seven hundred Sons of Nippon, making no attempt at concealment, came singing up the road toward Henderson Field. The

Marines were waiting. When the firing stopped there were six hundred and ninety-four dead Japs and six prisoners. There were seven dead Marines.

The cave on Tulagi which held a group of twenty-three Japs who were out of ammunition. The Marines called out to them to surrender. The Japs came back with a shrill yell: "No surrender. Give us more bullets." The Marines did.

The day on Guadalcanal when we were given one of the first examples of Jap treachery. Colonel Goettge, with a handful of men, went forward to receive the surrender of a Japanese Detachment that had sent an officer to our lines with a white flag. As the Americans approached, they were mowed down by machine-gun fire.

The young Marine who crouched in his foxhole as a Jap tank came roaring toward him. Just as it passed overhead he reached up and thrust a grenade in the treads. Finis for the tank; Navy Cross for the Marine.

The Marine who was driving a truck over an almost impassable road near the front lines. The truck slithered off to one side and bumped a coconut tree. A Jap sniper fell out of the green foliage that crowned the top of the naked trunk. Thereafter the Marines made a game of bumping trees, to see what might drop besides coconuts.

While Foster Hailey was aboard we asked him to write a piece for the Fantail Gazette about Guadalcanal, from where he had recently returned. Here is his contribution:

Guadalcanal Vignette

First there is the mud, black as sin and as inescapable. It rolls up on your shoes, fouls your clothing and is spattered on you from head to foot by every passing truck and jeep. By midday, around the airfield, it has dried into dust that hangs in the air waiting to cover your food, sift down your neck and up your nose and into your bed. It rains every night.

Then the heat that sears you like a flame in the open and hangs in the coconut groves and the jungles like a wet blanket. You walk around dripping, looking as though you had just taken a shower bath with all your clothes on.

Finally, as you near the front — now only to the west — there is the smell of rotting Japanese bodies. The Marines bury their own dead immediately, in shallow graves along the beach, scooped out with a helmet, until such time as they can be moved back to the well-tended, palm-shaded cemetery near the airfield. The Japanese dead are left where they fell until burying details of Japanese prisoners can be sent out to stow them away. When they become too numerous, as they do occasionally, a long ditch is dug and they are shoveled in with little ceremony. The Marines call the dead ones "stinkers;" the burying details "termites." The casualty ration has been 15 to 1, so the "termites" have been kept busy.

Where the fighting is now, to the west, the beach runs back only a hundred yards, sometimes less, where cliffs rise sharply some 200 to 300 feet, to grass-covered ridges that are as hot as hades from 10 a.m. to sunset. This escarpment is cut by deep ravines, or draws, all densely wooded. The cliffs and the sides of the ravines are honeycombed with caves. As late as two days after they have driven the Japs from an area the Marines find stragglers playing doggo in some of these caves, or hiding under logs. They root them out of the caves with grenades, but waste no powder on those they catch under logs.

The Japs fight only defensively in the daytime. At night they attempt their bayonet charges and their infiltration tactics. Heretofore this has proved demoralizing to the troops opposing them, but the Marines don't scare. They stay put in their foxholes and fire at anything that moves. It must be very discouraging to the Japanese. They never met first-class fighting men before.

As you may have heard, the Marines are great souvenir hunters. One American-educated Japanese prisoner put it succinctly when he said: "We fight for the Emperor. You people appear to fight for souvenirs." One sergeant who hopes to be promoted has collected a whole bag full of Jap flags. Small Rising Sun flags are a dime a dozen. Every Jap soldier has a home-made one, covered with good-luck stitches made by his friends. He carries it in his helmet. They are supposed to protect him from harm. They haven't been very efficacious.

These Jap troops are probably the crack troops of the Son of Heaven; veterans of Malaya, Singapore, the Philippines, Sumatra, Java or New Guinea. They are well-fed when they land. The bodies I saw were all of stocky, well-muscled fellows. I do not confirm this, but one Marine is supposed to have found on a dead Jap, souvenirs apparently taken from his brother who was a Marine on Wake.

The Japs really do yell "Banzai" (which means "Good Luck for a Thousand Years" or something like that) when they start a charge. And their officers lead the charge waving samurai swords. The Marines love their charges. It permits killing them more rapidly, which they can do with cross fire. Once they start they keep on coming, until they all are killed.

When captured, the Japs are abject prisoners, feigning lameness and illness while they are being watched. Once they learn that they are not to be tortured and killed they continue to be sullen but brighten up a bit.

Several years ago American newspapermen in Japan, tired to death of all the "banzai-ing," organized a drinking club whose challenge and reply apparently have been adopted in toto by the Guadalcanal Marines. The challenge was merely "Banzai." The answer was "Banzai yourself, you bastard."

FANTAIL GAZETTE

At sea we were unable to use the radios in the wardroom and crew's spaces for fear they might generate emissions that might be picked up by enemy detection devices and give warning of our approach. For our news of the world we relied on the press that was transmitted by Morse code from home stations. But there came a time, when the Commodore was on board and the G was functioning as destroyer flagship, that all of our receivers were needed for copying fleet affairs. We had long been mailless, now we were newsless, and we missed the mimeographed sheets that used to be brought around each morning with the latest information of the International Scene, The Home Front and the baseball scores.

To fill this void the Communication Officer resorted to a practice as old as the newspaper business; he manufactured news. The first issue of the Fantail Gazette made its appearance on a morning when our Task Force was ploughing north to hit Japanese fleet units that were threatening Guadalcanal. We had been underway continuously (I don't count two 4-hour periods at an advance base) for seventy days; we had action or the threat of action every day around the clock; we were tired. The Fantail Gazette gave us a new lease on life. It made us laugh, and laughter is a pleasant thing to see among men whose nerves cry for rest; men who are so worn out that they can drop on a steel deck and be deep in sleep while their fingers still fumble with the strap of a helmet. Ship's papers are part of the routine in battleships, carriers and cruisers. I had never seen one in a destroyer. The Fantail Gazette appeared at unstated intervals throughout our remaining months on the station. It was not a professional publication; it didn't lack for typographical errors; many of its points of humor were wholly local in their application, but it gave us something to think about, something to talk about, outside of our job and the war, and, in letting us poke a little fun at each other and at the world in general, it was a useful safety valve for thoughts and feelings that might otherwise have become burdensome. Our gossip writer, "Voltaire Vinchell," may have had a brand of humor that would be classified as "corny" by people who can pick up a dozen magazines on the news stand and select their choice among all the movies in town. We had no magazines or movies. The crew had damned little except weariness and a job to do and a temperament that let them make candid acknowledgment, under the headline The War Today: "From where we sit, the war today isn't a hell of a lot advanced over the war yesterday."

A self-proclaimed "Personal Organ of Prejudiced Opinion," the Fantail Gazette was a wholesome tonic for the officers and men of the G.

Fantail Gazette

"For Those Who Want the Straight Dope."

Due to the recent conversion of the Galloping Gee into the Fleet Flagship, and the consequent manning of all radio circuits in the Pacific Area plus Seattle Police Calls, it has been necessary to obtain our Press from the underwater sound machine. The following extracts were dredged off the bottom yesterday.

The International Scene:

Major trends in the fighting fronts yesterday led commentators to the conclusion that important new developments may be expected any day now. Smart money back in the States (the States, lug — you remember the States) has it that the Second Front can be anticipated soon. Britain already has 4,678,324 troops, including the Twiffenham-on-Twine Volunteer Pitchfork Battalion, poised for the invasion. This number, plus the American Army in England, is considered sufficient not only to defend the Land of the Big Boiled Potato and the Cold Pork Pie, but is thought to be enough to establish a beachhead on the Continent. Corporal Joe Doaks of the U.S. Marines has volunteered to clean up the general area surrounding the beachhead if he and his squad can get a day and a half off. His offer is being seriously considered. Corporal Doaks says, however, that he will probably need an extra round of ammunition.

The Home Front:

Things were quiet yesterday back home. The usual state of affairs prevailed. The rubber shortage is so critical that it was thought it may be necessary to cut down on the supply of beach balls for the summer.

Mayor LaGuardia donned his Volunteer Fire Fighter's hat and directed his boys in putting out the three-alarm blaze that threatened the local fire house.

A Congressman made a speech yesterday in which he said that things would get a lot tougher before they got any better, and that it is always darkest before the dawn.

Wendell Willkie, arriving home from his trip around the world, announced that most of the fighting fronts are characterized by fighting.

Musings from the Captain's Chair

It has been slightly more than six months since I had the privilege of taking command of this ship. Since then we have been so busy that I have had no opportunity to talk to you as a group. Just how busy we have been I didn't realize until this afternoon when I re-read our War Diary for the past few months. Before then you were performing your duties in the North Atlantic. You have had little time for rest or relaxation. At the present writing the G has been on this Station longer than any other destroyer, and there is no reason for believing that we will do other than remain here and continue to operate as efficiently as we can.

So far luck has been with us. We have a cherub on the yardarm and I hope he stays with us. He probably will if we don't rely on him too heavily. For my part I've never been shipmates with men who went about their work as quietly, as capably, as enthusiastically as you do. I like your attitude and I like your spirit. That goes for All Hands, with a little something extra for those whose battle stations keep them from seeing the action — the engineers, the radiomen, the magazine and handling room crews, ——, the sound operators who, like the kettle drummers in a symphony orchestra, must wait a long time before their turn comes to be heard.

In future Engagements, as in those we already have fought, I have every confidence in you. There is much work ahead of us. You need have no worry about getting into the thick of things when our time comes. When it is over let us hope that we will have so conducted ourselves as to merit a "G, Well Done."

In the Old Navy a standing toast in officers' messes used to be "A Bloody War and a Sickly Season," for either of these catastrophes meant rapid promotion. Between wars promotion was so slow as to stultify a man's ambition. My Naval Academy roommate's father (who was an Ensign for thirteen years, and then rose rapidly to the rank of Rear Admiral in 1917) used to tell the story of two Lieutenants on the quarterdeck of an old steam frigate in the dead days following the Civil War.

"Father," said the younger officer, "who has the midwatch; you, or I?"

"Neither of us, son," replied the older man. "Granddaddy has the midwatch. You and I have all night in."

War has always brought speedy promotions. Stephen Decatur was only 24 when he commanded "Old Ironsides" in the Tripolitan Wars. Edward Preble, at 42, was considered an old man when he commanded the American Squadron that "paid the tribute through the mouths of cannon." Napoleon, at 27, led the Army of Italy. Beatty, a Vice Admiral at 37, was an aggressive leader in Britain's navy. And so it goes in a Bloody War or a Sickly Season.

One reason for rapid advancement in war is that the rare individual who is a born leader has an early opportunity to prove his genius under conditions of combat. The other, and more general reason, is the simple one that armies and navies multiply, and a vast number of officers and petty officers are required. In this category are many men who are promoted before they have had an opportunity to prove their fitness — either to their seniors or to themselves. They are promoted as a wartime necessity, and suddenly they find themselves faced with new and strange responsibilities. Those who are worth their salt knuckle down and learn their jobs. A small minority feel that their new insignia has, in some miraculous fashion, endowed them with a wisdom and a knowledge of their rating that they did not possess yesterday. They soon learn, to their sorrow, that it takes more than a crow on the sleeve to make a petty officer.

For two years, during the Navy's lean years in the early nineteen-thirties, one of my duties was the allocation of ratings in Battleships, Battle Force. In fairness to all, we gave competitive examinations, with additional weight for Total Service, Service in Grade, etc. But there were so many men — and so few advancements. I will never forget the resigned expressions and frustrated attitude of men who were taking an examination for perhaps the twelfth or fourteenth time. They were good men, and able petty officers. It was their misfortune that, at the time, the Navy had little money and less promotion. Now, in the terrific waste of war, money has lost much of its significance, and man is significant only in the degree that he contributes to the National Victory.

Those of us who are promoted before our time have a real and personal responsibility to ourselves, our shipmates and our Service. Napoleon told his troops that each man had a Field Marshall's baton in his knapsack. In a like manner each of us has an Admiral's four-star flag in his sea bag. But it will remain there, furled and unused, unless we work to learn our jobs, study to fit ourselves for our rating, prove our worth by doing more than is expected of us. In the Navy there are few higher words of praise than to say of a man: "He knows his job and he stands a good watch." If each of us will do that, he will have a well merited sense of personal satisfaction and the knowledge that he is building towards a Greater G —

The Glory Road

Have you heard of the marvelous B.T.&B? It's now the route of the Galloping G.

Daniel Boone made a trail, so they say.
And blazed it on trees to show others the way.
When Christopher C. defied others' opinion
He up and discovered another dominion.
Hendrik Hudson was much the same —
He found the river that bears his name.
And so it went in the olden days.
People left home to explore new ways.
But of recent years this has declined,
I don't know — maybe folks are resigned
To the paths they know, the familiar route
That has borne the weight of their sluggish boot.
But one exception — for all to see,
Is the soon to be famous B.T,&B.
This is a new road, important as any —
A trail for the few, not for the many.
For not every ship that sails the sea
Could handle the dangerous B.T.&B.
It remained for the gruesome Galloping Ghost
To steer a course for that perilous coast,

To make light of hourly raids from the air
And never give bombers or cruisers a care.
To take what may come from the J-A-P
Is part of the job, on the B.T.&B,
And what, you ask, is this wretched route,
This way of death, and boredom to boot?
Where does it lie, where does it go —
Is it high, or is it low?
It isn't mysterious — the B.T.&B.
Is "Basket — Tulagi and Back," you see.

Lieut. (jg) Brundage, having been responsible for giving the Gazette its start in life, passes the management over to the crew:

After today the Gazette passes into new hands. From now on J. H. Collins will be the Managing Editor. I'll stick round to keep the Wardroom from being ribbed too unmercifully and to offer contributions now and then on various technical subjects such as "The Cultural Development of the Bronx Zoo During the Early Nineteenth Century," but the active work of publishing is now up to all of you.

Speaking for the topside management I'll say that we are tremendously pleased with the enthusiasm All Hands have shown for the Gazette. It was started to give the Skipper a poor substitute for the Morning Press, but it will continue, I think, as a real part of shipboard life.

After all, the possibilities are tremendous. You won't be able to convert the old Galloping G into a windjammer, and you probably won't be able to wangle yourselves a ten-dollar raise, but maybe Adolph will give up a little sooner, because of the Gazette. I don't think the Japs will be affected very much, though. Somehow I don't believe they would understand the spirit behind it.

I'll buy a copy any time.

Flash — Flash — Flash — Flash

The Cards lead the Yanks three games to one in the World Series. Unable to get any more dope on how the various games came out.

The Inquiring Reporter:

The question: "When do you think we will get back to the States?"

The place: The wardroom.

Lieut. (jg) Garrett: It is imperative that we arrive in the U.S. before the 23rd of February, 1943, or my wife will never forgive me for forgetting our first anniversary. Of course this is based on the premise that she remembers what I looked like.

Lieut. Linehan: (Guns for Hire) In seven years. I have recently revised my original estimate of eleven years, in view of the decided increase in the number of destroyers down here. I think we can look forward confidently to relief in seven; well, it might be even six, years. Besides, I like this place.

Doctor Peek: (Blasting, Inc.) Pretty damn soon. Maybe two years.

Lieut. (jg) Brundage: (The Secret Kid) They say that the Black Hawk stayed in China for over 20 years. The Maine has been in Havana now for almost fifty years. I think we can beat these records.

The Question: Do you think that women should be enlisted in the Navy for sea duty?

Fulp: (Signalman, First Class) Yes, I certainly do. They would be extremely useful. We need women aboard, especially to do the laundry.

Abritani: (Seaman) No! Women have a mind of their own. They couldn't take orders. Frankly, I wouldn't let one of them in my radio shack.

Mulno: (Chief Boatswain's Mate) They couldn't be worse than most of the people they get in the Navy these days. Just take a look at that First Division. Besides, women are useful for other things, like cooking.

One of the most consistent contributors to the Fantail Gazette was "Voltaire Vinchell" — who seemed to have a highly developed faculty for digging out the dirt — whether in the wardroom or the crew's quarters.

The Home Front:

The Washington Situation is getting pretty bad. Some folks are saying that we already have a Second Front right in the Nation's Capital. Any invasion of the continent will be small pumpkins compared to the invasion that is now underway in the Congressmen's country seat and the Senators' summer home. Contingents of fierce troops are arriving daily. The city designed to house half a million (if pushed) is already busting a gusset trying to give ten times that many hungry homesteaders half a shingle apiece. Some of the newcomers who got the word before they left home are bringing tents with them. This would be O.K. if they had made some arrangement beforehand for room to pitch them. As it is now, they are throwing up their canvas cottages on top of each other, and a fellow is lucky to move in on the third story. Of course Congress has the situation under advisement and is considering setting up an Emergency Housing Committee to handle the problem. To this end they have arranged to bring in another 10,000 head to staff the Housing Bureau. I heard of a man the other day who had the nerve to walk into a hotel and ask for a room. They told him they'd put him on the list and he could look for accommodations about the middle of next March, if he wasn't superstitious about sleeping thirteen in a bed.

The War Today:

There are two ways of looking at this war proposition. Either we stand to win or we're going to be licked. It's a free country so you can take your choice. Let's see what's against us. The Japanese can count on about a million and a half mad-hatters who have been fighting for ten years, either in China or back on the homeland, on reduced rations. (And a Japanese reduced ration is considerably reduced.) They are probably getting just as tired of it as you will be five years from now. Of course, you say that they are a militaristic people, and like nothing better than a barbed wire sandwich. (This may be due to hunger.) But the cigar store indian was once a belligerent savage and where is he today? So much for the Japs.

Now take the rest of the Opposition. Il Duce's troops, for instance. On second thought suppose you take them — sometime when you're Dummy.

That leaves the soldiers of Der Fuehrer. The Russian situation being what it is, Der Fuehrer's men are getting fuehrer and fuehrer. Like the Yanks, they once had a pretty good outfit. But there will always be someone around, like the Cards, to knock off the champs.

And when the present champs are chumps we'll all go home and take up where we left off. Seems to me I was right in the middle of a double chocolate malt.

Oscar, our trained seagull, just returned from an extremely hazardous mission to Frisco, which he modestly termed a "Routine Reconnaissance Flight," brought with him an urgent appeal from the USO for whatever contributions we can afford. The following is an excerpt from the letter from Mrs. Gerty Ginsberg, Pres.: "How we girls envy you brave heroes out there in the broad Pacific. It must be marvelous, visiting all those tropical Islands, and I'll bet you boys have such fun with those native girls! But we back here in the States are having a mighty dull time. Of course we try to 'Mother' the little soldier and sailor boys as the war is very hard on them. (Some of them are over a hundred miles from home, and they only get to visit their folks on week-ends), and the USO girls are giving their all for the Service.

"We would appreciate any contribution you boys could make, especially as you have nowhere to spend your money."

Mrs. Ginsberg also sent twelve tickets to a social gathering to be held at the Hospitality House tomorrow night. Too bad, gang, that the Mighty G is so low on fuel. We will have to miss this rare treat, at which will be served tea and cakes. But as an alternative we can go on a hiking trip.

Oscar also reports having made a low-level bombing attack along Market Street, and though it is hard to ascertain exact results at such low altitudes, he is pretty sure of one Army Sergeant and two Corporals. Explaining the daring attack Oscar said he came in at high speed and so low that he could observe the expressions on the faces of the victims. (And what expressions!)

Oscar is the only seagull, to our knowledge, equipped with the improved Norden-Sperry bomb sight, and this probably accounts for his remarkably successful bombing record.

Oscar is a cross between a seagull, homing pigeon and parrot. He speaks very good English; in fact, better than most of our bridge phone talkers. We are considering further crossing him with a woodpecker, so he can send Morse code. Oscar thinks he should have something to say on this matter, however.

On hearing of all these medals that the Navy is giving out, I wonder if they forgot the USO one. I guess it's pretty monotonous sitting in one of those Clubs letting Betty Grable pour coffee and Carol Landis feed you doughnuts. I, Voltaire, couldn't stand it, I don't believe. So let's strike a medal for that. After all, it's dangerous. They might spill hot coffee and scald you, or a hostess step on your foot, or you might get smitten with a wild ping pong ball. There are so many ways of getting hurt that the writer could go on forever, and I guess it's a bad risk for the Insurance Companies.

A lot of our plough jockeys, apple knockers, pumpkin rollers and share croppers are joyous in the fact that they are going to let farmers go home and raise crops. But as most of the G's ex-farmers didn't raise anything but dust, maybe we'll get to keep them.

One of our signalmen, Drake, came from the Wisconsin town to which was attributed the following quotation, which I hope will not bring forth an irate reply from The Chamber of Commerce.

Social Notes

Spooner, Wis. — The population of this quiet little mid-western village were almost hysterical today as the first news of the bombing of Pearl Harbor came in via mule train. They were reassured, however, when a Mr. Drake, one of the original settlers, pointed out that Admiral Dewey is very competent and quite capable of handling the Japs.

Lieut. Linehan chooses the Gazette to emphasize a number of careless habits that bring grey hair to the Gunnery Officer.

The Gunner's Lament

The first question asked when we drop the hook is not, as commonly believed, "How much Liberty gives here?" but "What are your requirements?" The last time I had a pot full of requirements, but this time only one — and the Tender can't be of much assistance in meeting it.

Since the commissioning, the official archives of the Ordnance Department show numerous entries mysteriously ending with the phrase "Cause Unk," just as the police records top off the end of a fruitless quest with "killed by a person or persons Unk." And so I submit my Work Request for the week: Investigate, determine origin of, classify, tag and dispose of Unk now existing in gunnery team work. Accompany with priced invoice. And to the investigator chosen for the job I described Unk thus —

In a recent target practice nobody turned off the rammer switch in Gun 1, yet it WAS off, and the rammer didn't work. Cause Unk.

In a total of seven firings the firing keys of different guns were closed, but failed to work. They worked O.K. in the morning routines and immediately after firing, however. Cause Unk.

One gun had a projectile catch in those light wires that are between the hoists, when the men were aiming at the projectile post — and hoisting it, too. Cause Unk.

A total of 92 phone talkers tested out and O.K.'d their phones: kept them on and then found them defective after a hot message had been missed. The phones were perfectly good when the electricians tried them. Cause Unk.

Six rangefinders made their adjustments when setting the watch, only to find that they were off when a good range was wanted badly. Cause Unk.

Machine Gun No. 9 was "cocked and loaded and ready" until "Commence Firing" was given, and then it didn't shoot. Cause Unk.

And so the mysteries pile up. So far no corpses have accompanied them, but who knows what Unk will bring in the future? The lookout didn't see the plane; the Soundman didn't ping the sub; the gun didn't match up for 40 seconds; the projectile never got to the gun; the signalman didn't see the "Enemy" flag. All Cause Unk — one ship sunk.

The investigator scratched his ear. "You don't need me. You need Two Hundred and Sixty men, all checking their instruments and themselves; striving for perfection. Unk is a very obnoxious personage, but he can be licked."

From the Birthday Edition of the Fantail Gazette:

Today marks the second anniversary of an historic event in the never-to-be-forgotten annals of seafaring men. On this most appropriate date the Galloping Ghost of The Atlantic Coast (now the Senior Charter Member, Escort Bureau, Pacific Fleet) was commissioned, and her crew made into a fighting, efficient unit. Since then new faces have appeared, old ones drifted away to other stations or duty. For the benefit of those who recently achieved the honor of becoming a part of this colorful, immortal crew we offer a kaleidoscopic glance into the past to reveal for perhaps the first time the unbelievable truth about a few of our plank-owners.

For instance, the fat old grouch who shoulders you roughly aside in the chow line and gobbles his food like a ravenous vulture was once the notorious Moon-Glow Wilson, of Charleston Gin Mill fame. We recall with reluctance how Moon-Glow used to lie prone, seemingly dead, all day long. Were it not for his boisterous snoring he oft would have been pronounced deceased. Then, as the first pale glow of a southern moon drifted over the housetops, this apparently inanimate mass of flesh would stir and moan as though prodded by some deep, prehistoric instinct. Suddenly, with a nerve shattering roar he would bound to his feet, eyes aglow, breath wheezing in cannibalistic gasps. "What time is it? Why 'n 'ell didn't somebody call me for chow This was invariably followed by a mad dash to the washroom, sans clothing of any sort. Hastily showered and shaved he would don his famous old steaming-blues, snatch a white hat from some nearby unsavory reserve and storm from the barracks. The hamlet of Charleston would echo and resound from his fast, gay rounds of night life. Stout-hearted minions of the law would cringe in doorways. The ever alert, fearless Shore Patrol traveled in sixes, doubly-armed, praying that Moon-Glow would not cross their path. As in merciful relief the red-gold beams of light announced the approach of another day. Hastily gulping his last case of Bee he would throw off the imprisoning arms of some fair damsel of the pubs, thunder into the street and bellow "Taxi.

Taxi!" Knowing full well they would not be paid, numerous cabbies herded their cars to him. Upon reaching the barracks he would leap agilely into his bunk (usually falling out the first two or three times) and lie dormant throughout the ensuing day. So ended a night of revelry, and a fear-ridden, apprehensive citizenry ventured forth once more to the comparative safety of the sun-bathed streets, confident that the leering monster would remain in his den until nightfall. Today's haranguer of the mess halls is a far cry from his former savage self. Take care, fellowmen, lest you once again rouse the beast in him.

Shift the scene quickly to the forward part of the ship. Deep in the bowels of the boatswain's locker we see a little gnome of a man, feverishly at work midst a background of hemp, marlin, thimbles, shackles, wire and, oddly enough, a hot-plate. His chunky, compact body aglow with sweat, he slaves away hour after hour trying to make Second Class. This, my awe-bound reader, is Mouse Matthews, czar of the boatswain's storeroom. This wizened, sour dipsomaniac was once the heart throb of the outskirts of Charleston, the scene of our reminiscence. He responded to the charming nickname of Dapper Dan. Immaculately attired in some shipmate's best suit of tailor made blues, he cut a swath through the blissful innocence of this southern town's young feminine circle without so much as a twinge of conscience. His running mate on many of these escapades was the infamous Round House Watson. He, too, was a debonair scoundrel of the bright lighted way. Now he sits drooping by the loading machine, his tumbling hair like a surveyed thumb-mat, his beady eyes aglow with avaricious glee, hopelessly entangled in a coil of wire, mumbling "Under three, under two, under one — Shift!"

Once we stood near the quarterdeck and watched a bright-eyed, eager young Ensign bound lightly up the gangway, execute a smart salute, leap in his car and zoom away, lost in the clouds, thinking of his beautiful young wife in their cozy love-nest. Today this selfsame man is a quiet, sedate Lieutenant, hard at work navigating his ship. Never-failing, he stands on the bridge at dusk and dawn, surrounded by his assisting staff of quartermasters. If you listen closely you can hear him mumbling "Venus, Aldebaran, Mars, Altair — gad, it's confusing!"

We end this saga by telling you that the author was found dead in his bunk, death being brought on by the administering in huge quantities of poison; stabbing, gunshot wounds, beating about the head and face with a blunt instrument after an indeterminate period of ancient Chinese torture.

There will be no funeral services — just an informal little celebration on the fantail, open to a select few.

Writing under the name "Lee Scupper," someone contributed the following verses to The Birthday Edition of "The Mouthpiece of the Mighty G."

When Nipponese are thick as fleas,
Behind each lurking cloud,
And bombs are dropping all about
While guns are sounding loud —
(The ——, big and grand
Is close aboard the starboard hand)
And the steersman shouts in sudden fright
"The rudder's jammed at thirty right!"
Will you be my Valentine?

When a voice has said "Condition Red!"
Over the Candy wire.
And the Jap Express is headed south
To back up the aircraft fire.
(The anchor lies buried deep in mud —
The anchor engine proves a dud)
And control calls down "What shall we do,
The —— just now broke in two."

Will you be my Valentine?
When we've swept the seas of Nipponese
And the Fleet is headed home,
And we flemish down within our sacks
For we'll no longer roam —
Then a signal comes "At Lat. Fifteen
(It's the damndest thing we've ever seen)
Detach the G — send her today
To patrol off Pallikulo Bay."
Will you be my Valentine?

When the Galloping G comes home from sea
(In Forty-Seven or Eight)
And the crowds mass close along the shore

That surrounds the Golden Gate,
To cheer the last of a valiant band
That fought the war in a distant land —
At thirty knots we'll back and stop
And take up then — anew
A little unfinished business from 1942,
Will you be my Valentine?

THOSE IN PERIL

Eternal Father, strong to save,
Whose arm has bound the restless wave —
Who bidd'st the mighty ocean deep
Its own appointed limits keep,
Oh, hear us when we cry to Thee
For those in peril on the sea.
Navy Hymn

We had entered a South Pacific port and anchored after a four-day sweep with our Task Force, and again we were short of destroyers because of the detachment of the N and Meredith on screening jobs to Guadalcanal. At this time we were using every possible means to send bombs, ammunition and aviation gasoline to our Marines. It was being delivered by transports; by destroyers with deck loads of gas drums and with bombs lashed in every available space; by flat barges that had been towed out from Hawaii, and by transport planes. We had a very real admiration for the sang froid of the pilots who took off in their unarmed transports, with cans of one hundred octane gas jammed into every nook and cranny of their planes, to fly several hundred miles over enemy patrolled waters with no fighter protection. But Guadalcanal had to have the tools of war and ComSoPac was delivering the goods in the determined and aggressive manner that marked his character.

Now it was one o'clock in the morning, and I sat in my cabin waiting for the Commodore to return from the flagship, to which he had been summoned by signal at midnight. There was something in the air, and apparently it would require action on the part of the G. So I drowsed over a late cup of coffee, envying my shipmates who were flemished down all over the topside, making the most of the first night in many weeks that they had been able to relax for a few hours.

We were once more full of fuel, and ready to cover long distances. But if the engines had food it was more than could be said for the crew. Our provision storerooms were virtually empty and in a few more days we would be reduced to beans, rice and coffee. At that we were better off than the Marines farther up the line, who were subsisting largely on supplies captured from the enemy. The thought of our storerooms took me back to the early months of the war when the Boise, after a week of rice, beans and coffee, entered the little port of Tjilatjap, on the south coast of Java, and the Dutch slaughtered beef for us that was delivered on board in so fresh a condition that some of the crew swore they saw the cattle take a few faltering steps before they collapsed on our decks in a welter of blood and black flies.

There was a knock on my door and the gangway watch poked his head in to report that the Commodore was returning. I went on deck to meet him. We came back to my cabin.

The Commodore eased his frame into a chair.

"Well, skipper," he said, "it looks like the Meredith has been sunk. Dive bombers and torpedo planes from Jap carriers that sneaked in from the north. She's a day overdue and this afternoon our patrol planes reported sighting a large oil slick south of Guadalcanal."

If this were true it was a tragic blow. We could ill afford the loss of a new destroyer, and moreover the Meredith was part of our own gang — one of the four ships of our division. Together she and the G had lived through the heavy weather and the cold discomfort of North Atlantic duty. They had known Iceland and the bone-piercing fog of the Denmark Strait. They had dragged anchor at Argentia and picked their way through ice floes along the coast of Greenland. They had been a part of Admiral Halsey's Task Force on the famous Shangri La raid to Japan. The Meredith and the G were buoy mates. Their officers and men were old friends, and I had known Harry Hubbard, the Meredith's Captain and the Number One man in the Naval Academy Class of '25, since we were Midshipmen.

The Commodore went on to explain that the Meredith had been escorting a minesweeper (which I shall call the Verity), and that the Verity had been towing a barge laden with bombs and avgas. A second ship, also towing a barge, had been able to cast off her tow and get clear of the area before the attack. Our orders were to search for survivors of the Meredith; to salvage the Verity if she, too, had not been sunk, and, at all costs, to locate the barges, if they were still afloat, and get them to Guadalcanal, where the shortage of ammunition and airplane fuel was now critical. The Task Unit would consist of the G, her sister ship, the Gwin, and, to tow the barges if we should find them, the new tug Seminole, which had recently arrived on the station.

Signals were sent to the Gwin and Seminole; the crew of the G were roused out, and with light enough barely to see the dim shape of anchored ships and the heavier darkness of the Jungle along the shore line, we got underway and cleared the port.

The exact location of the Meredith's last position was unknown. If we were to find the survivors and barges without delay it was important that we estimate correctly the effects of wind and sea and, by resolving these components, decide what allowances to make in laying our course. Our frequent passages to Guadalcanal had given us an opportunity to determine within narrow limits the prevailing set and drift of the current in this portion of the Coral Sea, so Frank Peters, after working over his charts for some time, was able to scribe a small circle and state with confidence that the rafts should be within its confines.

Held back by the slow speed of the Seminole, we could not go charging to the north in the manner that destroyer sailors like. Even the Commodore, who was a man of notable patience, seemed to feel that our progress was tortoise-like, so he sent a gentle hint to the effect that we would be delighted to see a higher wave along the Seminole's bow and a larger expanse of white water under her stern. She replied in aggrieved tones that she was making engine turns for more than the designed speed of the ship.

From: Commodore

To: Seminole

You are doing all right. We hope to do our part as well.

All the same we were reminded of the admiral who with growing impatience had waited for a destroyer to sortie from Guantanamo and take her station in the formation. When finally she was in position, after making many unnecessary maneuvers at speeds that would have been sedate even for a battleship, the admiral sent the laconic message: "Your movements are majestic but very slow."

During the forenoon we checked the details of our Survivors Bill, which had been designed to meet the situation that was now apt to arise. It provided for certain men to stand by the life nets that lined our bulwarks along the main deck ready to be lowered over the side, while others, with lines around their waists, would swim out to help any injured men. It assigned a few expert riflemen to take station along the upper decks and keep a ready eye out for sharks while we were picking up survivors. The ship's cooks on watch were to prepare hot soup and coffee; stretcher bearers would stand by; the Doctor and his Mates ready at the Battle

Dressing Stations, while in the washrooms a working party with soap, towels, soft rags and diesel oil would prepare to bathe the less seriously injured and cleanse the survivors of the heavy fuel-oil sludge that is a concomitant of almost any sinking.

Early on the morning of the second day we sighted several patrol planes, but none of them could give us any information as to the location of survivors or the Verity, although it was obvious that we were in the area of an action, for all three ships sighted life jackets, bits of flotsam, and the bodies of several Japanese aviators in dark-brown flying suits and life jackets.

At 0955 a plane ahead of us dropped a smoke pot and the G stood in at flank speed to investigate. Two minutes later we had a half-submerged destroyer-type raft in sight, with seven ebony-black, oil-soaked figures huddled inside. We backed the engines and maneuvered to bring it alongside. As the realization that help was at hand dawned on them the men in the raft came to life. Holding one another up, waist deep in the oily water, they lifted dull eyes toward the G and gave the most valiant and pathetic cheer that I have ever heard. "Meredith!" they shouted, and "Meredith!" again. One voice, stronger than the rest, called out asking us to "Have Dr. Peek standing by." Someone on the bridge said "That sounds like John Bowers." Later, when the fuel oil had been scrubbed off, we found that it had been Dr. Bowers, the Medical Officer of the Meredith, whose sole thoughts and actions, in spite of intense shock and complete exhaustion, had been directed toward giving immediate aid to his shipmates, whose wounds he had treated as best he could during the three days and nights they had spent on the raft.

By the time we had brought the seven men on board and carried them below, the patrol plane was again dropping smoke pots ahead. We had the next rafts in sight when suddenly there was a yell from somewhere out on our starboard hand. Through our glasses we saw a lone swimmer, without benefit of clothing or life jacket, racing toward the G at a pace that easily made him the speed and distance champion of the Coral Sea. We dropped him a line. He caught it and took a turn around his waist. We hoisted him aboard and he collapsed instantly in a dead faint. Later we learned that he had left one of the rafts two hours earlier, thinking he saw land and that he could swim for help. (Nearest land 400 miles.)

The next group consisted of three rafts lashed together, and contained the remainder of the survivors from the Meredith and Verity. They represented a regrettably small percentage of the crews of the two ships, for the attack had come with suddenness and ferocity. Captain Hubbard had taken the crew of the Verity on board the Meredith, expecting to clear the area at high speed in view of the heavy air menace that was impending. The enemy struck with dive bombers and torpedo planes, and while the dead Japs that we sighted, and two live ones that we captured, testified to the fierce resistance of the Meredith, the odds were too heavy for one destroyer. The ship sank in less than five minutes. Jap planes remained for some time, strafing the survivors in the rafts and in the water. Almost every man had wounds and bums in varying degrees of seriousness.

There were two men — a Lieutenant and a Boatswain's Mate, who especially attracted our attention. Lieutenant J. C. Legg was the Commanding Officer of the Verity. He was a man in his fifties who had come up from the ranks and had entered the Navy long before most of the men in the rafts had been born. In obedience to Captain Hubbard's orders he had abandoned the old ten-knot Verity and gone on board the Meredith with his crew. During the attack he had been on the bridge of the destroyer. Just before she plunged to the bottom he cut lengths of halliard and made them up into descending lines, down which the bridge crew slid into the water. When all of them who were still alive had gone down in safety, he helped Captain Hubbard, who was blinded and badly burned about the face. Once in the rafts, his quiet humor, sound common sense and good seamanship kept up the spirits of the men and held them together. He made small mention of the fact that his hands were severely burned and one knee dislocated. All of the survivors had thrown away, or lost, their steel helmets when they entered the water. Jimmy Legg had not bothered with a helmet, but in some mysterious way his uniform cap had stayed with him. When we went alongside the rafts he was sitting up, erect as a young cadet, his cap perfectly adjusted, its gold untarnished.

Some of the survivors were able to pull themselves part way up the life nets. Most of them had to be lifted. With few exceptions all of them collapsed when they reached the deck. But there was one man who not only required no assistance from the men of the G, but who remained in the raft, passing lines around his comrades and helping them to safety. When his raft was empty he clambered aboard the G and joined my crew in pulling up more survivors, waving aside the suggestion that he go below and turn in. Finally, when everyone was aboard and the G was backing clear of the rafts, he pulled out his knife, cut the lashings from his heavy, oil-soaked life jacket and threw it far out into the sea, remarking in a matter-of-fact voice, "That son-of-a-bitch weighs forty pounds."

He was Wesley H. Singletary. He was a Boatswain's Mate, Second Class, a big, blond boy from Georgia. Later we heard more about his hardihood from his shipmates. During the three days and nights in the rafts he had been a tower of strength. He had hauled the three rafts together and lashed them in place, insuring that they could not drift apart in the darkness. It was Singletary who, under Captain Legg's direction, rationed the food and water and saw that the shares were distributed evenly. He established a watch — not only to keep a lookout, but to make the men take turns sitting inside the rafts and floating outside, holding on to hues, for there were too many men and too few rafts; if all of them climbed inside, the rafts would have sunk. Later, when the sharks came, and some of the men demurred at getting into the water, Singletary dove over the side, pushed the sharks away with his foot and announced with a confidence that he surely could not have felt, "See, them things can't hurt you." It was fortunate that the men of that group did not have open wounds. In the other rafts several survivors were attacked and bitten by sharks, one of which came over the coaming of the partially submerged raft and floundered around inside until he was picked up and tossed back into the sea.

Two hours after the last survivor was aboard we sighted the first barge, and the Seminole stood over to take it in tow. A few minutes later we spotted the Verity, and the Gwin was directed to inspect her and report whether or not she was capable of being gotten underway. Meanwhile the G swung around in large circles, keeping an underwater ear open for Jap subs, and hoping that we would be fortunate enough to get one. The sight of the Meredith and Verity men had put us in a frame of mind where we wanted badly to find some way of paying back the Nips in a hurry. At two o'clock that afternoon, while we were making a short sweep to the north, we found some live Japs, but the circumstances made our discovery anticlimactic.

The lookouts reported what appeared to be another raft on the horizon and we charged up to investigate. It was a raft, true enough, but through our glasses we could see that it had broad red and white stripes. Two monkeylike figures in flying suits and helmets sat on the gunwale and cast baleful looks in our direction. We went alongside and our deck force, overcoming an understandable reluctance, hove lines which the Nips caught and pulled their raft alongside our sea ladder. Suddenly one of them whipped out a pistol from beneath his jacket and shot himself between the eyes. We snaffled the other one aboard in a hurry, to discourage any similar action on his part, but I doubt if it was necessary, for he was tractable enough, and gazed with indifference at the body of his companion. Our Mr. Moto was a slender youngster of about twenty, and well above the average Jap prisoner in appearance and intelligence. He had been in the raft for three days, ever since his torpedo plane crashed or was shot down by the Meredith. Dr. Peek dressed the burns on his legs and we gave him a regular crews' ration which he attacked hungrily after gazing at it with suspicion for a few seconds. We couldn't give him the dried fish and sea weed that are staples of Japanese diet, but he seemed to thrive. He gained about five pounds during the eight days we had him on board, and he developed a craving for navy coffee — probably the first he had ever tasted.

By this time the Seminole had the barge in tow, so, the Gwin rejoining, we headed for Guadalcanal. The Verity was in good shape. We would take care of her on the return trip. The Seminole reported that one of the men she had picked up was developing a gangrenous leg, so we sent a boat and brought him on board the G; another patient for the doctor and his Pharmacist's Mates. But the treatment of survivors, like so many things in a small ship, proved to be an all-hands Job. The Medical Staff could treat the more serious cases; our crew took care of the remainder.

The oily sludge was a nuisance. It was hard to wash off; it ruined almost every blanket we had in the ship, but unquestionably it saved the lives of many Meredith and Verity sailors, for it formed a seal that kept in the body moisture and acted as a protection from sunburn and water blisters.

That evening Dr. Peek came to the bridge and reported that he believed all of our passengers would live, with the exception of three — Lieutenant D. R. Cockrill, U.S.N.R., and two Seamen — J. E. Maynard and William S. Marks, all of whom had been unconscious for two days, and in very serious condition from wounds, shock and exposure. The seventy-odd other survivors were in bad shape, but, barring complications, they should pull through, though it would be many months before any of them would be fit for duty.

Two days later we advanced slowly through Indispensable Strait, and in mid afternoon entered Lengo Channel on the north coast of Guadalcanal. We were reasonably certain that we had been sighted by Jap snooper planes, which at that time covered the Eastern Solomons and the northern portion of the Coral Sea pretty thoroughly, but none had closed in to give us a shot at them. As we passed Hutchinson Reef the loud-speaker in the pilot house blared forth with "Condition Red over Guadalcanal. Condition Red. Many planes." The ship was already at General Quarters. We passed the word among the passengers that there would probably be some shooting. Sure enough, there were many planes, but fortunately for our barge load of bombs and gasoline, and for the peace of mind of the survivors, they concentrated on the shore defenses, apparently overlooking us in the gathering darkness of late afternoon.

Just at dark we delivered the Seminole and her barge and, with the Gwin, departed on the next phase of our task, able once more to settle down to a good destroyer speed that ate up the miles.

It was the last we were to see of the staunch little Seminole. A few days later there was another Condition Red in which her luck failed her and a bomb found its mark.

Despite the efforts of Dr. Peek, aided by Dr. Bowers of the Meredith, our three most seriously injured survivors continued to grow worse. Lieutenant Cockrill, a splendid young officer from Nashville, Tennessee, was in very grave condition, and at nine-thirty on the evening that we left Guadalcanal, he died. The next morning, while his shipmates of the Meredith gathered around the flag-draped figure on the fantail, I read the Burial Service and a Psalm, and we committed his body to the deep.

Our ten-day experience with the Meredith and Verity was such an emotional cocktail as I do not want to repeat. To the survivors themselves it was a shattering experience. Generally when a destroyer is sunk in action there are other ships around to pick up the survivors immediately. Rarely are they in the rafts more than a few hours. There have been several cases of aviators drifting for many days, but their rubber life boats are luxurious in comparison with the doughnut shaped destroyer raft with its open grating. Even when you are in the raft you are up to your waist in water and covered with fuel oil from your ship's tanks. The senior survivor of the Meredith, Lieutenant John Z. Bowers, Medical Corps, U.S.N.R., wrote his account of the episode while he was still on board the G. He completed it when he was convalescing in an Advance Base. The pages that follow are his.

The Doctor's Story

October 12 — Sailed with the A and B (each towing a barge of aviation gasoline and bombs) and the Verity.

October 13 — A large Jap surface force shelled Henderson Field, Guadalcanal. Many shell holes in the air field. Weather clear and warm. This was our first intimation that the situation was becoming acute in the Solomons. It appeared that the Japs were starting another push, and that we would be in the middle of it. Our carriers are known to be in the area and we understand that we have a large group of planes at Guadalcanal. However, the Japs have been shelling the place nightly and bombing it daily, so the defenders are in poor physical condition. They have been living in fox holes, eating two field rations a day and fighting like hell for over two months. There is an Army field-artillery unit on the Island, but the remainder are all Marines, many of whom took part in the original landing on August seventh.

October 14 — Continuing toward Guadalcanal at a speed of about 8 knots. Joined last night by the N (a destroyer). Received message this morning that Henderson Field had been bombed twice by the Japs. On the first attack the planes came in at about 12,000 feet, and our fighters couldn't reach them before the damage was done. The second attempt was met by our fighters who shot down six bombers. However, we have very few flyable planes left on the island. Simultaneously the Japs began to land heavy reinforcements.

We all realized that if we were to continue in to Guadalcanal our chances of returning would be quite small. We could envision Jap cruisers and other ships patrolling the channel that we were about to enter, and Jap planes covering the sky above us. There were many of us who had been yelling for a fight, but these were not exactly the odds that we had anticipated. We suddenly became very quiet. The Captain said: "You gents who were looking for a scrap have certainly quieted down."

At dinner that evening the Captain told us that if we were not ordered back that evening we would not be able to turn back. We went to Evening G.Q. at about 1745, and later we received orders to return to port until the situation cleared. Before dark we were turning about.

October 15 — A message arrived ordering the Verity to take in tow one of the barges of aviation gas and bombs and to proceed to Guadalcanal with the Meredith as escort. Avgas was badly needed — their supply was almost exhausted.

It was several hours before the tow was finally passed to the Verity. I stood the mid watch and turned in after Morning G.Q. I had only been asleep a short time before the General Alarm went off. I had just gotten both feet on the deck when the main battery started firing. I walked into the wardroom and started getting out my first-aid equipment — spray guns for burn cases, basins, splints, etc.

The guns fired only about 15 rounds, and by then I had learned that we were shooting at a Jap reconnaissance twin-float seaplane at about 12,000 yards. The plane turned off and went out of range.

The Jap plane continued its observations and soon another plane appeared and we fired on it. It took up a position on our starboard beam, so now we had a Jap plane on each beam, out of gun range.

Messages continued to arrive telling of enemy landings on Guadalcanal. We received reconnaissance reports on two Jap battleship-carrier-cruiser Task Forces, whose courses were such as to converge on us. We were making about 6 knots and the tension was terrific.

About an hour later the guns started firing again: the planes had come within range, but only for a short time. The First Lieutenant commenced breaking out mooring lines and fenders. He said that the Captain was debating the advisability of taking the men off the Verity and trying to out-run the Japs.

Then one of the Jap planes disappeared. A message was received from Guadalcanal stating that the gas situation was critical.

We passed close beside the Verity and the faces of her crew told of their anxiety. The Captain called out: "Don't worry. I will see that you men get through this all right." It was apparently at that time that he decided to take the crew off the Verity. We began to approach her on her starboard side.

I was standing on our forecastle deck amidships as we came alongside and the Verity crew climbed over the side. We were expecting those two heavy Jap Task Forces to hit us at any minute.

Then we pulled away from the Verity. At the same time we sighted a large group of planes.

I went to the bridge to see the Captain. We were attacked viciously by a large group of Jap carrier-based planes, about 26 in number: 12 torpedo planes and 14 dive bombers. My first knowledge was when someone shouted and I looked up to see a dive bomber coming out of his dive about 400 feet above us. The first bomb hit by Number Two gun and went on down through the decks. Another went past me and exploded just forward of Number One stack. These two severed all communications and blew out the plotting room. Another bomb hit near the fantail and a fourth by the carpenter shop.

At about the same time that this attack began a group of torpedo planes made runs. A torpedo hit the forecastle and blew it off, while another hit on the starboard side near Number Three gun, and overturned that gun. A torpedo exploded on the starboard side just forward of the break of the bridge.

At each explosion the ship would be lifted out of the water and thrown to the side. The air was full of hot steel, smoke, flames, and water. I was thrown to the deck and each successive explosion would lift me up and throw me down again.

Our main battery fired one salvo at the planes as they dove, and thereafter were firing by local control. The 20 mm's were firing constantly, and all in all we hit about five planes, knocking down three of them.

After the torpedo planes dove they would come over the ship and strafe us, concentrating particularly on the bridge. We called down to the torpedo battery for the men to fire the torpedoes (in order to decrease the topside weight, and give more buoyancy to the sinking ship) but only the forward mount was able to do so. They trained out about 20 degrees and fired the fish into the water.

The Captain called out "Send a message — 'Meredith sinking,'" but there was no radio room. This was about two minutes after the attack began. His next words were: "All hands. Abandon Ship."

The only exit from the bridge was by the ladder aft, for the pilot house was ablaze, I walked to the ladder and looked down. All that I could see was a mass of smoke and flame. I climbed down to the forecastle deck, where the Paymaster was standing. I jumped off and started swimming out. I swam a few strokes and the cold water must have brought me to my senses, for I stopped and removed my helmet and my glasses. I looked back at the ship and she was under, forward of the superstructure, with the stem in the air — a twisted and battered wreck.

Just then someone shouted: "Look out!" and I turned to see a number of Jap planes coming at me with machine guns blazing. I grabbed a mattress and put my head in the water beneath it. I could hear the bullets sizzle as they hit the water around me. I tried to dive, but my life jacket prevented it.

As the planes passed on bedlam broke loose. A lad hanging to the mattress beside me had his hand shattered and begged me to pull it off. All around there were men, in groups and singly, crying for help. Two men brought the Chief Yeoman to me, his face badly torn and his arm broken. He said: "Oh, Doctor, please help me." His face was white and his eyes were pleading. I said: "You men try to get him to the raft and we'll fix him up."

I saw four rafts about 75 yards away and wondered whether I should join them. I thought the planes would come back and strafe us again, and certainly concentrate on the rafts. Floating near them was the Verity and the barge, and I knew that if the barge was hit we would be goners. But there were a lot of men on the rafts and I thought that was my place. How glad I am that I so decided.

I struck out and found that I could do all right, despite the life jacket. As I passed over the spot where the ship had sunk there was an explosion deep down in the water and I felt as though someone had pumped about two gallons of water into my rectum. I remembered the Hamman and her blast cases, and floated on my back for a while. (Note: When the Hamman sank, at least one of her depth charges exploded as they were carried down to the depth for which they were set. Many men were injured by concussion.)

After resuming the jaunt I passed many men dead or dying in the water. Someone called from a raft: "Doctor, here's the Captain," and I swam to the raft. As I came alongside I realized that we were all covered with fuel oil.

Lying or sitting on the raft were about 14 men, all moaning and groaning. I could only recognize one or two — the others were so full of fuel oil, and so badly burned, that I did not know who they were. They were piled one on top of another, and no one seemed to care.

I found the Captain, who was sitting along the edge with his face and arms badly burned and swollen. He was being held up by a boy who claimed that his legs were paralyzed. I doubted it, and found later that I was correct.

The Captain said: "Is that you, Doc?" As I answered in the affirmative he said: "I'm badly burned and I can't see. You sure were right about those flash burns."

Meanwhile several of the rafts were trying to make it to the Verity, which was slowly drifting away from us. The Captain said: "Tell them to trip the pelican hook on the tow and get a boat over here to help us." Just then someone shouted "There's a Flying Fort!" and I looked up to see a B-

17 flying over us at about 12,000 feet. He gave no evidence of having seen us.

I looked around and there were about 20 of us hanging to the sides of the raft. I saw the Gunnery Officer sitting erect and pulled myself over to him. He said: "Doc, my belly is hurt inside." Near me in the water I saw the Paymaster, who seemed intact; the Torpedo Officer, unhurt, and an Assistant Engineer unhurt. We heard a roar in the distance and saw the Jap planes in formation. I thought My God, don't strafe us again. They flew off in the distance and two of our own dive bombers appeared, circling and blinking their lights. We all cheered and waved, thinking now we will be picked up. They flashed a recognition signal as they circled the Verity, and then flew on when it was not answered. (Note: At this time the Verity, crewless and drifting, was moving rapidly away from the survivors in the rafts. Later that night six officers and men, after a long and desperate swim, got aboard her. They lowered the boat and searched for their shipmates, but were unable to see the rafts which, in any kind of a seaway, are almost impossible to see from the surface. The men in the boat set a course for Espiritu Santo, 400 miles away. When they had the island in sight a patrol plane saw them; landed and took them to safety. They reported the sinking, but by that time those survivors who were still alive had been picked up by the G, the Gwin and the Seminole.)

Already the fuel oil was burning our eyes and it was difficult to see clearly. I noticed another raft beside us with many men hanging to it. Some of them swam to our raft and we were afraid there would be too many of us. We asked them to stay where they were.

Someone called out: "Doctor, Silva is dead." Silva was about 30 years old, a very nice little fellow who had just been made Chief Storekeeper. I could feel no pulse or heartbeat, so pulled him off the raft, removed his identification tag, cut off his life jacket and towed him out a short distance from the raft before letting him slide away into his final rest.

During the next two hours three others died and I repeated the procedure. They had all been badly injured and there was nothing to be done for them. All had been badly burned.

Meanwhile we were making repeated efforts to drag the raft towards the Verity, but we could make no progress. One side would pull while the other pushed. Men were trying to climb on to the raft, but they would only trample and crush the injured and it was necessary to pull them off. We were all certain that we would be picked up the next morning, so we were not concerned.

Darkness soon descended and a chill set in. I was a bit cold, but not to a troublesome degree. There were now about 35 men on and about the raft. Most of them were uninjured, but some were becoming panicky, and continued to try and climb aboard the raft, and it was necessary to pull them off. Only a few were uncooperative; the vast majority were true blue. The other raft continued to drift into us and men switched back and forth between them. They looked like hobgoblins with their black shiny faces and anxious eyes.

The night wore on slowly and every few minutes I would look up at the moon, to find out its position. I knew that it should set at about one a.m., but until it disappeared below the horizon it did not seem to have moved. At intervals I would hear someone calling for help in the distance and, after a few minutes, silence — a dreary, significant silence — another shipmate dead. I hung on beside the Captain throughout the night and he seemed fairly comfortable. At that time there were men two and three deep hanging on to the lines leading out from the raft.

Finally the sky lightened and we started another day. We had water and rations lashed to the plywood grating that formed the bottom of the raft but I said nothing about breaking them out. I felt certain that we would be picked up within thirty-six hours, but if we were not, we would have to conserve water as much as possible. The sun was very warm, but our fuel oil "skin" protected us and we were not uncomfortable.

As the day progressed two B-17's flew over on a N.W. course. They were very high and gave no sign of recognition. The Captain was in poor shape and was unconscious after mid-morning. Poor fellow. He had so much to give the Navy and his Country.

We kept wondering when the ships would be out to pick us up. The men talked about it incessantly. Several men died and were given our simple funeral. The seas were calm and we were still floating in a heavy scum of fuel oil.

As evening approached, the realization that we must spend another night at sea fell heavily on all of us. It was as though we were children getting ready to enter a dark closet alone and have the door locked behind us.

I had not been on the raft at any time, and I was beginning to feel quite weak. I did not look forward to the approaching night with any relish.

The Captain died at about eight o'clock. We cut off his life jacket and he disappeared. The Gunnery Officer said: "We are giving them a good man this time." As the Captain's poor, burned body slid beneath the waves a great silence descended on all of us. He had been an understanding Captain, brilliant yet plain, and a great fighter.

After about ten minutes — announced that he would try to get us to Rennell Island. I thought that he was talking and acting rather strangely, and I crawled into the raft, as I was very tired.

—— had the water breaker unlashed and before we realized it he had tossed it over the side, saying: "It's no good. It won't work." We could have used a pen knife to open it and were sorry to lose it. He then grabbed me from behind and lunged overboard with me in his grasp. He was shouting and cursing and I realized that he had snapped. I managed to break his grip and get back aboard the raft without too much difficulty. We got him aboard, but he must have lunged over again, for I dozed off for a few minutes and when I awakened he had disappeared.

Sleep was impossible, but the mental and physical exhaustion was so great that consciousness would be lost for a few minutes. I would not dignify it with the name "sleep." These periods were filled with wild dreams, all centered about being picked up by a ship. I must have dozed off four or five times and each time I dreamed of another ship picking us up. I know that I was desperately tired.

The next day I felt somewhat stronger. One of the men went out about ten feet from the raft, apparently to cool off. He suddenly screamed and came back to the raft with a large wound in his arm. We had opened the first-aid box, thinking to find something with which I could clean our eyes, so all of its contents were oil and water soaked. About an hour later one of the men who was a few feet from the raft screamed, and we pulled him aboard. His entire left buttock was bitten off. Both men died within a few hours.

We opened the rations and fished out a can of malted milk tablets and opened it. We would scoop out one on the blade of a knife and jiggle it down our throats. We also opened some spam and hardtack and ate it. I found that both made me quite thirsty, so settled for about five malted milk tablets. We cut loose the canteen on the bottom of the raft but were unable to open it. I punched a hole in it with a knife and we each had a sip of water — about five drops per man. However, I was not particularly thirsty at any time.

Through the night men had disappeared and now it was possible for practically all of us to be on the raft. The men sat without talking and all seemed depressed. I said: "Men, let's say a prayer." I prayed with all the fervor that was in me, asking God to send ships or planes to pick us up. From then on, without request, men would start to pray. Two B-17's flew over, but at their usual altitude.

I dreaded the approach of night, for mornings always found so many familiar faces missing. The moon set at about two o'clock and we used that as an indicator of the progress of the night. As darkness fell a hush descended and we set our teeth for another night. The —— was irrational and kept begging me to show him the hatch so that he could go down in the mess hall and rest. I dozed off and dreamed that buccaneers had come aboard. The night dragged oh interminably and seemed as though it would never end.

As the day dawned I saw fourteen men sitting in the raft, and all the others gone. My strength had picked up and I was feeling rather chipper. We broke out the paddles and attempted to rig a sail, using a shirt that one of the boys donated. We broke out the rations and all ate heartily of malted milk tablets and spam.

I prayed again for succor and at about 1030 we heard a plane approach. It was a PBY and flew over at about 800 feet while we waved our paddles madly. He flew on, then turned and came back over us at about 70 feet, dropping a smoke bomb as he passed. It is impossible for me to express the feelings that ran through me as this happened. He flew off, then came back and dropped another smoke bomb. I paddled madly to keep the raft near the bombs. Several of the men wanted to go over near them, saying that they probably contained a message for us, and some water.

About fifteen minutes later one of the men called out: "Here comes a destroyer!" I looked up to see the G headed for us. We came alongside and I held the raft while the other men crawled aboard. I reached over and grabbed the net but could not climb it. The life jacket felt like it weighed 50 pounds. They lashed a line around my chest and pulled me over the side. I flopped on the hard, hot steel deck. It felt like a beautyrest mattress.

The men of the G were going about in their life jackets; very busy; well organized; moving along the decks supporting figures covered with fuel oil.

We were taken aft to the temporary first-aid station where we were given any necessary immediate treatment and wrapped in blankets. As I approached the station the men supporting me called out: "Here's the Meredith's doctor." The fuel oil covering our eyelids made vision difficult, but I could discern the face of Dr. Peek, whom I had last seen at the Officers Club in Pearl Harbor, where we sat dressed in spotless khaki discussing Medical Schools and Hospitals. We wasted no time in formalities, for I could see that he was very busy. All that he needed was one look at me. He wiped the fuel oil from my face and placed mineral oil and cocaine in my eyes to alleviate the incessant burning.

We were taken to the wardroom and on the way I could see other oil-soaked survivors being brought over the side of the ship. After a glass of cold water we fell asleep undisturbed by now unnecessary dreams of being picked up.

After several hours I awakened to find other survivors sleeping on the deck and on the transoms. As they too awakened we exchanged congratulations on being alive, and then came the inevitable summing up of the fate of our fellow officers and enlisted men. They told me how a young boatswain's mate had lashed three rafts together and how his indomitable spirit had served as a stimulus to them all.

After more water and another nap I awakened to find two young seamen looking me over. I asked them if they would help me to the shower. They left the wardroom and returned in a few minutes with a bucket of diesel oil, wash cloths and several bottles of shampoo. Thirty minutes later I stepped from the shower, having shed my fuel oil skin. The bucket and the shampoo bottles were empty and a goodly portion of my fuel oil now covered the dungarees of my seamen-in-waiting.

As the officers were cleaned up they were placed in bunks belonging to the officers of the G, and the crew of the G turned theirs over to our surviving enlisted men. So, for the next ten days, we dressed in the clothes and slept in the bunks of the men of the G. While we rested in their comfortable quarters they slept in blankets on a hard steel deck. We asked for nothing, for everything that we needed was given us or done for us without request. The life of a destroyer man in the South Pacific is at best a difficult one but there is always the knowledge that when a long watch is over a bunk is waiting below, and a chance for a brief rest and a change of clothes. This they sacrificed while fighting off attacks by Japanese bombers and reconnaissance planes. To them the men of the Meredith owe a debt that can never be repaid.

The following morning we entered Guadalcanal, where fierce fighting, land, sea and air, was in progress. Despite the exhaustion a feeling of intense anxiety pervaded us all. One man told me "Hell, Doc, if I'd known we were going to Guadalcanal again I'd have had the G drop me a canteen of water and some cigarettes where they found us, and pick me up when they finally got back out."

For three days we had floated about, dreaming of steak and turkey dinner. Now that food was available none of us could eat. The fuel oil that we had inadvertently swallowed made us ill and we were forced to subsist on broth and toast. During the brief period when our ship was being blown apart we had all felt burning, searing pains in our arms and legs. Now, on examination, we found these members covered with painful wounds produced by small pieces of flying red-hot shrapnel. In addition the salt-water fuel-oil combination had covered the unaffected areas with small boils.

The third day we were resting comfortably and beginning to feel a lot more chipper. One of the officers had started to talk about what he was going to do when he reached San Francisco, when we suddenly felt the G speed up and heard the guns training out. We grabbed for our life jackets as the general alarm sounded and, somehow, stumbled out of the wardroom while the watertight doors clanged shut behind us.

Within the minute the guns were firing and a look of anxiety and fear — which I had never seen before — passed across the faces of the men and, I am sure, my own. We knew now what could happen, and the first sound of gun fire brought it all flooding back to us. We knew that destroyers can sink fast and we also knew that whatever happened we were unable to help ourselves to any appreciable extent. We lay down on the decks. An officer said: "They've done enough to us already." Another looked at me and said: "Doc, if we only had something to do!" I understood his feelings, for in action the doctor waits at his battle station while the fighting goes on. After one such experience I always found something to keep my mind occupied.

For the next five days the G was under constant Japanese air reconnaissance. These days were spent at General Quarters and we either sat or lay on the decks of the wardroom, hoping that somehow Commander Bell and his men would get us through. The Japanese planes over us were the same type that had found the Meredith for the kill, and we were not encouraged. However, the officers of the G laughed it all off, which helped considerably.

Finally there came an afternoon when our harbor was in sight and the planes overhead were friendly. In a splendid piece of work a group of men had been put aboard the Verity and gotten her underway under the very noses of the Japs. She was returning to port with us, her barge retrieved. With so many mouths to feed, rations were getting low, but the Mess Treasurer somehow found a turkey and the steward managed a freezer of ice cream. I dressed for dinner — a pair of white shoes donated by Chief Crane, dungaree trousers from Scotty Etheridge and a khaki shirt from Dr. Peek.

Soon after, boats came alongside to take us to the Naval Hospital on shore. We said good-bye to all and tried, although inarticulately, to express our appreciation. As we pulled away from the G and I looked at her riding at anchor my mind went rushing back to the events of the past two weeks. We had walked through the Valley of the Shadow of Death, and had hoarded away the memories against a long winter of forgetfulness.

Salvage of the Verity

Our course had been laid for the second barge that had been cast off by the towing ship when the heavy Jap attack developed. It had been adrift now for five days and was many miles from its original position, but the Navigator was adept at judging the vagaries of wind and current and we sighted our quarry, rolling deeply to a long southeast swell, within forty minutes from the time that Peters had estimated.

The problem now was to fix the position of the barge; rediscover the Verity; put a crew aboard her and get her underway, then bring her to the barge and let her tow it to an advanced base. Captain Legg assured us that his ship had ample fuel for the four-hundred mile passage to our destination and that the provision storerooms of the Verity were well filled. This knowledge was consoling, for we had left our base with very little food aboard, and the presence of our passengers had proved an additional embarrassment to the Commissary Steward, who prided himself on serving ample and excellent food, and who was afraid that our guests might gain the wrong impression of the kind of chow we had on board the G.

The Commanding General, Guadalcanal, asked for us to return and carry out a fire-support mission by bombarding the Jap lines from close in to the beach. Nothing would have given us more pleasure, especially at this time, but the old Verity, and that drifting barge of bombs and gasoline, were too important to be disregarded, so, with reluctance, we were forced to postpone our Coconut Shoot to a later date.

We were again in the area to which the Fleet had given the name Torpedo Junction and there was a good chance that we might get ourselves another sub. We redoubled the lookouts and kept our ears tuned for the welcome sound of propellers far below. Extracurricular tasks were not devoid of interest but they distracted us from the real job of a destroyer in war, which is to cruise always with a chip on your shoulder, and search out the enemy — whether he be over, under, or on the surface of the sea.

Three days after leaving Guadalcanal, and just a few hours before we again sighted the Verity, there occurred one of those heart-breaking incidents that can happen so frequently in war. A plane was sighted from the bridge. The lookouts and the gun-control officer both reported it at the same time. All stations identified it as a Douglas Transport. That type of plane was a common sight, so, busy with our preparations for handling the Verity, we paid little attention to it and Control did not commence tracking.

In a few minutes I noticed that the plane had changed course and was circling, gradually drawing nearer. Further, while it looked almost like a DC-3, there seemed to be certain barely discernible differences. I called to Collins, one of my signalmen and a man with a fine pair of eyes.

"Put a glass on that plane and see if he's got a white star on him."

Collins looked, and reported, excitedly: "No, sir — he's got a red ball."

The Officer-of-the-Deck and I leaped for the General Alarm; the Ready Guns trained on the plane, and Control commenced tracking.

Our Jap DC-3 drew closer. He was now in to 4000 yards and by all odds he should have been a dead duck on our first salvo. Then and there, with a fine, fat bomber ready to become another trophy flag painted on our gun director in a matter of seconds, we dubbed the putt; we let the ball slip from our fingers; we fell flat on our face within inches of the finish line. To be specific, one of our key gunnery men tripped over his telephone lead and, breaking it, severed all voice communication between the gun director and the fire-control instruments. At that instant I gave the order to Commence Firing.

The results were startling, both to me and to the Jap pilot who, possessing more curiosity than good judgment, continued to close. Our first salvo was all around him. The second tore a hole in his wing and he dove for the water. Despite the inaccurate shooting, which I could not understand, it looked as though we'd clipped him for fair. I heard the Commodore say "You've got him!"

But we hadn't. He skimmed inches over the water, then gradually gained altitude and made off at high speed. The broken phone was replaced in a few seconds, but things happen quickly when you're shooting at a plane, and the Jap was out of range when we commenced to pump out the rapid, well-grouped salvoes that are expected of a destroyer. It was a disappointment. At any rate it taught us to run duplicate telephone leads to some new stations. We wouldn't get caught that way again.

Just before that comedy of errors I had granted permission for Mr. Moto to be given a bath. When we secured from G.Q. a seaman came on the bridge and approached the O.O.D. "Sir," he said, "I had the Jap under the shower when the General Alarm sounded, so I run him back to his cell. If the shootin's all over I'd like to get him scrubbed up." The O.O.D. nodded his head sadly. Like all of us he had expected that we would shoot down some companions for Mr. Moto.

In the meantime the Verity was wallowing in the trough of a sea that was rapidly building up. We put a salvage crew aboard, by boat, then tried to go alongside with the G in order to pass a steam line and decrease the time necessary for getting her underway. We got alongside all right, but the Verity showed her resentment by tossing her heavy bow against our thin plating and punching a hole in our side. There was nothing for it but to take her in tow while the salvage crew lighted fires under her boilers. We sent a working party over, with our Chief Commissary Steward in charge, to dig into the storerooms. We were getting awfully tired of beans, crackers and coffee.

While we were getting the tow line secured, and while our boat was shuttling between the two ships with provisions, I received the first of a series of messages from Lieutenant Superfine, the First Lieutenant of the G, who had been sent in command of the salvage crew. Evidently he had inspected the Verity and discovered the difficulties that lay before him in raising steam with so few burnable materials at hand. In shore language, there was darned little kindling.

From: Verity

To: G

MSG Captain. Am thoroughly convinced that General Sherman was right.

The sea made up rapidly. We hoisted our boat with difficulty, leaving the Commissary Steward and his working party on board the Verity. Shortly after 2200 Superfine reported that he had raised steam, and was ready to test out his engines. We continued to tow for ten hours with both ships working up to higher speeds, until, at 0415, the tow fine parted and the Verity went ahead under her own power. Aboard the G we reeled in what was left of the towing hawser and moved out to a screening position.

From: Verity

To: G

MSG Captain. Good Morning. Still have Commissary Steward as guest and more provisions for you. If impracticable to effect transfer suggest you utilize Jap's services in galley. As matter of curiosity would like to know where we are and what our visual call is. Hope you enjoy eating food for breakfast.

From: G

To: Verity

MSG Captain. If conditions favorable may send for stores and Comsy Steward today but do not slow down for our boat. Mr. Moto says so sorry cannot cook. Will send 0800 position. With regard your call sign I do not wholly agree that we should assign you call for quote Garbage lighters under my command unquote. By food do you refer to the substance we used to eat some weeks ago.

Shortly before 0900 both the G and Gwin sighted a plane that came in close enough to be identified as a Jap twin float seaplane. This was our introduction to the shadow that came in to see us at frequent intervals for the next four days, staying out of gun range except for two brief intervals.

In exchanging information about the Jap plane the two destroyers must have worried the Verity for she signalled over to say "Have only one pair of binoculars but would like to know if enemy aircraft are actually in sight."

From: G

To: Verity

MSG Captain. Suggest advisability making two monoculars from present pair, then four one-eyed men can stand watch and watch. We have been shadowed by twin-float seaplane for two hours. Now bears 160. Situation fluid.

From: Verity

To: G

Refer you to Saint Luke 6/25. (Woe unto you that are full, for ye shall hunger. Woe unto you that laugh now, for ye shall mourn and weep.)

Presentiments of woe on either score were wholly unnecessary, for our bellies, if partially satisfied were still far from full, and the circumstances were not conducive to laughter. Two more of our survivors had died and were buried off the fantail while the Jap snooper circled just out of range and our crew stayed at G.Q., hoping that the shadow would come in. It was reasonable to assume that he had informed his friends of our presence, and that we could expect at any moment the same form of attack that the Meredith received.

Our other passengers were in grave condition. They were now in the secondary stages of shock and exhaustion. They had been with us for a week and we were no closer to our destination than when we had rescued them. They spent their days struggling into their life jackets when the General Alarm sounded, and trying to keep clear of the blast from our guns. It was definitely not the type of treatment that they needed.

There was a group of them on the superstructure deck one morning when I came down from the bridge to try and get a bath during a brief interval of quiet. To my inquiry, "How are things going?" a husky six-footer raised his eyes and said, in a voice quite devoid of expression, "Captain, I want to go home."

Let the fictioneers write of flag-waving and the glamor of gore and battle. These were fighting men and they would return to fight again. They had proved themselves in battle. They spoke up with candidness and affirmed that for the time they had had enough of action. They possessed no mock heroics.

We picked up the other drifting barge and the Verity took it in tow, receiving a "Well Done" from the Commodore for smart ship handling. We were fortunate in that Ensign Enzweiler, of the Verity, had volunteered with the salvage crew. He was familiar with her characteristics, and was a great help to Lieutenant Superfine. Captain Legg, and many of his men, wanted to go back to their ship, but their injuries made it out of the question.

Our shadowing Jap seaplane continued to keep us company.

From: G

To: Verity

MSG Captain. Please join in singing the first verse of Me and My Shadow.

From: Verity

To: G

MSG Captain. Have never won a prize for singing but we have been vocalizing for several days. Our song — San Francisco Open Wide your Golden Gate. Incidentally when you fire would like to know whether for practice or the real McCoy. How was breakfast.

The days settled down into a kind of watchful monotony. General Quarters most of the time; a few rounds at the Jap when he came in close enough to give us the slightest pretext for firing; efforts to make our passengers more comfortable; a semi-nudity — in some cases approaching indecent exposure on the part of our crew, who had delved into their skimpy sea bags to outfit the survivors. Searching for a sentiment that would indicate our state of mind we referred the Verity to St. Paul's Epistle to the Hebrews, Chapter XIII, verse 8, (Jesus Christ, the same yesterday, today and forever) to which they replied that the quotation was a gross understatement. There were more days of five-knot steaming, with empty fuel tanks and storerooms bringing the G's salt-streaked sides high out of the water. Then, one afternoon, the mountains of our island destination shoved their summits over the rim of the horizon.

From: Verity

To: G

What is the song for today with the barn in sight. Sorry you were unable to come over yesterday for the apple pie a la mode.

From: G

To: Verity

Hamlet gives us the thought for today quote One woe doth tread upon another's heels so fast they follow unquote. Hope you have not recovered from indigestion brought on by gross overeating.

Our arrival off port the next morning provided the complete anti-climax of the cruise. The G took station in the van. The Verity, after bringing the barge to a position for towing alongside and sending a pert signal telling us to "Lead on. Whither you go I go," fell in astern and we started up channel through the mine field.

We were midway through the field when the shore station flashed a message: "Stop. Do not enter. A ship has just sunk at the head of the mine field."

That put us squarely on the horns of a dilemma. We could not go forward; there was no room to turn, and backing through the narrow path between mines is not a sport that makes for longevity. We passed the word to the Verity, and both ships went astern in a most gingerly fashion until we were once more in the clear.

From: Verity

To: G

MSG Captain. Whew — Repeat — Whew!

Later in the day we were allowed to enter. With food for only one meal; with oil for a bare two hundred more miles' steaming, the G slid up to a tanker for fuel, and dispatched a Commando Unit in search of meat and vegetables. The Commodore and I, from information that we had been able to piece together, would now prepare a report giving the details of the Meredith's loss and the salvage of Verity and barge.

We turned Mr. Moto over to the Marines on shore. After dinner, boats came off to remove our passengers. As they cleared the side they raised their voices in a cheer for the G, then disappeared in the darkness, leaving us with oil-soaked blankets, few clothes, virtually no shoes — and memories of fine courage.

DUNGAREE SAILORS

In a large ship it is possible for a few men to slide by with a minimum of effort; to stand their watches, man their battle stations, but contribute little to the general welfare. In a destroyer there can be no deadheads; a man pays his freight, does his job and more besides, or pretty soon he finds himself at the gangway, waiting with bag and hammock for transfer to another ship. There are no union hours anywhere in the Service or for any person from apprentice seaman to admiral, but in a large ship a man can feel reasonably confident that a certain set routine will be carried out. He knows that, after a fashion, certain days bring certain drills; certain hours are taken up with previously prescribed duties. In a destroyer there is no such adherence to plan, and that is one reason why destroyer duty is hard duty — and why it holds a fascination.

The destroyer is a triple-threat weapon, designed to carry the offensive against submarines, aircraft or surface vessels. Its guns are "double purpose" — high angle for planes, hard-hitting, flat trajectory for surface work. Its torpedoes make it the most dangerous type of ship in the fleet for its size. Commenting on its strictly offensive character. Rear Admiral Tisdale, who commands the destroyers of our Pacific Fleet, closed a recent letter to me with the words: "I consider the destroyer the fightingest thing afloat." Its action in the South Pacific bears out the description. They're the hottest, coldest, fastest, rough-ridingest ships we have; they are uncomfortable and wet; they have a hull so thin you could break through it with a hammer; they have the horsepower of a battleship and less armor than our newest bombing planes; they carry three hundred officers and men packed in a slender streamlined form that is designed to strike hard and strike fast. Gun for gun, ton for ton, they are the fightingest things afloat.

In destroyers responsibility comes early. The Chief Engineer Officer has charge of a plant as powerful as a battleship; the Gunnery Officer is boss of a fire-control system as intricate as any in the fleet; the Executive Officer is second-in-command and navigator. All of these officers, as Lieutenants, are responsible for the care, upkeep and operation of Departments in which, in a larger ship, they would be well down the line of seniority. If a young officer takes to responsibility and proves that he can work hard; if he can do a little more than is expected of him, and if he has the type of judgment that makes for quick action and proper reaction in emergency — he'll get along. If, in addition, he is the fortunate possessor of a personality that makes officers like to work with him, and his men like to work for him; if he can be reasonably cheerful after six months of day-in, day-out cruising, and keep his eyes open when it has been seventy-two hours since he last saw his bunk — he'll be welcome aboard any destroyer in the fleet. But if he's just a little better than run-of-the-mine; if he figures that the end of the day means the end of work, and after watching him awhile you see he's not the type to whom men come with their troubles and their little personal triumphs — then it will not be long before his face is missing around the wardroom table. Lack of training in a new officer is expected — we'll train him; intellectual shortcomings are capable of adjustment — we'll find a place for him. But lack of effort we haven't time to cope with. If he won't try, we ease him along, and get someone else "in his room," as they put it in the Old Navy.

In the G we were blessed with earnest, industrious officers and the finest crowd of men I ever worked with. We spoke of the cheerful cherub that stayed on the yardarm, and gave this little angel credit for the bombs that missed us, and the torpedoes that went past the stem. But no self-respecting cherub would have hung around a destroyer so many months unless he had gained a feeling of affection for the people on deck below him, and unless he could get an occasional laugh from watching them and listening in. Certainly, there must have been times when he came down from his perch to join the crowd that gathered around the anchor windlass on a quiet evening when Mulno, the Chief Boatswain's Mate, held forth. I've met many able raconteurs in the Navy during the past twenty-three years, but Mulno is the only one who never repeated himself. There was always "no bottom" when he sounded his sea of stories, and he had a personal anecdote for any occasion. The first few years of his naval service resembled a sign curve as he was alternately promoted and reduced in rating. On one of the up portions of the curve he was made the coxwain of an admiral's barge. One day there was an early trip and, caught before he had waxed the linoleum and woodwork, Mulno gave it a quick rub down with butter. It was beautiful and shiny and all was well until the admiral stepped aboard. His feet slipped from under him and he rocketed into the air. "I guess he was right much surprised," Mulno admitted, "but he kept his head. He managed to say, 'Mulno, you're fired,' before he ever hit the deck."

As Chief Boatswain's Mate it was Mulno's job, under the First Lieutenant, to take general charge of the deck force. On a destroyer rust is a persistent enemy. The main deck is under water on all but the calmest days. At any speed the ship dips her nose under, and tosses water aft along the forecastle — over the bridge, in a moderate sea. On a sharp turn the fantail submerges like a startled porpoise. It is the endless duty of the deck force to combat the rust and corrosion, and the Chief Boatswain's Mate is the boss.

One night at anchor I asked the Captain of a destroyer alongside if he had room for a newspaper correspondent whom we had as passenger, as the G was getting underway at four in the morning. "Send him over," he said. "We'll put him in the Professional Men's room." "You'll put him in what?" "Oh," he said, "I've got a banker and a doctor and a couple of lawyers over here, all in one room. We'll put the newspaper man in with them."

After working for two years with the officers of our Naval Reserve I am continually amazed at the rapidity with which they learn their jobs, the conscientious manner in which they perform their duties and their all around ability and interest. In every way they have brought a new breath of life to the Service, and the Navy is fortunate to have them. Professional training and knowledge aside, the principal difference between the Naval Academy graduate and the college man lies in the manner in which they carry out an order, and the degree of supervision that they require. Give the Naval Academy Ensign an order and he will reply "Aye, aye, sir" and get it done, though he may not know beans about it — he'll find out, and do it with no follow-up on your part. The college man is inclined to be more analytical. He wants to know the reason. And he has an understandable tendency to pass the order along to a subordinate and accept his explanation for modifying it or failing to carry it out. He requires more supervision — but not for long, if his shipboard training is properly monitored. Should he belong to the fractional percentage who will never learn, you check him off as a mistake and get rid of him, in the same manner that you would a Naval Academy Ensign if he failed to carry his share of the load. Our Reserves make mistakes; they do weird things to the language of the sea, which is as foreign to them as their business jargon would be to us professional sailors, but for my part it makes little difference if a man gets mixed up in port and starboard; if he calls the bow of the ship "that part of the boat up front," and uses the handy word "gadget" to cover an ignorance of naval nomenclature, provided he can load a gun or fire a torpedo or feed water to a boiler. As a matter of fact they fall in with naval routine so easily that after a man had been in the ship a month or so, I didn't know — or care — whether he was regular or reserve. We were put on our mettle to train them, but it's easy to train men who want to learn, who are interested in every phase of naval life, and who, because of their diverse civilian accomplishments, bring a fresh and inspiriting atmosphere to shipboard routine.

Among the officers four of us were regulars and graduates of the Academy. In our intercollegiate wardroom, there were graduates of Yale, Princeton, V.P.I., U.S.C., Stanford, Northwestern, St. Mary's, V.M.I., Vanderbilt, Tulane, and the Universities of Virginia, North Carolina, Texas, Oklahoma, California, and Michigan.

All were in their early twenties; all had practiced a business or profession after leaving college, and before receiving a short course as Reserve Midshipmen. In consequence, our wardroom small talk went far beyond the usual limits of "shop," for we numbered in the mess men who had experiences as:

Journalist

Mining engineer

Manager of a textile mill

Student of animal husbandry

Raiser of pedigreed cattle

Clothing merchant

Lawyer

Instructor in public speaking

Efficiency engineer

Aviation engineering designer

Broker

Surgeon

From the tip of her pointed stem to the center of the rounded stern beneath the depth charge racks, the G measured a few inches over 348 feet. At the broadest portion of her beam she was 36 feet across. The result gave her the streamlined shape of a racing whippet, with the same nicely rounded rib-line, and no excess flesh. She was made for speed; she was designed to carry the maximum fighting power in her slender hull, and there was no wasted space. In fact there was so little unused room that when it became necessary to find a new location for a motor unit that measured about four feet by one, there was great head scratching and figuring before we finally found enough room in a compartment on top of the keel.

The engineering spaces — firerooms and enginerooms — are amidships, and use about half of the ship's inner spaces. As originally designed, the crew would mess forward and sleep aft — an innovation that did away with the old four-stacker arrangement where a man swung his leg from the bunk and found himself in place at the mess table. The war requirements of a larger crew did not permit us to continue having separate dining rooms and bedrooms. We put bunks in the mess halls in every possible place in tiers of three, but even then there were a dozen or more men who had to sleep catch-as-catch-can, and who kept their clothes in sea bags because there was no more room for lockers. In the wooden ships each man was allowed eighteen inches of swinging for his hammock. In destroyers he has about the same amount, but it is vertical. He can slide into his bunk, but he can't sit up in it without striking his head on the one above or, in the case of the topmost man, the pipes and wires that run along the overhead.

I don't remember anyone falling out of his bunk in the G. Perhaps tin-can sailors are better bronco busters. In the Boise we rarely had a surprise night General Quarters that some unfortunate didn't turn up at sick bay with a broken head. It became routine to ask Dr. Stelle "How many sutures tonight?" when we gathered in the wardroom after securing from Battle Stations, and generally we found that someone had taken a swan dive from an upper bunk, or banged his skull against a hatch. On one occasion a sleep-befuddled sailor stepped off into space and landed on the hangar deck twelve feet below. The surgeon had a good deal of patch work to do that night.

On each bunk is a hair or kapok mattress inside a muslin cover. Every man has a pillow and a couple of warm woollen blankets. We don't bother with sheets, the seagoing laundry situation being what it is, and pajamas are something that officers wear when the ship is not in a battle area. That's one thing about a war — you save money on dress uniforms and gold lace and pajamas. I slept "all standing" for a year — slipping below after dawn General Quarters for a bath and fresh clothing. It worked out pretty well — I got caught only once in the shower when the General Alarm started bonging. On our flagship the Commodore directed the movements of the squadron wearing nothing but a rapidly drying covering of soap — just soap — the morning of a vicious sub attack when one of our large ships caught a torpedo and the G, on the opposite side of the formation, put on a fine show of broken field running to dodge three others that slid by close aboard.

We are never greatly concerned about clothing aboard destroyers in wartime. The crew wear the blue denim shirt and pants to which a village in India has given the name of dungarees. Their caps are dyed the same color — we avoid white in combat waters. Khaki is the uniform for officers. At sea we cover our heads according to the temperature and how easily we blister in the sun. Overseas caps, visored caps, pith helmets, or the inner detachable portion of a steel helmet — that looks like the hats women wore in the early twenties — which resembled an article of Victorian bedroom crockery without the handle. After our first visit to Wellington, the troops blossomed forth in high-peaked campaign hats, pinned up at the side with the badge of the New Zealand arm. That phase was brief — we catalogued shore headgear, with beards, as something to be abjured in the G. Some ships go in for beards — on the China Station they are invariably bushy and red, but we decided that the officers and crew of the G would appear to better advantage without the concealing shrubbery of a frontal hedge. There's something in the Navy Regulations that permits a man to have a beard and mustache provided they are not grotesque. There is no criterion set forth as a yardstick for measuring the aesthetic effect, but a destroyer Captain with whom I once served devised his own standards. Whenever a man appeared at inspection with the beginnings of a shaggy dog face covering, the Captain would look at it with care and then pass judgment. "It's grotesque," he would declare flatly. "Shave it off." In the G we followed the same rule. Facial fuzz was, ipso facto, grotesque, just as side burns and a hat hanging on the sternmost hair of the head are marks of the Hollywood sailor and the Vine Street Commando. Your deep-water seagoing man wears his uniforms with an air of distinction that the novice, who knows no better, attempts to imitate by putting on a skin-tight jumper and ridiculous pants, cocking his hat on the back of his head and rolling along the streets in what he conceives to be the manner of an old salt. The real Navy man will have a fling on the beach — and who wouldn't — but he chooses privacy for his celebrations and he doesn't bring ridicule on his uniform by blustering in public or wearing his clothes like an extra from the Yo-Heave Ho movie set on his way to the studio cafeteria for lunch.

Clothing and shoes were difficult to replace during the early months of the South Pacific Offensive. We had a full allowance on board but after four months of wear and launderings our shirts tore whenever we thrust an arm in the sleeve, the bottoms of our trousers began to have a natty fringed effect, and our shoes looked like the property of a corn-field hand with sore feet. A man with two pairs of socks was something of a dude. When we picked up the Meredith's survivors we outfitted them as best we could, and found ourselves in a condition approaching mass indecent exposure. In one of the storerooms we carried an outfit of anti-gas protective clothing that consisted of overalls and hooded jumper. We broke out the jumpers and, because they were white, sent them to our miniscule laundry to be dyed blue. It was a good idea, but there was a shortage of dye, and the results were garments of a pale, baby-blue tint. We wore them, because it was chilly and rainy, and the long sleeves and hood would be a protection against flash-burns, but it was excruciatingly funny to see a half dozen broad-shouldered, hairy-chested sailormen crouched around their gun looking for all the world like children in bunny suits waiting for the Easter egg roll to start.

The bunny suits bring to mind the Boise, and Easter Sunday, 1942, when the Japanese moved into the Bay of Bengal and raised merry whatnot. We were a few hundred miles to the west, expecting to escort a very slow convoy from Bombay to Colombo, but when Colombo was raided and stations from Rangoon to Trincomali began sending reports of attack, we were diverted from our route and told to proceed alone.

A few days earlier, on board a British cruiser, one of her officers asked if we had much trouble with men adrift when we went to Battle Stations. We hadn't heard the word used in that manner. "What do you mean by 'adrift'?" we asked. "Well —" he answered, "if a man's adrift he's not closed up." That was another poser. "Closed up?" The Britisher looked baffled — it was difficult to explain things to us, it appeared. "If a man's not closed up he's — ah — he's adrift!" he told us, triumphantly. Adrift — not closed up; closed up — not adrift. We nodded our heads and changed the subject.

On that Sunday morning someone found an Easter card, and sent it to Captain Moran:

As the Boise sails the Arabian Sea the Easter rabbit seemed to be Adrift and not closed up —

Yet in some mysterious yogi way he came on board us just to say Happy Easter, Captain M, from we and they and those and them — The Boise boys, that fortunate crew, who'll take her there and back, with you

So cheer the Easter rabbit, cheer Colombo and Bombay —

Cheer the six point five knot convoy — if we must —

This Easter Day.

In destroyer life the percentages that customarily apply to the time spent in working, eating, sleeping and enjoying recreation suffer a considerable upset. Work is never ending; sleep is a luxury that you clutch at odd times and hours; recreation means an hour or so without general quarters, and food is a source of conjecture, reminiscence and planning for the future. It is also one of the two greatest morale factors — mail from home being the other. Even in peacetime, men will ship over or extend their enlistment if they are in a "good feeding ship." When two ships are alongside, and sailors lean over the rail chatting with men next door, one of the first questions is always "How's the chow over there?" A good Commissary Steward and cooks who know their business can go a long way toward promoting happiness and contentment among a ship's company. Sailors don't go in for a soup and salad luncheon, or a skimpy breakfast of toast and coffee. They want a man-size chow, and they need it, for many of them are boys in their teens who sprout in all directions and outgrow their shoes and clothing in the course of a few months — in a good feeding ship.

Our navy, in ships of the destroyer class and larger, uses the cafeteria system of feeding the crew. It has many advantages over the older method of trying to serve ten or fifteen men at a table; bringing them food from the galley at the same time for everyone. Wartime watches prevent more than half the crew from eating at the same hour. The cafeteria system. with steam tables, keeps the food hot and allows each man to select as much or as little as he wishes. The usual breakfast includes fresh fruit, cereal, and either eggs — with ham or bacon — creamed chipped beef, or hot cakes and syrup. On Wednesday and Saturday breakfast means fruit, baked beans, sweet bread or buns of some kind. There is always coffee, unlimited.

The noonday meal is a working man's dinner. There will be soup, at least two vegetables, and pork chops or veal chops or roast beef or fried chicken, dessert and a beverage. Supper is a lighter meal. In the tropics it includes a cold salad, cold sliced meats, dessert and coffee or tea. The noon meal on Saturday is invariably a New England boiled dinner and baked ham — a holdover from peacetime when Saturday morning meant Captain's Inspection, and the cooks, consigning the noon meal to bake oven and boiling-coppers, could turn to in the galley, polish their knives, scour the ranges and be ready, in spotless white hats and aprons, when the Master-at-Arms stepped in and shouted "Attention." Parenthetically, every Captain enjoys this part of his inspection, for it gives him an opportunity to nibble a slice of ham fragrant with brown sugar and cloves, and say to the baker: "Let me see if this cake is as good as the one you made last Saturday."

When the fresh provisions run out, and this takes only a few days in a destroyer where our icebox space is limited, the cooks are put on their mettle. Dehydrated vegetables and boned tinned meats have been a great help to the commissary department, and so long as there is flour and sugar, something in the way of cake can be baked, but after a few weeks the day comes when it is possible to walk around in the storerooms that were filled to the overhead when you left port; when the cans have been transformed into flat strips of tin, bundled for shipment home as salvage and stowed in the deck lockers that are empty now of onions and potatoes and cabbages. It is not often that you get down to bed-rock staples like rice, beans, flour, sugar, and coffee. It happened only twice in the G, and that was early in the campaign. Toward the end the crew had fried chicken every Sunday and ice cream every day in port, and we were inclined to be critical if there was a shortage of celery and fresh lettuce at the advanced bases. You get soft in a hurry.

In a destroyer, food is served in three places — in the mess compartments for the crew; in the C.P.O. mess room for the Chief Petty Officers, and in the wardroom for the officers. The chiefs have the same food as the crew, with a little something extra that they pay for out of their own pockets. They have their own mess cooks — who do not cook, but who bring the food from the galley, serve it, and clean the compartment. The younger seamen are assigned this duty in rotation — as mess cooks for the crew as well as for the C.P.O's, and they receive extra pay while they are mess cooking. They take turns, also, as scullerymen, another extra-pay job.

The officers have a tiny pantry adjoining the wardroom, and a section of the galley is assigned for their use. For them the cooking, serving and room cleaning is done by members of the messman branch — who have no other duties except, of course, at General Quarters, for every man has a battle station. The messmen are Filipinos, Chamorros (natives of Guam) or Negroes. Filipinos have not been enlisted in the navy for several years. Those who were already in the Service were allowed to remain, and to receive promotion when due. The Chamorros were quiet and capable, but that source of supply is not now available, with Guam in Japanese hands. So the majority of the stewards and stewards' mates are Negroes. Their battle station in the G was in one of the lower handling rooms and magazines — sending powder and shell up the hoists of the gun. They did a good job; we had no worries that their gun would be slow in loading, for they "passed the ammunition" with the same equanimity and quiet efficiency with which they passed vegetables in the wardroom.

The officers, of course, pay for their own food, which they buy on shore or purchase from the general mess. To plan the menus, and collect mess bills and keep the accounts a member is elected as Mess Caterer. He sits at the opposite end of the table from the President of the Mess (the Executive Officer in large ships, the Captain in destroyers), and serves for a term of office that is dependent upon his own ability and interest, and the state of abdominal contentment of his messmates. Some mess caterers go on and on like the brook; others are voted out at the end of the month, if the mess bill has taken a sudden and unexplainable rise, if the mess share has dropped out of sight, or if the unfortunate caterer has sought to swing the mess toward his own particular culinary affectations. I once served in a cruiser where the navigator complained constantly about the food. In any ship this is tantamount to election on a "let's see what you can do" basis. He brought the mess bill down by locking the icebox and pantry to keep out the mid-night snackers, a most damnable violation of naval usage which we accepted because we were saving money, but when for four consecutive days, lunch consisted of calves brains and a red apple, we threw him out and elected, by popular acclaim, a Lieutenant whose platform included three courses for lunch, and tasty bits for the midwatch and, inevitably, a five-dollar extra assessment at the end of the month.

In another ship, a four-stack destroyer, our Ensign mess caterer attended a cocktail party just before our departure for five months in the tropics, and, fascinated by the taste of anchovies, ordered the steward to lay in a good supply. He did. We had anchovies on toast, anchovy salad, minced anchovy and bacon (there's a neat dish!) and, as a frightful climax, anchovies stewed up in a kind of bouillabaisse that tasted like something you might pick up along the shore at low tide. We begged the doctor for something to soothe our salt-parched throats, and held an election on the spot. The new mess caterer, after going into a huddle with the steward, announced with pride that there would be home-made cherry pie for dinner. But the steward, too, had come under a spell. His pie was a beautiful St. Patrick's creation made entirely of green maraschino cherries.

Every ship has its mess boy stories which, as a rule, center about the difficulties of an island boy with the English language, or the more homely problems of a young Negro on shipboard. My favorite has to do with a Chamorro who was being examined for promotion. Invariably the first question is to define the difference between an order and a command. The Training Course tells them, in effect, that an order allows the recipient some initiative in how he carries it out; a command is arbitrary and inclusive. The youngster from Guam had his own ideas, based on a few weeks' experience around the wardroom. "An order," he wrote, "is ham and eggs. A command is Bring 'em in."

The G's reputation as a good feeding ship was enhanced by the ability of our bakers. In a four by four affair of a bakeshop, they turned out light, crusty bread, delicious pie and cake. The exhaust from the bakeshop led up near the bridge. On nights when baking was in progress the midwatch was a hunger-provoking experience and the officer of the deck had great difficulty keeping his mind on his job. At intervals he sent scouts below to "see how they're coming along in the bakeshop," and at about three in the morning a plate of fresh cake, or a large wedge of apple pie still bubbling from the oven would appear on the bridge, for the O.O.D., with more waiting in the galley for the men when they came off watch. Mid-watch snacks are a part of the navy. When the night came that I couldn't put away a double slice of hot pie and two cups of coffee, and fall asleep as soon as I hit the bunk, then I knew I was growing old.

Despite all of the high-powered glasses and the fancy gadgets for increasing and improving vision, we can always use a man with good eyesight. In the South Pacific, where a periscope may bob up at any moment, or enemy planes come swinging in low on the horizon or rocketing down from the overhead, every man on watch on the topside is a lookout, and frequently first information of a contact will come from a seaman who, without benefit of binoculars, spots the flicker of sunlight on a bomber's wing before the bridge has picked it up.

Some of our best lookouts in the G were the men on depth-charge watch, way aft on the fantail. From this unfavorable position, so close to the surface of the sea that the men had to do a human fly act and climb up the vertical surface of a bulkhead to dodge the waves that rolled across the stern, we received accurate and first-hand information that caused the regularly assigned bridge lookouts to get a little red around the ears.

Talker: "Fantail reports a plane bearing 175 relative; position angle twenty; looks like a B-17."

O.O.D.: "Very good. Ask the lookouts why they haven't picked up that plane."

Lookout: (10 feet above the bridge level where he has heard the O.O.D.'s order to the talker): "B-17 coming in on the starboard quarter."

O.O.D.: "Yeah. You let the fantail scoop you again."

On one occasion the lookouts were vindicated. The torpedomen on depth-charge watch reported a plane. Neither the bridge nor the lookouts could find it in their glasses.

O.O.D.: "Ask the fantail if they still see that plane."

Fantail: "We still see it" — pause, then, disgustedly, "It's flapping its wings."

Airplanes that flapped their wings were not the only thing that fooled the lookouts, and sometimes caused us to bring the guns to bear. Porpoises leaping through quiet water make realistic periscope tracks; blackfish submerging in a whirl of foam become submarines in a crash dive; tree trunks and branches, and lone coconuts that abound in the northern Coral and Solomons Seas — all of these give a thrill to sailors who are looking for trouble. On a bright, cloudless day a planet may become a prankster. We were going south in the Sulu Sea a few days after the outbreak of war. It was a quiet, sunny morning with unlimited visibility. A destroyer had just gone up to a tanker for fuel. A mile or so ahead, the Langley began firing into the sky. The destroyer cut its lines, cast off the fuel hose and forged ahead to lend assistance.

Destroyer: "Request bearing and position angle of target."

Langley: (Whanging away with every gun she had): "Bearing 270; position angle nine-oh."

Destroyer: (After a careful scrutiny of the sky): "Believe you are firing at Venus."

Langley: (After a long pause and a quick cessation of fire): "Return to your station. Resume fueling."

We were about five hundred miles west of San Francisco a few days after I had taken command of the G, when Gun Control reported sighting an object overhead that looked like a barrage balloon adrift. We swung the guns up to get a little practice firing, but the target was very high, well out of range, and hanging stationary in space. "It's Venus," the Navigator announced, and the Gun Boss admitted that it would strain our main battery if we tried to bring down this particular barrage balloon.

There was one young sailor in the G whose eyes must have had an adjustment to take care of the earth's curvature, for on at least three occasions he reported sighting ships long before the tips of their masts came over the horizon in the field of our binoculars. This youngster was unique in other respects. An orphan, and a product of the city streets, he was sending his sister to college, after Heaven knows what personal privation in his early teens to see that she received a good elementary and high-school foundation. He was cheerful, and popular with his shipmates, but I never saw him smile and when he talked he did it without moving his lips, in the manner of a child who had been forbidden to speak. His duties required him to make frequent reports by phone, over which he spoke in a low-voiced monotone that was impossible to understand. After a good deal of instruction he broke himself of the habit by exaggerating the pronunciation of every syllable. He was a good boy and an asset to the G.

In a ship's company made up largely of reserves the composite background of the crew is not what you would consider a normal preparation for seafaring life. We had ex-farmers and policemen and horse trainers and salesmen, clerks and municipal employees, school teachers and deacons. The educational standard is high, for regulars and reserves alike, and this remains a source of perplexity, a cause for envy, and an early topic of conversation, among all foreign officers with whom we come in contact, for no other navy has men who possess the American sailor's initiative, intelligence and all-around adaptability. The crew of a ship is a team on which the mistakes of any member may effect the final score. Among the entire ship's company, from the Captain to the greenest seaman, there must exist a well-balanced cooperation, mutual trust, and a knowledge that the other fellow can be relied upon to do his job with minimum supervision. In war and peace, at anchor or underway, in the frozen waters of the north or the tropical heat of the Solomons, the shipboard routine continues, and while we are not so polished and shining these days as we used to be, the problems of ship's housekeeping, like those at home, seem never ending. We decentralize the work load, and split it into as many parts as there are members of the crew, with each man responsible for a bit of the deck, a belowdeck compartment, a storeroom or the area around a gun or torpedo tube. In the Biblical manner we have captains of ten and captains of hundreds, and while there may be minor differences in the assignment of shipboard responsibility — "different ships, different long splices," in the Old Navy term, a man going on board a ship of any type may be reasonably certain of being given the same watch and the same cleaning that he had in his former duty.

The pilot house and chart house are the province of the quartermaster for routine upkeep, and for the more specialized duties concerned with navigation. The chief quartermaster is the navigator's assistant. He sees to it that the chronometers are wound each morning, and this momentous bit of news transmitted to the officer of the deck, so that at noon the O.O.D. may inform the Captain "Twelve o'clock, sir; chronometers wound" in the way it has been done in our Service since Paul Jones and Thomas Truxtun. He looks after the navigator's own, personal instruments, watching that young officers under instruction do not commit the grievous naval offense that causes the navigator to leap into the air and shout "Who the hell has been using my sextant!" Young gentlemen have been known to use the navigator's dividers for stirring coffee, in the dim hours of the midwatch, but this breach of tradition is so horrible that it is spoken of only in whispers.

Every mail brings booklets of correction for Charts and Sailing Directions, Notices to Mariners and other bits of information that must be inked on charts and pasted in books. In peacetime you stock up with charts of the area in which you are working. A ship on the Mediterranean Station wouldn't clutter her storerooms with charts of the Antarctic or the China Sea. It's different now, when you use a sheepskin coat today and a sun helmet tomorrow, and the lookouts are equally adept at spotting icebergs or palm trees, and Charts and Sailing Directions no longer fit in the cozy five-foot book shelf above the chronometer case. They have suffered a wartime inflation; they block the passage to the Captain's Emergency Cabin, they fill the space beneath the navigator's mattress, and if the quartermasters had their way, we'd find charts in the ice box and in the Commodore's bureau. They view the mail orderly's return with misgivings, for each pouch holds more charts, more corrections.

At General Quarters, and during Emergency Drills, a quartermaster takes the wheel and steers the ship. At other times this duty is performed by seamen, all of whom must qualify as helmsman. Usually there is a "lee helmsman" — a young seaman under instruction who, if unwatched, has been known to become so fascinated with the graduations on the gyro repeater that he puts the wheel the wrong way, and keeps trying to catch the little marker, which results in the ship chasing the compass — an interesting pastime, but unprofitable.

The Quartermaster of the Watch records routine weather information in the ship's log and keeps a notebook in which he jots down items of interest as a help for the officer of the deck in writing his log at the end of the watch. There, again, is a chance for self expression, and green quartermasters, if given the opportunity, may devote pages to describing the approach, passage and retirement of a mild rain squall, while avoiding any mention of fleet changes of course and speed, and the fact that so-and-so made a depth-charge attack.

In an exposed position near the mainmast there is a duplicate wheel, compass and engine telegraph. At General Quarters a quartermaster is stationed at this "after steering station," ready to take the wheel if the pilot house suffers damage. In the very stern of the ship, over the rudder, is the steering engine room — another spot where a quartermaster is on watch at all times, for a steering failure may bring quick and unpleasant results, and aboard ship we like to have a spare at hand. Drill in shifting steering control from bridge to steering engine room is a part of the day's routine.

Extending around three sides of the chart house is the signal bridge, home of the "flag wavers" and "bunting tossers" — the signalmen, who look after the visual communications between ships. There are three general methods of making polite reply to a senior or asking a contemporary for the telephone number of that girl in Wellington. It can be done by signal searchlight, using the Morse code; by flag hoist, using flags and pennants that have, singly or in combinations, arbitrary meanings that are found in a signal book; or by a pair of semaphore flags waved around so violently that you don't recognize it as the same thing you used to do in the old Beaver Patrol.

In peacetime a signalman jumped for the small searchlight whenever there was a message to be sent, but searchlights, even in daylight, make you more conspicuous than you like when you hope to stalk a submarine, so these days we rely principally on flags and semaphore. For every second of every minute around the clock a signalman keeps his eye glued to one end of a telescope pointed at the signal bridge of the senior ship present. He is the signal spotter. Another man holds a snap hook on the end of a halliard (a small line rove through a block on the yardarm) ready to snap it into the eye of a flag. He is the bender on. A third holds the other end of the halliard, waiting to pull the flags up at the word "take it away." He is the hoister. There is an operator at each light, and a recorder, with message blanks and pencil. This is the signal team at General Quarters during daylight. For routine watchstanding we do the best we can with a skeleton signal outfit. At night, if we must send signals by visual, we use miniature lights shaped roughly like a rifle.

Visual communication is highly competitive, with every signalman, like every cribbage player, certain that his team is the best in the fleet. If you can hoist a signal before the ship ahead has run it up you feel a glow of triumph and you are apt to hear someone on the bridge say "Scooped him, by God." On the other hand, if your mania for speed is more compelling than your desire for accuracy and you notice that every other ship has up a red and yellow flag and at your own yardarm a blue and white one flies boldly — then you have been "skunked," and your signalmen have very little to say.

If your spotter is able to read the flags as they come out of the flag bag on the flagship (that's a lot of flags, but I don't know how else to phrase it) so that your own hoist is two-blocked ahead of the ship that originated the signal, your performance is notable and you wear a self-satisfied smirk that lasts until you answer the Commodore's searchlight and he says: "I have been calling you for five minutes." Ships have no alibi equivalent to "wrong number" or "sorry, sir, the line is biz-zee."

On a big ship the signalmen have a spacious bridge and a steady platform. To acquire a reasonably accurate picture of a destroyer signal spotter in action, put a small telescope to your eye, let two people shake you violently from side to side while a third tosses water in your face, and try to identify the color combination in a flag three feet square, whipping in the wind on a building three miles away.

To send a message by semaphore from a destroyer a man must be a seagoing cowboy. Bracing his knees against a tee-shaped support on top of a gun mount or some other exposed position that gives an unobscured background, he leans into the wind and waves his flags, reading the message from a paper tucked in his waist, or trying to hear as someone calls the words to him against the noise of a gale.

Intensely jealous of their ship's reputation in communications, signalmen spend all their waking moments on the bridge, lending a hand to the men on duty, criticizing the slowness of a neighboring ship, drinking coffee which they brew in a percolator that is kept in a small locker along with the portable sewing machine for flag repair, lengths of bunting in various colors, and the leading signalman's personal long-glass, wrapped in green felt and stowed in a special bracket. In the evening, when canvas covers are hauled over the flag bags, and the searchlights are secured, the signalmen off watch gather in a corner of the darkened bridge for low-voiced argument on minor points of communication procedure and to tell a new member of the gang about famous "busts" in signaling. "We were making twenty knots, and we catapulted two planes and the old man says to make the signal 'I have launched two aircraft.' So this chief signalman runs up a hoist, and pretty soon the admiral sends us a message 'How do you do it at this speed'? The Old Man smells a rat and he says 'Chief, check the meaning of our hoist.' And he does, and it means 'I have two divers below.' And boy, did the Old Man run him up the mast!"

The most cliquey rating in a destroyer is that of torpedoman's mate, for these men are super-specialists. Everyone in the ship knows something about signals, knotting and splicing and general seamanship. All the deck force have battle stations in the gunnery department — either in magazines, gun control or at the guns themselves. The firemen know something about the engines, and the machinist's mates understand boilers. But none except the torpedo crew and officers who have attended the torpedo school has a working knowledge of those lean, wicked-looking, highly complicated mechanisms that we call "tin fish." Torpedoes have changed a great deal since 1925 when I attended the school at Newport and learned to take them apart, put them together, using dozens of tools, each known by number, and, with a little prayer that they wouldn't sink, fire them on the practice range. The tin fish are different, but the technique of the torpedomen is unvarying, and they still play to a capacity house when they haul a torpedo from the tube, lay out their tools and open it up with the precision and confidence of an experienced surgeon commencing a major abdominal operation. The senior torpedoman is the operator. He is surrounded by assistants, and damn their eyes if they hand him forceps when he wants a sponge. "Gimme a 141." A weird-looking tool is slipped in his hand. Back from the tube a torpedoman explains. "He's gonna take out the gyro housing." The spectators nod. The gyro housing is as meaningless as the theory of relativity, but it's a swell show. Now the chief is up to his elbows in the innards of the patient. He calls for more tools, wiggles his arms — and pulls out a shiny object. "That's the gyro, see." Around the crowd there are smiles of admiration. "Boy, he pulled out the gyro."

In the last war, when we seldom met a surface enemy, there were few opportunities to use torpedoes. In the four night actions off Savo and Lunga Point our destroyers sent more torpedoes crashing into the Japanese Fleet than the navy had previously fired in warfare since the tin fish was invented. The G carried quite a few torpedoes. One torpedo, properly placed, will put a cruiser out of action — may well sink it, and a salvo of two or three will whittle the largest battleship down to a boy's size. In a naval engagement the ideal situation is met when, simultaneously, the destroyers reach their attack position, the bombers arrive at the dropping point, and the battle line opens fire. This triple combination will throw any enemy fleet into confusion. It is rarely accomplished, even in Fleet Problems, but a destroyer torpedo attack, alone, if pushed well home, forces the enemy to maneuver and places him at a tactical disadvantage. To combat the Torpedo Boat of the late nineteenth century a larger type, with heavier guns, was devised. This was the "Torpedo Boat Destroyer," of which our modern destroyer is an improved version with a shortened name. Depth charges were added during the last war; the guns became "double purpose" to fit them as AA weapons, and the method of computing ranges (the "fire control system") has grown more complicated and far more effective. The modern destroyer has become a small cruiser, but she is still the deadliest killer in the fleet, for her size — because of the tin fish that she carries in tubes on deck. And the men in dungarees who adjust those torpedoes, and clean them and fuss around them and keep them ready for instant use are skilled specialists who labor to the end that, when their fish leave the tube and the propellers bite the water, the track toward the enemy will be "hot, straight, normal."

A fire-controlman has nothing to do with putting out fires. It is his business to start fires — aboard the enemy. With tools ranging from the finest hair's-breadth calipers to an open-end wrench that weighs ten pounds, the fire-controlman keeps in working order the range computers, the gun directors, the delicate optics of the rangefinders — and all the wiring, the tiny motors, the massive calculators that make up the fire-control system of a ship.

Naval gunnery has problems that are not shared by shore ordnance — except possibly in tanks operating on hilly ground. Before the guns are used you must compute the effects of own speed, target speed, wind — both along and across the line of fire — the target's movement during the time of flight of the projectile, temperature differences, which influence the powder. As the ship rises to meet a wave the forward guns are above their normal level; the after guns lower. This introduces errors which must be corrected in setting up the fire-control problem. After a number of salvoes the gun barrels become hot, raising the temperature of the powder, which imparts more velocity to the shell and sends it farther than when the gun was cold. Other variables add difficulty to shipboard markmanship — and make naval gunnery a subject that fascinates all of us who work with it, for accurate shooting is the Navy. Pause while the engineer says "If it weren't for us you never get within range," and the Damage Control Officer speaks up with "You can't keep 'em shooting unless you keep 'em floating." No argument there. It's the old question of teamwork — within a ship, as within a fleet.

We've come a long way since someone revolutionized naval gunnery by hanging a pendulum amidships and ordering the crews of the long toms and carronades to set off the powder train when the ship was on an even keel. We still do not hit with every shot, but the lightning calculators and wizard instruments used by the fire-controlmen help to make American naval gunnery the finest in the world today.

The fire-controlmen look after the instruments; the gunner's mates take care of the guns, and no twelve year old ever tended his first shotgun more carefully than these men clean and oil and adjust their shooting irons. There can be no rust or dust, no moisture or frozen parts in the gunnery department.

We have abandoned the practice these days, but in peacetime the keys to the magazines are kept in the Captain's cabin, where they are obtained each morning by the gunner, and returned by him to the Captain when the magazines have been inspected, powder temperature checked and necessary tests conducted. I once served in a ship with a captain who was as kind hearted as, he was absent minded and vague. In port, when he was in his cabin to receive the keys from the gunner late each morning, we missed the show, but at sea, with the Captain on the bridge, we used to enjoy a little scene that was regularly enacted. The gunner would come into the pilot house and approach the Captain, who sat in his sea-chair watching the fleet and smoking with nervous rapidity.

Gunner, saluting and extending keys: "Good morning, sir. Here are the magazine keys."

Captain, taking keys and putting them in his hip pocket: "Good morning, gunner. Yes — ah — fine morning — ah — I suppose you want the keys." Removes them from pocket and hands to gunner.

Gunner, in a firm voice — anxious to go below to the warrant officers' mess for a cup of coffee: "Magazine inspection completed, sir. Here are the keys."

Captain puts keys in pocket, lights cigarette from butt and puffs rapidly. Gunner salutes and starts to leave. Captain spots him: "Oh, uh, there you are, gunner; little late this morning — yes — ah — well here are the keys. Be sure that all magazines are locked when you bring them back."

Gunner, desperately: "But, Captain —"

Officer of the Deck, to gunner, in a low voice: "Shove off. I'll take care of it."

To Captain: "Sir, have you noticed that Captain So-and-So's ship is 'way behind position this morning? Here, sir, let me get your glasses."

Captain: "Yes, ah — so it is. He's apt to get a 'posit' from the Admiral. Now, young man, you be sure we maintain our station to within a yard — a yard. No getting out of position. I won't have it."

O.O.D., who now very definitely has the ball: "Aye, aye, sir. Helmsman, mind your steering."

In our ships today there is, aside from clothing, and life jackets, mattresses and paper, very little inflammable material. The furniture is made of metal, as are the lockers, bureaus, mess tables and galley equipment. Except for boat repairs the ship's carpenters have small opportunity to use the tools of their trade. Instead, they join the shipfitters in forming the nucleus of repair parties that function in the control of battle damage. Effective Damage Control has saved many ships in this war and kept them in the fight, on an even keel, despite gaping holes and torn bulkheads. I am not at liberty to give the extent of damage suffered by the Boise in the Far East, but the work done by her repair parties is considered to be the largest "ship's force" job ever accomplished in our navy. In the night action off Savo her Damage Control Organization again distinguished itself in making repairs to serious battle damage. She, and many of her sisters, lived to fight again because the men of the repair parties, working in darkness, in oil and rushing waters, were able, during battle, to strengthen bulkheads, stop leaks and put out fires. Away from the guns, unable to watch the battle, the repair parties lie flat on deck, far below, waiting for the bombs or shells or torpedoes to strike. Then they go into action. They know every valve, every hatch and door and pump. In drill they are blindfolded and sent three decks below with orders to find their way through smoke-filled compartments. They are skilled welders and pipefitters and repairmen who know the inside of the ship as thoroughly as the inside of their lockers.

We were being repaired at a port in India. The ship's force had cut and trimmed the plate, made the templates and performed the welding. Now the riveting was being done by a gang of Pathans — well-built men, Mohammedans, from the Northwest Frontier. They were noisy workers. A vociferous conference and much shouting of "Allah — il allah" preceded the driving of each rivet. By the time three men tucked their robes between their bare legs, pushed their turbans back on their foreheads and picked up the air hammer, the rivet, heated to a pale pink in a hand forge, had cooled and stood a good chance of being crystallized at the first blow. Ski was one of our shipfitters. He watched the punishment of cold rivets as long as he could, then stepped in. "Here," he said, "gimme that hammer." The three men who held the hammer passed it over, and Ski yelled for rivets. In about ten minutes he drove more, and better, rivets than the grinning Pathans had averaged for the morning. At the end of the day Ski was standing on the dock coping when the workmen came up. As they saw him, each man raised his arms, bowed low and murmured, "Sahib. Salaam, Sahib." Ski loved it.

Several times each day all work stopped while the Pathans went up on the dock, kicked off their slippers, faced Mecca and performed fifteen minutes of arduous religious rites. Checking through the shipfitter's log I found the entry: "1140 — Natives knocked off. Left the dry dock. Went up to do their daily dozen."

While the forge was in the bottom of the dock, alongside the plating to be riveted, the rivets were kept on top of the dock, some distance away. We learned the reason behind many obscure native actions, but we never found out why the crane didn't pick up a week's supply of rivets and send them down at one time. All day long, a thin Mohammedan, robes flapping about his ankles, climbed the muddy stone steps, picked up four rivets, and descended again into the dock. We called him Ali Ben Rivet, and his companion at the forge Ali Ben Bolt — which shows the effect of wartime cruising on an otherwise normal sense of humor. The civilian overseers — sons of Scotland, all — were as bewildered by the nicknames as they were by many of our actions. "Why d 'yee call 'em thot?" they demanded. "Thire nawt Toor-rks."

Ali Ben Bolt was not a Toor-rk but he became a colorful Pathan one morning when the end of a manila line hung in his forge. He brushed it aside repeatedly — it swung back. Instead of moving the forge a few inches he reached up and gave the line a yank. What followed was a perfect Keystone Comedy sequence. The line led up to a bucket of red paint on a staging at the waterline. Ali was vermilion from turban to toes. Unfamiliar with Mohammedan reaction under the circumstances, we tried not to laugh, but Ali roared, and with shouts of glee the riveting gang piled out from under the ship and rolled in the bottom of the dry dock. In a drab company of grey and brown robes, Ali stood out like a lone ornament on a faded Christmas tree.

"Personnel Damage Control" in a destroyer is in the hands of a Doctor and two Pharmacist's Mates, There is a small sick bay and dispensary, but no operating room. At General Quarters the Doctor and one assistant set up shop in the wardroom; the Chief Pharmacist's Mate takes charge of the After Battle Dressing Station, near the stern of the ship. In all ships the crew receives a great deal of first-aid instruction. They are taught how to apply battle dressings and how to use the morphine syrettes that are carried by all officers and many petty officers, and found, in addition, in boxes at each gun and important battle station. Any feeling of indifference toward learning elementary first aid disappears after a man has once been in action. Let the crew see some poor devil with the flesh peeled from his hands and arms and you never again have trouble enforcing the ruling that the body must be well covered against flash burns. Stretcher bearers come from the repair parties — unless the ship is badly wounded, when material takes precedence over men, except for the immediate use of dressings, tourniquets and drugs to deaden pain.

In the matter of general ship sanitation the Medical Officer works with the First Lieutenant. Together they inspect the galley ranges and equipment, the scullery and dishes, the storerooms and bakeshops and pantries, to eliminate roaches and bugs and make certain that food is untainted. You can imagine the effect of even a mild epidemic of food poisoning on board ship in wartime. Not long ago a destroyer used vegetables that were improperly canned; fifty men and half the officers were out of action for two days — not, fortunately, in time of battle. Such occurrences are rare. Food is good, and well cooked. Ships are clean and sanitary.

The first destroyer in which I served had just returned from five years on the China Station, following two years in the Mediterranean, where she had been sent in the late days of the last war. I joined her at the New York Navy Yard on a cold January afternoon when the snow was thick on the ground and my new ship crouched unhappily in the bottom of the drydock. I went aboard and stepped down to the wardroom. An officer was sitting on the starboard transom with an air rifle in his hands. As I entered he motioned me to be still; brought the rifle to his shoulder and fired. There was a squeal from the overhead on the port side, and a rat fell at my feet. The officer made a chalk mark on the bulkhead, then rose to greet me. "Lots of 'em," he said, "damn things all over the ship." Rats don't like us these days. I haven't seen one in a ship the past fifteen years.

The engine room of a destroyer is a marvel of stowing the "mostest" in the "leastest" space. High-pressure steam lines dart from the overhead to carry a message from the boilers. Wires and pipes spread in a metallic maze over the condensers and pumps and motor generators that add their individual throbbings to the rhythmic beat of the ship's heart. Here in this world of shining steel the machinist's mates move silently, watching temperature readings, checking gauges, ears tuned for sounds that might indicate trouble within the turbines where the strength of fifty thousand horses joins in the cycle that converts a drop of oil, a speck of water, a breath of air, into power that spins the bronze propellers.

In the firerooms, on the floorplates in front of the boilers, petty officers known as watertenders watch the height of water in the gauge glasses, check the temperature and pressure of oil that is fed into the burners, and regulate the supply of air from the blowers so that the three elements will achieve efficient combustion and generate steam in the most economical manner. We must not waste oil; we must not make smoke. A perfectly clear stack may indicate an excess of air. It is inefficient and wasteful. A boiler is steaming properly when there is a light brown haze from the stack.

Bridge scene:

Chief Engineer, watching another destroyer from whose stack a light plume of smoke is trailing: "Huh, she looks like she's laying a smoke screen."

Captain, pointing to own stacks, that are making the same amount of smoke: "Take a look at ours. Chief. What do you call that?"

Chief Engineer, moving toward the engine room telephone: "Oh that's just a little light brown haze, sir — very efficient combustion."

Together with firemen and electrician's mates, the machinist's mates and watertenders constitute the engineering ratings. A senior watertender is given the duty of keeping accurate accounting of fuel oil used and oil remaining on board. He is called the Oil King, just as the shipfitter who supervises the pumping and distribution of fresh water is known as the Fresh Water King. We no longer have the fresh-water troubles that were part of the navy before the present excellent evaporators were installed. There is plenty of water in the showers for everyone — provided they remember they're aboard ship, and don't leave the spigots on while they soap. In the G, because the crew cooperated, we never had to establish hours for using the washrooms. On our Midshipmen's cruises, in the old coal-burning battleships, we were allowed a quarter of a bucket of water a day — for everything. I remember one classmate who acquired a reputation through his proven ability to brush his teeth, bathe and shave, using one cup of water for the entire operation. Later he claimed that there was enough water left over to wash a hat and a suit of whites, but that was sheer boastfulness and gross exaggeration.

In those coal-burning days a watertender was a barrel-chested toughy who could, and would, wrap a Johnson bar around the head of any unfortunate fireman who couldn't strike down coal from the bunkers and heap it on the floor-plates as fast as the boilers could use it. And they were the hungriest boilers I have ever seen. Getting rid of ashes at the end of the watch was another nightmare. There was an ash hopper in one corner of the fireroom. It was an invention of the devil. In theory, you opened the cover, turned the valve and shoveled in the ashes to be carried outside of the ship's hull by a strong jet of water. It never happened quite like that when I was on watch as Midshipman-Fireman. As soon as the cover was lifted, the ocean entered with a rush — flooding the fireroom, covering you with clinkers, and bringing red-hot curses from the watertender whose professional pride was wounded if he couldn't turn over a spotless fireroom to his relief.

The question of discipline in a destroyer is closely related to that mixture of common sense and understanding that masquerades under the name of morale. Men of the navy have never been mollycoddles. They would resent a captain who raised a banner of sweetness and light and who beamed happily on the misdemeanors of "his boys." The American sailorman is an individual who can think for himself. He wants to learn his job; he wants to get ahead in his profession, and no organization in the world provides more, in the way of schools, training courses and specialized instruction, than our navy. It is to our advantage that the men of the fleet increase in knowledge. It is to everyone's advantage that the ship's company consist of a group of hardworking men who are reliable and alert. Troublemakers are a nuisance to all. Among three hundred men there are bound to be a few who do not measure up to standard. There are a couple who drink too much on shore. There may be one or two who find it difficult to outgrow their adolescence. But these men are rare exceptions in a Service where, until recently, we have been able to pick and choose, and which, for years, has had a waiting list six months long.

Should trouble arise, the man involved is placed on the report, either by an officer or petty officer. At the first opportunity the Executive Officer investigates the circumstances. In case they are wholly trivial the Exec will dismiss the charges. As a rule, though, a man is not put on the report unless it is warranted, and in a few days he finds himself brought to "mast." Here he confronts the Captain, who makes painstaking inquiry into his case. Here, too, the culprit learns the enormous benefit of having a clear record. If this is his first time at mast the chances are that he will be given a "Warning." The Warning stays in his record for six months, then, if he has not again been brought to mast, it is removed, and his record remains clear. But if the Captain thumbs through the pages of the Service Record and finds it liberally salted with offenses — then there is punishment to be awarded if the man is found guilty of his present misdemeanor.

The Captain is authorized to assign extra duty and restriction to the ship; he may award confinement, up to thirty days, and, in especially aggravated cases, up to ten days' solitary confinement on bread and water (provided the medical officer certifies that the man's health will not thereby be endangered) with a full ration every third day. The Captain may decide that the man deserves more in the way of punishment (or he may feel that the evidence is not conclusive enough either for acquittal or punishment, without further investigation) and he awards a Deck Court or a Summary Court Martial.

A Deck Court consists of one officer, of or above the rank of Lieutenant. He is authorized to assign confinement, or loss of pay, within narrow limits. The Summary Court Martial consists of three officers and a recorder who acts as prosecuting attorney. The accused is permitted to have counsel — any officer whom he may select — to represent his interests before the Court. The Members of the Court take an oath that they will "well and truly try the case now depending before this Court in accordance with the evidence which shall be adduced, The Laws for the Government of the Navy, and your own conscience." A Summary Court Martial is a strong instrument of naval justice. It may sentence a man to confinement for three months, it may fine him the equivalent of three months' loss of pay; it may recommend that he be given a Bad Conduct Discharge from the Naval Service. Beyond this is the General Court Martial, which is reserved for the trial of offenses that are extremely serious. The specifications which list an offense for trial before any court martial these days close with the ominous words, "the United States then being in a State of War."

In destroyers it doesn't take long for the crew to size up an officer, be he captain or ensign. We live too close to one another, and we are too mutually interdependent, for a man to be able to throw a bluff.

In matters of discipline a sailor is like any other man; he wants to know where he stands; he wants to feel sure of how his seniors will react to any situation. In short, he wants a feeling of security. A captain who vacillates, who blows hot and cold, who is tolerant today and intolerant tomorrow, cannot obtain the loyalty of his crew. He can be a strict disciplinarian, but he must be one consistently.

Among intelligent men — and our dungaree sailors are intelligent and alert, well mannered and efficient — "hope of reward" is vastly superior to "fear of punishment." In other words, a pat on the back brings better and happier results than a kick in the pants. For a few weeks we worked with an officer who belonged to the pants-kicking school. His signal lights blinked all day with querulous little stabs. "Expedite. Why the delay? You are too slow." The destroyer captains were goaded constantly with that sort of thing, and no one was happy. He was succeeded by a man who was also a perfectionist, but who took it for granted that you were doing your best, and who occasionally sent a "Well Done," reserving his criticism for airing at a conference when we returned to port. We worked doubly hard for that man. We were determined that we would never let him down in the eyes of the admiral. Human nature and character and the attributes of leadership are alike, ashore or afloat. It is only in their application that men differ. There are no "old women" left in the navy; petticoats are a hindrance in the business of running a war. Our captains understand that they will have no worries over discipline if they so organize their command that it is known as "a taut ship and a happy ship."

CHRISTMAS, 40-SOUTH

When we left our base the orders said that the G would accompany the transports to Brisbane, but we wouldn't have taken any bets on our chances of carrying out those orders, for there was a little matter of going first to Guadalcanal with reinforcements, then bringing out the first Marines to be evacuated since the original occupation. And, as we had discovered, much can happen to orders while you are in the process of steaming a couple of thousand miles. So we thought a great deal, kept our fingers crossed, and said little. We wanted to believe in Santa Claus but we couldn't scuttle the suspicion that at the last moment the benign old gentleman would snatch off his false whiskers, make a little Nipponese bow and hiss politely through his buck-teeth "So sorry, preez. Orders changed. You stay Guadarcanar."

Except for eight days alongside the tender, which can scarcely come under the heading of "leave, liberty and recreation," and a few hours in port, standing by to get underway on thirty minutes' notice, we had been at sea five and a half months. In that time even the most enthusiastic sailor is driven to the conclusion that one wave looks much like another; that there is a certain unmistakable sameness to all seas, oceans and straits and that it would be pleasing to reassure one's memory of trees, green lawns, the smell of beer in a dark, cool barroom, and, most unmistakably, the reality of beings that had so long existed as a constant but never-tiring subject of conversation in our mermaidless world.

The trip up the line was the old familiar story of screening, patrolling, searching for planes, listening for subs, sleeping on a catch-as-catch-can basis. For a change the Japs were off somewhere licking their wounds or celebrating Boy's Day. We had alarms, but no direct attacks on the convoy. That may have been why our own troops fired on the and why another destroyer of the Escort went to General Quarters at three in the morning and made ready to hold a little gunnery drill with the G as target.

When we neared the southern entrance to Indispensable Strait the G was sent ahead to scout in advance of the Convoy during darkness, with orders to pass Taivu Point an hour before dawn, have a good look at Lengo Channel, and search for subs in the vicinity of Lunga Roads prior to the arrival of the transports. At midnight we were on our way. At four a.m., with Taivu a black splotch close on the port hand, we entered Lengo and commenced a short-legged zigzag to cover both sides of the channel. The cool, pre-dawn breeze was on our faces, bringing with it the heavy, sweet fragrance of Cape Jasmine that we will always associate with Guadalcanal in the early morning.

We were opposite Barande Point, fifteen miles from the Japanese shore positions, when the stillness was broken by gunfire, and a handsome stream of tracers rose in a crimson arch from the beach, ending in a series of splashes a few yards from our port side. Machine guns joined in the fun, zinging their bullets across our decks.

"What the bloody hell goes on?" exclaimed Lieutenant Brundage, who had come under the influence of New Zealand small talk.

"Those bastuds are shootin' at us!" remarked a signalman, who had retained the vernacular of his native Virginia mountains.

Below the bridge and along the port superstructure there were sounds of activity as our port 20-mm crews prepared to go into action, though still wavering between training and discipline, and an understandable impulse to "shoot at the guy what's shootin at us," whether he be friend or foe. I stepped into the pilot house and pushed the "cease firing" gongs, as a preventive measure to discourage our marksmen, and ordered our recognition lights to be flashed on. The firing stopped at once, and we continued quietly on our way.

"Well," said Brundage, "it took eleven trips to Guadalcanal before our own Army started taking pot shots at us."

"They missed us," Frank Peters said, "and that's news."

Yes, they missed us, and the G hereby absolves whoever it was along that section of coast that got a little trigger-happy early one December morning. Everybody was that way for the first two or three days in the bush and it must have been a temptation when a black shape appeared suddenly, a few hundred yards off the beach. It was darned seldom that you birds missed. We're glad it was that way when you were firing at the G.

There were no subs off Lunga that morning. Our transports came in and anchored in the usual fashion — steam to the throttle — and landed their Marines and troops with their field guns, tanks, motor vehicles and all the accoutrements of mechanized armies, so quickly that we had scarcely settled down to our routine patrol before the signal was made to get underway.

During the night we steamed in the Strait, to return at dawn and embark the marines. Again the G was the advance guard and scout, and for the second successive day there was a fiasco involving our own forces. We peeled off from the formation at the appointed hour and turned back to repeat the search and scouting mission of the previous night. At five minutes past three I was awakened by a squawk from the TBS.

"Strange ship bearing three two five; range twelve thousand yards."

One of the mixed blessings of sleeping in a homemade bunk on the starboard wing of the bridge was that I heard the voice radio as soon as it commenced to talk. "Who made the report?" "It was the N, sir," replied the Officer of the Deck, naming a ship commanded by Bill Brown, a classmate of mine. The O.O.D. sounded a little perplexed. "I think he's talking about us, sir. We have sighted a ship on the reverse bearing that he reported. It's where the N ought to be."

We held our course and waited to see what would develop.

The N informed the Unit Commander, "I'm going in to investigate the strange ship."

I picked up our phone. "This is the G. Believe you have sighted us." There was a pause, then I recognized Bill Brown's voice. "It's quite likely," he said. "We will challenge."

We saw the N's light and answered with the reply that was in effect. Bill spoke up again: "Ship is friendly. N is rejoining."

We learned later that he had gone to G.Q. and was approaching us with guns loaded. Always a smart ship, no one ever caught the N napping. She was certainly wide awake that night. We began to suspect a put-up job to keep us from going to Brisbane.

The next afternoon we received orders detaching Lieutenant Commander F. M. Peters, my Executive Officer and Navigator, to command another destroyer that was then in company. This was a distinct loss to the but we were delighted to see Frank Peters given his own command. His new ship also expected to go to Brisbane with the transports, so Frank would continue to be near us a little longer.

Lieutenant Irving J. Superfine, the First Lieutenant and Damage Control Officer, was appointed to relieve Peters. A few months earlier I had sent "Supe" to command the Verity when we were called upon to salvage that unfortunate ship, and for his excellent work on this task he was awarded the Silver Star Medal. Lieutenant (jg) John Garrett fleeted up to the important and never-ending job of First Lieutenant.

It took only a few hours to embark the Marines who were being evacuated. They had been on that damnable island since August 7th and they were ready to leave. In their four months on Guadalcanal they had seen enough close combat, hand-to-hand fighting, air raids, naval bombardment and just plain hell to last any fighting man the rest of his natural life. There were not many of them; a bare handful, as armies go, but they had left their mark on Japan as no one ever had done before. To speak of these men as brave, heroic, magnificent, would be inadequate as well as meaningless, for descriptive words and phrases have been over-worked in the writings of this war. Someone on the bridge of the G, watching the weary men in faded green and brown as they climbed aboard the transports stated our feeling for them in a brief, heartfelt sentence. "Jesus," he said, "those guys are good."

Our passage southward, otherwise uneventful, brought disappointment when the N was ordered to leave the Brisbane convoy and proceed to an advance base. As Bill Brown took his ship out of the formation he signalled to the G: "Ain't it hell. Have five or six for me." We assured him that we would, but we were sorry to lose the company of the N and her skipper.

With the departure of the N the screen was so reduced that we knew we would go all the way with the transports. At least we would be in port long enough to fuel and look around for fresh vegetables. In the knowledge that they would not be let down the crew broke out their blue uniforms and sat around the decks with buckets between their knees, scrubbing, soaking, rinsing. We rigged gantlines on the fantail and they blossomed with clothes like the peacetime navy before admiral's inspection. The wardroom became a tailor shop as several ensigns who had become junior lieutenants since we last wore blue crouched over the table, jabbing themselves with needles, swearing and sweating at the highly important task of bending on that extra quarter inch of gold braid. All of our gold had suffered a sea change and the silver eagles on our caps were fierce birds with green tail feathers and black wings. Everyone had his pet mixture for removing this corrosion. Our table talk became a scientific discussion of formulas involving vinegar, catsup, brightwork polish and cyanide of potassium. It sounded (and the results probably tasted) like an interchange of cocktail recipes in the prohibition era. The fumes of these witches' brews filled the air, and together with the odor of mothballs made the wardroom an excellent place to test a gas mask. The only bright spot was that the flavor of camphor gave a new taste to the coffee. It needed it.

As we made our way up the approaches to Brisbane River at a joyous speed to beat the turn of the tide, Scotty Etheridge brought his Engineering Log to the bridge and we did a little figuring for the record. Not counting eight days alongside the tender we had been at sea one hundred and seventy-seven days, and it had been exactly six months and two days since the crew had set foot on shore on liberty. We had steamed 51,123 miles (twice the distance around the world) since the engines had been secured with boiler fires died out. We didn't bother to check the weight of every man, but we estimated that everyone had lost an average of eight pounds. There had been no illness; none of the colds, catarrhal fever and minor ailments that usually bring half a dozen men to Sick Bay each morning. In that respect we were healthy; trimmed down to good staunch bone and muscle, but as I looked about me I realized for the first time how drawn and haggard we were, how hollowed-eyed and tense we must appear to the curious gaze of the Brisbane pilot. A run on the beach was the best medicine we could have.

We went alongside Frank Peters' ship, already moored to the oil dock, and received a Boarding Committee of American and Australian naval officers who brought the usual information about liberty hours, places of recreation, hotels and restaurants, and the location of the one or two hot spots that were out-of-bounds. Half the officers might go on shore leave; half the crew on liberty expiring before midnight. The hotels were crowded and could not promise overnight accommodations for the men. In a few minutes our contingent left the ship; spotless in their well-tailored blue uniforms and white hats; pockets filled with money they had been unable to spend for half a year; swinging down the dock with heads up and chests out as if the mere sight of the beach had given them a new lease on life.

Frank Peters and I were able to get ashore by dinner time and meet Foster Hailey at Lennons Hotel where, after a judicious employment of cocktails (we were badly out of training) we dined in such an atmosphere of bright lights, unaccustomed delicacies and the startling sound of female voices that we felt like small boys on their first visit to New York. General Vandegrift and his Staff, at an adjoining table, appeared to find as much pleasure as we sailors in the situation.

The following morning, in the enjoyment of using my cabin for the first time in many months I lay abed late, and so missed the little scene next door that might be entitled "Frank Peters and the Wallaby." A wallaby is a junior-size kangaroo — not a baby one, but a perpetual flyweight, whereas a kangaroo often develops into a promising welter, and on one occasion at the Fleet Finals in Guantanamo I saw one knock a colored heavyweight champ clean out of the ring.

Some of Frank's men, in that mellow alcoholic state that fills the heart with affection for mankind discovered the wallaby in a perfectly comfortable zoo, and decided that he would be happier aboard an American destroyer. In a skillful but most unorthodox fashion they got him out of his cage, returned with him to the ship and locked him in the chart house.

At breakfast time they smuggled a ration from the mess compartment and carried it to Brother Wallaby. He sniffed at the eggs and bacon; stuck the tip of his nose in the coffee, then, with a snort of indignation, leaped high in the air, cleared the bridge railing by five feet, and landed in the river. Two sailors dove to the rescue and with a good deal of tussling managed to pass a line around their disheveled pet and hoist him once more to the bridge.

They turned to with turkish towels and gave him a brisk rub-down. As they stepped back to admire their handiwork the wallaby's hind legs and tail went again into action and he sailed off in space in a magnificent bound that would easily make him a dangerous contender in the East Australia Finals. (Class C, for wallabies under four years of age.) Changing direction in mid-air he descended toward the well deck just as the Captain stepped out to pass judgment on the morning. The impact was violent; the surprise mutual. Peters collected himself to see two of his men dive from the bridge and swim toward a furry animal that seemed to be hard put to keep its head above water.

When the second rescue of the morning had been effected the Captain made it clear, very, very clear, that the ship was not large enough for himself and a wallaby, and that he had no intention of leaving. Even to the sailors the wallaby no longer prompted any feeling of sympathy or affection. He was an ungrateful beast and the hell with him. Taking their pal back to the zoo in the light of day was not half so pleasurable as rescuing him from prison in the middle of the night.

Two of my own men were returning to the dock on a tram, and singing. The conductor protested. They said: "If we pay everyone's fare it will be our tram, and then we can sing if we like." So they gave the conductor a pound, paid all fares, and everyone in the tram, including the conductor, Joined in the singing.

The local leather shortage was brought home to two signalmen who went to sleep in a hotel lobby and awoke to find that their shoes had been removed and made off with.

A couple of our farmer boys saw a sandwich horse, with large advertising posters suspended from his back. They paid someone the usual pound and took turns riding the horse through the main streets. They were perfectly — well, almost, sober.

After the first night at Lennons, Foster Hailey found the war correspondents' headquarters, and invited me to stay there with them. These men, when they were not covering the war in New Guinea and our army activities in northern Australia, lived in a large, comfortable, old-fashioned house on the outskirts of Brisbane. The driveway is guarded by a stone lion with a lecherous expression; a veritable Don Juan of the jungle whose glass eyes carry a perpetual glitter of invitation and appraisal. But most real animals of the antipodes must have been produced in their creator's light-hearted moments, for all of them are weird and strange. The kangaroo and the wallaby, the koala bear and the kiwi bird and, above all, the duck-billed platypus, an object that resembles a flattened-out dachshund wearing a false face, and guaranteed to give D.T.s to a Deacon.

In front of the house is a sign which reads "War Correspondents' Convalescent Home" to which the ladies of Brisbane react by bringing gifts of cake, homemade candy and nourishing broths. During the three days I spent there we convalesced each morning, but by nightfall we were again in pretty good shape.

Frank Prist of Acme News and Marty Barnett of Paramount had recently come back from accompanying General MacArthur's army on its first big push across eastern New Guinea. Al Noderer of the Chicago Tribune had covered most of the east. I believe he was one of the last to leave Singapore. Jack Turcott of the New York Daily News was a musical wizard as well as writer. Bill Chickering, whom I had known in Honolulu and who, the last I had heard, was living in Mexico and writing another book, now represented Life and Time. Jack Kahn, a slender, rather pallid Army Private, moused through the house in a bashful way and went upstairs early in the evening to turn out those excellent articles on Army Life for the New Yorker.

Two Army Medical Officers, Doctors Swartz and Yeager, drove out with us on my first visit to the Correspondents' Home. Both were from Baltimore, so the evening began in a "do you know" vein, as my wife is from Baltimore, and it is my own second home. With Dr. Swartz giving new life to the piano while Jack Turcott played the violin and the rest of us sang in a manner that sent the little Australian maids rushing from the kitchen, we had a grand evening until Marty Barnett, the "house mother" and mess caterer, decided it was time to turn in. It seemed that I had just had time to roll over in that soft four-poster when Marty was again at the door, shouting that if anyone wanted breakfast he'd better come and get it. What a blissful sensation to look out of the window and see green foliage, to hear birds whistling and chattering, and know that for the first time in six months there would be no General Quarters, no "Condition Red," no "get underway and proceed immediately." For breakfast on this December morning in Australian midsummer there were fresh peaches, plums, cherries and strawberries. Then an hour on the broad porch, listening to the behind-the-scenes stories of the Correspondents, leering back at the stone lion in the driveway and drawing new strength and tranquility from the sun that flooded the lawn, before returning to the ship and seeing my own comfortable state of mind reflected in the eyes of my shipmates.

I dined one evening at the Queensland Club with old friends from cruiser days who were now on the staff of our Admiral commanding in the Southwest Pacific. At a nearby table several civilians were engaged in a discussion of ranches, sheep stations and horses. As I wanted to buy a present for my daughter, who is a keen young horsewoman, I went over later and asked if they could advise me where I might have a saddle made.

Mr. R. W. Heggie not only told me a great deal about Australian leather, but volunteered to meet me next morning and take me on a tour of the various saddlemakers' shops. We found one firm who thought that, despite the scarcity of labor and material, they could meet the specifications. Some months later, at about the same time that I came home, the saddle and bridle arrived from Australia. They were beautifully made and immediately took their place in my daughter's affection, along with a stuffed koala bear that I had brought from Melbourne a year earlier. We put the bear in the crotch of a tree so he could watch us fit the new gear to my daughter's mare. While Barbara found her seat in the saddle and pulled the reins through her fingers I regarded our Australian purchases and felt satisfied with my ability as a bearer of gifts. "Daddy," said Barbara, "the next time you come back from a cruise, please bring me a duck-billed platypus." So stand by, Mr. Heggie, here we go again.

We had three days of soft living, then received orders to accompany the transports to Wellington, New Zealand, an unexpected break that promised to add at least a week to our vacation from the forward combat area. In some more first-hand experience of this geographical war we learned that the antipodes in midsummer can be cold. Crossing from Australia to New Zealand we used all the hip-high woolen stockings, jackets, sheepskin coats and knitted helmets that we could find, against the wind that sweeps unhindered from the antarctic, chilling your bones, kicking up a high, short chop in the shallow waters of the Tasman Sea and keeping a destroyer underwater most of the time. It was an unhappy experience for those newer members of the crew who made the mistake of judging destroyer antics in the reasonably smooth waters of the Solomons and Coral Sea. At the end of a four-hour watch they could echo the words of Francisco and greet the next man with "For this relief much thanks; 'tis bitter cold and I am sick at heart."

In the steep cross-seas of Cook Strait we lived a page from Victor Hugo when a depth charge got adrift and took charge of the fantail, forcing us to lie to for an hour before it was captured and secured by a half dozen nimble seamen.

We entered Windy Wellington two days before Christmas, and immediately came under the charm of New Zealand. (This book is no travelogue. There were times, it is true, after a week or ten days with two hours sleep a night that someone would look astern and murmur "And so, as we sail into the setting sun, we say good-bye to Beautiful Guadalcanal, peerless pearl of the Solomons.") But in Wellington, the officers and men of the G found a warmth, a friendliness, a genuine pleasure in our presence that was all the more welcome because it came at Christmas time, and all the more impressive because the war was an old story to the citizens of this remote British Commonwealth.

On Christmas morning I received Communion from the Bishop of Wellington. There were few men at that early morning Service, but the cathedral was filled with women whose husbands and sons and sweethearts had gone from home two years ago to fight and die in the deserts of North Africa and the Middle East, along the beaches and among the mountains and vineyards of Crete and Greece. Many of them wore black; none were in diamonds and fur coats. The tired brave figures of these New Zealand women, kneeling on Christmas morning with their heads bowed over work-scarred hands meant things to me that we had not yet seen at home, where we have so much to be thankful for; so many blessings to count that occasionally they get adrift, and then, like the quaint animal in the children's story, we are filled with folly and we dance in the moonlight.

One of our first callers at Wellington was Major Kirk, who fought in the last war, and whose three sons were now in the service in England, in the Middle East and in Africa. The Major was retired. He and his gracious wife got up a Committee of Hospitality when the first Americans came to, or through, Wellington. Two elderly ladies of the committee approached a group of American soldiers who were wandering in aimless fashion along the street. "Would you young men like to come home with us for a cup of tea one of them enquired. The soldiers stammered and looked uncomfortable, but not, as the kindly old ladies discovered immediately, because of bashfulness or the fear of dropping a tea cup, for one of them replied in brusque tones: "Gwan, scram," he said. "We've been warned about women like you."

Major Kirk had a call very shortly from his greatly distressed and perplexed committeewomen. Perhaps it would help to avoid misunderstanding, he considered, if his committee wore a distinctive button; one that could be described to American chaplains, and by them to their men, so they would not confuse dear old ladies and an invitation to tea with sinister implications of the giddier fife.

I had Christmas dinner with Major and Mrs. Kirk. The Major had been at the docks most of the morning to meet a well-known transatlantic liner, now a transport, that was loaded with American troops from whom their itinerary had been so well concealed that they leaned from the rails and shouted "Hey! Where are we? What do you call this place?"

The Major arranged, too, for all the men of the G, except a skeleton watch, to have Christmas dinner in the homes of the citizens of Wellington. The Major said: "I like to feel that we are doing only what the people of America are doing for our own New Zealanders who may be there today." Our men of the G had a wonderful time. Each took with him from the ship a small package of sugar and coffee for his host and hostess of the day, but no gift could repay the mothers and fathers of Wellington for the warm friendliness that won the hearts of sailors from overseas.

The Kirks' big house that sat on a hill overlooking the harbor frequently had been the scene of entertainment and home-cooked meals for American sailors. "They are always so outspokenly genuine in their comments," the Major said. I knew what he meant. An American bluejacket, wandering through the rooms of the Kirks' house, inspecting the pictures and the furniture and the statuary, would not lack for words in expressing his pleasure and appreciation. There was one youngster who collapsed in a soft chair after a dinner that included turkey and all the trimmings. "Boy, oh boy," he said, "I'm going to write my mamma and tell her how I'm suffering!"

On Christmas Eve we lighted a big red star that our carpenters had made and which shone from the masthead of the G until it was time for the blackout. We bent Christmas trees to the mastheads and jack staff, and after dinner there were carols and a little present for each officer from Foster Hailey, who had spent hours in the ten-cent store finding a little boat for me, a miniature hammer for the First Lieutenant and appropriate gifts for the rest of us.

Captain Jeffries, the naval commander of the port, and Mrs. Jeffries, had us in for a glass of sherry and to meet the New Zealand officers of his staff. There was a dance for the crew, and another for the officers. I met a stout, jolly Paymaster Commander of the British Navy who said, "I have the two hundred and fifty most beautiful girls in all New Zealand working in my office." After seeing them we agreed that he had much more than a fair percentage for one man.

On the morning after Christmas we sailed from Windy Wellington to return to our duties in the tropics to the northward. We were rested and relaxed by the ten days away from the combat area. Aboard the G we were of one opinion — we were leaving a country that we hoped we would be able to revisit after the war. Our Christmas, 40-south, had given us a lasting affection for New Zealand and her people.

COCONUT SHOOT

Along the northwest coast of Guadalcanal the mountains tumble toward the shore in a series of wooded ridges and rocky escarpments that form the foothills for the seven-thousand-foot peaks of the Kavo Range.

It is difficult country to fight in. The valleys are jungles, matted and twisted with vines and rotting logs; steaming hot. A hundred feet above the undergrowth the tree tops of the forest entwine their branches and hold in the oppressive heat and the rank, humid air that soaks the body in sweat before bringing on the ague and chills of malaria.

It was among these mountain-jungles along the fifteen-mile section of coast between Kokumbona and Cape Esperance that the Japanese were trying to hold off the slow, steady advance of the American troops. The Japs were sick. Medicines were scarce and they were running short of food and ammunition. For weeks their supplies had come to them in wooden boxes or watertight rubber bags tossed over the side by destroyers in the night, to drift in to the beaches to be picked up at dawn. They were losing the fight, but they hung on with the tenacity that we knew so well, taking advantage of their strong natural defensive aids to make us pay dearly for every foot of jungle, through which our army sloughed and cut its way, every spiny ridge that we had to scale with ropes and mountain gear in the face of a nasty fire from mortars and machine guns.

There was an easier way to get at the Japs, and when General Patch decided to use it he gave the G and several other destroyers an assignment that was a welcome diversion. Along this portion of the island the mountain ridges are perpendicular to the shoreline. Steaming close in to the beach a ship can make a clear and easy target of the reverse slopes and enfilade the long, deep valleys that give a roller-coaster effect to the entire range. The Marines had called for destroyers to make shore bombardments when they were pushing their way east from Lunga, but now that most of them had been replaced by the Army we were not being invited to the party.

When we took our transports to Guadalcanal we patrolled around them by the hour, watching the puffs of white smoke rise up over the hills on shore, listening to the sound of artillery and the rattling fire of machine guns. And while the patrol almost invariably brought action against either aircraft or submarines, we wanted to get into the scrap on shore and throw a few hundred rounds of 5-inch into the Japanese positions for which we had a grandstand seat.

One morning when the transports had departed, and our remaining convoy consisted entirely of merchant ships, I found what I considered to be a reasonable excuse for going ashore on Guadalcanal. For the time being I was the senior destroyer officer of the escort; the merchantmen were being unloaded very slowly and were falling farther and farther behind schedule. The mechanics of unloading were none of my affair, but I did have to make a progress report to my own admiral each evening, so he and his staff would be able to keep track of the schedule and the prospective movements of destroyers and cargo ships. It was not difficult to persuade myself that I was duty bound to consult the senior naval officer on shore in an effort to speed the unloading. The fact that I had long wanted to spend a day on Guadalcanal (which sailors other than those stationed there were rarely able to do except when they drifted up on a raft after a night action) and that I wanted to receive permission to give the G a coconut shoot were wholly subsidiary causes — I hoped.

We closed the beach, put the whaleboat in the water and I proceeded shoreward while the Exec returned the G to her station. A continuous fine of tank lighters and landing craft were ferrying supplies from the merchantmen. When we were close in to shore I hopped aboard one of them and found a seat on the mountainous stack of cases of fruit and vegetables that filled the boat. We hit the sandy shore, the propellers drove us forward, the gate dropped and an army truck backed its rear wheels into the lighter. Even before I clambered over the truck for a dry landing the supplies were being rushed ashore.

Standing under a coconut tree directing the loading of trucks I found a Major who offered me a Jeep for the five-mile trip to our Navy Headquarters. The driver, a young soldier from Kansas who had, oddly, an accent of the deep south, was a new arrival on the island and eager to learn all the details of earlier fighting. For the Marines he had a feeling little short of hero worship. Right there you have an example of a basic reason why our Services work together so smoothly in the South Pacific. It is not a mutual admiration society — the reaction is deeper than that. There is a wholesome respect for what the other fellow is doing; you rely on him in the knowledge that he will carry his share of the load; there is no diminution in your own Pride of Service or Corps or Regiment or Ship — that is everpresent, but you are determined not to let the other fellow down and you go about your duties with the certainty that — in our case — the Marines or the Army will operate according to plan. On the wall of an army quartermaster office in one of our South Pacific bases is a large sign — "No one is allowed to say 'No' to any request, except the Commanding Officer." Red tape is one commodity that all of us left at home. Nor have we seen anything of our old peace-time friend who insisted that requisitions be submitted in quintuplicate. Bureaucracy has been scuttled for the duration. We would like to think it's gone for good, but that pleasant prospect could exist only in Utopia.

Back from the red-clay road over which our jeep bounced and slid, beneath the coconut trees that stretched in long, evenly planted rows, were the stores for our army of occupation. In marked contrast with the Japanese, who were eating on a catch-as-catch-can basis, our troops were doing very well indeed. Gone were the hungry days of the preceding August and September when the Marines existed as best they could on two thin meals a day from captured enemy rations. Now the boxes were stacked high under rudely painted signs nailed to the trunks of trees. We drove for a mile past mounting piles of dried fruit, vegetables, preserves and jams, tinned meats, cereal, flour, sugar and coffee. Near the airfield we passed a few thatch-roofed storehouses that still held a few hundred sacks of Japanese rice and barley. My driver motioned with his head. "I'm glad we don't have to eat that stuff, like the Marines did," he said.

On every hand was evidence of the bombardment by our own and Japanese ships. There were great holes in the ground; the few trees left standing near the airfield wore deep scars in their sides. We crossed the Tenaru by a log bridge that our people had built. In the muddy waters, fifty feet below, soldiers were bathing or scrubbing their clothes and putting them on large flat rocks to dry. Here was the narrow road along which the Japs had marched one night in a bold attempt to recapture the airfield. On the far end of the bridge we pulled off the road to allow a column of troops to pass. They were bathed in sweat as they trudged along in the mud that lay beneath the top coating of thick red dust. They had another six-mile climb before they reached the front lines. We met other groups on their way back from the rocky defiles to the west. They looked tired. They weren't smiling. It was significant that most of them carried a Japanese rifle or sword in addition to their own arms. They weren't so weary that they had neglected to collect souvenirs.

Further along the road we came to a sign "U.S. Navy, Construction Battalion." Here were the Seabees, those indefatigable men-of-all-work who will build a road, throw a bridge across a river, construct a dock or, if need be, drop their tools and use their rifles and machine guns — all in a very matter-of-fact fashion without any fuss or feathers. The driver pointed again. "Them Seabees sure put out the work," he said.

We took the wrong turn and found ourselves at the end of the road, our way blocked by the Post Office. Army, Navy and Marine mail clerks were sorting the mail that our transports had brought to the island. There were hundreds of bags, for it was almost Christmas and the gifts mailed from home in October were arriving. While we were asking directions to Navy Headquarters another truck drove in, piled high with more grey and blue bags. Half a dozen jeeps were parked under the coconut trees beside the post office. Their drivers, waiting to take mail to their units, leaned against the wooden side of the one-story building and passed the time of day like farmers at home, gathered about the country store. It was very hot and very quiet. We could hear a plane warming up on Henderson Field, but the sounds of firing, so audible aboard ship as we patrolled along the coast, did not penetrate to the post-office clearing beneath the trees.

We reversed our way, found the proper road and crossed the Lunga river. More soldiers were bathing and scrubbing faded green and khaki clothes. We drove up alongside a neat low fence bordered with flowers. A gravel path led from the gate and wound around past the brown tents and camouflaged wooden buildings of Navy Headquarters. I don't know whether the Seabees or the regular naval contingent made this oasis which rested in such trim, shipshape fashion among the fox holes, the shell-torn trees and the mud and dust of the main roadways.

In one of the tents, with the sides rolled up to give cross ventilation, I found the officer for whom I was looking. He was seated in a packing-box chair working at a sturdy table made from cases that once had held canned tomatoes. There was a mosquito bar over his cot in one corner. On another homemade chest was a white enamel wash basin and toilet articles. Beside it, on the wooden floor of the tent, was a galvanized bucket half full of water. On the work table were half a dozen books and some family photographs. A pistol, flashlight, canteen and steel helmet hung from the back of the chair.

This Commander and I were old shipmates; we had served together in the Maryland several years ago. "For Heaven's sake," he greeted me, "where did you come from?" He gave me the canvas guest chair, held out a cigarette and shoved a coconut-shell ash tray where I could reach it.

"You've got quite a place here," I said.

"Not so bad." He smiled. "After all, I've been here five months. It wasn't so comfortable at first." He pointed to a fox hole just outside the tent. "We spent most of our nights in those for some time."

I explained that I wanted to see if anything could be done to hasten the unloading of our cargo ships. "And what about a little shore bombardment?" I asked. "We're getting pretty tired of steaming up and down so close to the Jap fines and not being able to go in where we can enfilade them."

We talked for thirty minutes or so. The Commander said he would see what could be done about giving us a coconut shoot. "Once the army sees what you can do with destroyer guns they'll want ships in there every day." I told him that was fine.

I said good-bye and went out to where the jeep and my Kansas driver were waiting. On our way back to the loading beach we picked up a couple of other soldiers who were stumbling along the muddy road under the weight of rifle and pack. They were new arrivals who had not yet been under fire, but they expected their outfit to move up to the front lines that afternoon. They were not particularly worried, but neither were they bragging.

On the road by the airfield we passed half a dozen Solomon Islanders wearing their customary brief skirt, and tightly drawn bands over the upper arm. One of them carried a Garand rifle slung negligently over his shoulder. They glanced at us impersonally and stepped off the road to allow the jeep to go by.

We pulled up along the beach and I thanked my driver and the Major. A few yards off shore my whaleboat was anchored while the crew enjoyed the novelty of a swim in the clear blue water. I went off in a landing craft, transferred to my own boat and we headed out past the cargo ships toward the destroyer patrol line. The G spotted us, swung in close to the boat, and we were hoisted in. Covered with red dust I headed for the shower and clean clothes.

We didn't have our coconut shoot on that trip, but a few days later, when we were with another group of merchantmen and transports, the signal light on Lunga Point began to blink. "Close the beach and receive Marine liaison officers preparatory to executing shore bombardment mission."

We slipped in toward the point, made a lee for a landing boat, and took on board Captain Oldfield and Lieutenant Young of "A" Battery, 10th Marines. They were brought to the bridge, and introductions made all around. "What about a pitcher of ice water?" we asked. They looked at one another and grinned. "Ice water! We haven't seen any for five months."

That detail arranged, Oldfield spread out a chart and an aerial mosaic of the coastline. "Our Command Post is at Point Cruz," he said. "Our front lines stretch back along the Poha River from Kokumbona. We believe that the Japanese General Headquarters is in this location, so that will be the first target."

He pointed to a spot a few miles to the westward. "Along this area, between the Umasani and the Segilau Rivers, we think the enemy has ammunition and supply dumps. It will be exploratory shooting, but we'd like to pay some attention to it in hope that we might start some fires."

He looked up from the chart. "After that, Captain, we can cruise along the coast as far as you like, looking for targets of opportunity. We may see only a few individual soldiers, or perhaps some small groups, but they're worthwhile targets, for they indicate the presence of larger units near by."

I turned to the gunnery officer. "Have you got that, Joe?" Lieutenant Linehan grinned happily. "Yes, sir," he said.

To the navigator: "Supe, lay your course three thousand yards off the beach, from Point Cruz to Cape Esperance."

One of the Marines spoke up. "That's a little close. Captain. The Japs have some six-inch stuff along here."

We knew that, but a six-inch gun could reach out farther than our own main battery; we would be within range of them wherever we chose for our off-shore track, and under the circumstances we decided that we might as well stay within easy binocular range of our targets.

To the Officer of the Deck: "Go to General Quarters."

The general alarm commenced to bong; the gun crews manned the battery, and those men whose battle stations took them belowdecks cast envious looks at their topside shipmates as they headed for the ladders.

On the bridge I took the phones from the yeoman who usually wore them at General Quarters, for I wanted instant communication with the gunnery officer. This was one time when I would not have to pay attention to the tactical situation. There were no other ships present and we had only to follow a straight path along which the navigator would keep our position plotted by taking bearings on charted mountain peaks and river mouths, and tangents on various points and islands.

We headed in toward the coast, the quartermasters at the peloruses making a running report of bearings to Lieutenant Superfine, who had moved his chart to the table in the pilot house, "You can come right, to course 279," he said. The helmsman moved the wheel and our bow swung to the right. Through our glasses we inspected the dark-green slope of the jungle hillside where we hoped to find some Japanese Generals with their Staffs.

"Control — the point of aim is the conspicuous tree bearing 210 true. Lay a box barrage, two hundred yards to a side. Report when ready."

"Bridge — Main Battery ready."

"Commence firing."

The tremendous initial velocity of naval ordnance gives a straight, flat trajectory at the close range we were using. The shells travel in a direct line, with none of the high arc of long range firing. The muzzles flashed and our first salvo tore into the jungle. The conspicuous tree kited high in the air. Linehan's calculations had been correct to the foot.

"Control — Nice salvo. Shift to rapid fire."

A continuous sheet of flame came from the guns as we poured salvo after salvo into the rectangle that held the Japanese G.H.Q. Clouds of dust and foliage rose up from the forest — then smoke, and the red tongues of fire.

Along the ridge back from Kokumbona our troops were waiting. As we ceased fire they rose up from their fox holes and moved forward.

The supply and ammunition dumps were next. At ten knots we slipped past the shore line, keeping a careful scrutiny through our glasses. The Umasani River, a coppery thread almost hidden by overhanging branches, dug lightly into the coral sand and emptied itself in the blue waters of "Ironbottom Bay."

"Control — The target area is the west bank of the Umasani, to a depth of two thousand yards. Commence firing when ready."

This was exploratory shooting. We walked the salvoes along the river bank, then spread them to the right. Suddenly, from deep in the undergrowth there was a heavy detonation. Flames and smoke curled above the trees. We had found our target. For five minutes we gave it a thorough going over until we felt certain no supplies remained that would be of any value to the Japs.

We repeated this procedure for four miles along the coast, until we reached the Segilau River. The main east and west mountain range is buttressed by ridges that run off at right angles with their rocky spines perpendicular to the beach. The Japanese entrenchments were clearly visible as we steamed by. Our gunners pounded the jungle, laid their shells among the enemy troops and gun emplacements, tossed trees and coconuts into the air and splashed Japanese over the landscape.

Captain Oldfield and Lieutenant Young wore pleased expressions. Each had been wounded; each had suffered from daily bombing and nightly shelling from the sea. Now, from the bridge of the G, they had a chance to get in their own licks, and the results were clearly evident.

Gradually we moved down the coast towards Cape Esperance on the northwest tip of Guadalcanal, directly opposite Savo Island. We were passing over the scene of some of the mightiest sea fights in naval history. Here Admiral Lee's battleships and destroyers smashed the enemy on the night of November 13-14. A few miles to the west Admiral Scott with his cruiser-destroyer force gained a notable victory. In this same restricted area Admirals Scott and Callaghan, fighting against great odds, crushed a major Japanese task force of battleships, cruisers and destroyers in mid-November. Four hundred fathoms down, on the coral sands of Ironbottom Bay, a vast armada of the Rising Sun rested in eternal eclipse. Near them, guns still trained out, are the graves of the Astoria, Quincy, Vincennes and Canberra; the Northampton, Atlanta; the Duncan, Preston Laffey, Walke, Monssen and De Haven; the Barton and Gushing. Beneath these quiet waters are thousands of American sailors; their watches over, their duty done. Here are more Japanese ships than were ever before lost in battle, and more American warships than we have lost since the invention of the ironclad.

When the day comes that our representatives take their places at the head of a table to dictate terms of peace — let them remember these ships and men on the floor of Ironbottom Bay; let them remember, too, the pseudo-surrenders of our enemy; the upraised hands holding grenades; the white flag that led our marines into ambush; the subterfuge, the trickery and deceit that are national characteristics of our foe. And let them remember, too, the fanatical bravery of the Japanese and their fierce national pride, a pride out of all proportion to the worth and the accomplishments and the culture of their country. And let our statesmen make peace with the same courage, the same dignity and the same ability with which our sailors made war in those black nights of battle off the coast of an island far from home.

Arriving off Esperance we hauled away from the coast and secured from General Quarters to let the crew have lunch. There was no hurry; we had plenty of time to complete our inspection of the shoreline in the afternoon. The marine officers and I were standing in my cabin when the officer of the deck phoned to report having sighted two canoes headed for Savo, and to request permission to close them for investigation. I went to the bridge shortly. Ahead of us were two Solomon Island log canoes — high prowed like Venetian gondolas, manned by friendly natives who were paddling at a pace that would shame any college crew. We didn't chase them, of course, once we knew who they were, but they were taking no chances. They beached their boats on Savo, leaped ashore and disappeared up a trail into the jungle.

After lunch we returned to our position at Cape Esperance, close to the ruins of the Roman Catholic Mission. We reversed our course of the morning and began to look for what the marines euphemistically call "targets of opportunity." At a distance of twenty-five hundred yards from the narrow strip of yellow sand we steamed slowly, keeping a dozen pairs of glasses trained on the dirt road that wound under the coconut trees a few yards back from the sea. Here the jungle did not run to the shore. This was plantation land, with cleared ground around the groves of coconut palms to a depth of about a quarter of a mile, before the level plain shot abruptly upward to the green walls of the mountains.

"Bridge — The target is a group of Jap soldiers with packs, moving along the road behind the coconut trees, bearing seven-oh, relative."

"Fire three salvoes when ready."

Our shells tore in and a pall of smoke and dust and wreckage came up from the road. Very slowly it settled and drifted away. Control reported "Three salvoes fired; the target has been destroyed."

Among the ruins of a native village we saw a solitary Japanese soldier poke his head around the corner of a house, debating, apparently, whether to stay there or run for cover. The problem was solved for him when we knocked down the house.

Two of our planes came over to spot for us. One of them dove sharply at a point a few yards below the summit of a rocky peak. Checking through our glasses we could see a faint discoloration in the heavy green foliage that covered the slope. We gave it a salvo and saw camouflage nets rip open. We fired twice again and watched a Japanese battery blow up and scatter itself along the hillside.

Along the beach were the skeletons of many Japanese landing boats and the scorched hulks of four large transports. It was possible that the enemy was using the masts of the largest transport to conceal a radio antenna. We removed the masts with the main battery, and gave the 20-mm crews, who had not seen action today, a chance to play a tattoo on the flanks and decks of the beached ship.

Other targets of opportunity presented themselves when small groups of Japanese soldiers, drawn to the beach by the sound of firing, remained there on the sand to watch us steam by. It was slaughter, but, thinking of the white flags and the bombs; the subterfuge and trickery of our enemy, we relished every blow we could strike.

Near Umasani, smoke was still rising from the supply and ammunition dumps that we had hit in the morning.

We arrived abreast Point Cruz, ceased firing, and secured from General Quarters. I turned to Oldfield and asked if he and Young would like to have a hot bath. The expression on his face was answer enough. We went below and they took turns in the shower, enjoying the first bath, outside of a muddy Guadalcanal river, that they had been able to have for months. When they left us they were shining and happy. For us, too, it had been a thoroughly satisfactory day. Five hundred and sixty nine rounds of 5-inch. It had been a fine coconut shoot.

NIGHT ACTION

It was five in the morning. The sun was coming up over the hills of the island on the starboard bow, and unless we left the big carrier, that showed no signs of preparing to enter port, the G was going to be late arriving. We had joined her the previous afternoon when we were coming south alone and she answered "affirmative" when we asked if she would like us to join her screen.

"Send a signal to the Task Force Commander and tell him we request permission to proceed now in order to meet our schedule."

The carrier blinked back with the admiral's reply: "Proceed at discretion. We have enjoyed your company." We changed course to the right, boosted the speed and headed for the Light and the narrow passage between the reefs.

Shore Station to G: "After fueling, anchor in berth 5, inner harbor."

We filled up with oil, asked the net tender to open the gate, then wound our way among the anchored ships toward our berth at the inshore end of the line.

In normal times this must be a pleasant place; a Gallic haven in the midst of the South Seas. In this war it is a ghost town. There are soldiers by the thousand. The traffic problem is an everpresent menace; the little water front is eternally busy. The town itself is dead; the shops barred and shuttered; the flowers in the plazas strangled by weeds. Though the paint is beginning to fade you still can read the signs above the doors, but no fragrance of baking comes from the boulangerie, no spicy and provoking odors fill the air around the épicerie, and especially no sound of scissors and sewing machines from the empty façade behind the door of M. Ishii, Tailleur; no sharpening of knives and beating of cleavers from the boucherie of M. Tonogawa. The ubiquitous Japanese tradesmen have joined the authentic French merchants in a tropical limbo that makes doubly difficult the simple amenities of life.

Despite the fact that there is little buying and selling along the main streets, the people seem not to have suffered. They are well clothed, well fed, and certainly the majority of them must be making money. The American Army and Navy cannot move into a small island in force without bringing prosperity to the populace. For the children the whole affair is a wonderful adventure. The world of New York and Hollywood has come to their little island. Their eyes are bright with excitement as they follow behind the nuns along the quiet avenue that leads them to the church that sits on a hill, overlooking the harbor and the walled prison on the island. There are many prisons — most of them in ruins. I spent an afternoon exploring one and reached the conclusion that it could not have been so horrible a place, despite the thick walls, the cubby-hole cells and the daily drudgery in the nearby mines, for the guards could not have had energy enough to strike very hard blows or to make excessive demands of the inmates. After all, everyone on the island was a prisoner, whether he spent his nights in a cell or in the stone house of the colonel looking toward the reefs and the blue remoteness of the Coral Sea.

The bare, brown hills, so reminiscent of Southern California, that surround the town have become cities of canvas and planking and corrugated metal. The troops are fortunate who live near the shore for there are wide beaches of yellow sand and cool waters lying within the protection of the barrier reef ten miles to seaward.

I went ashore to see the personnel officer about getting replacements for a dozen petty officers who had been ordered back to the States to help put new ships in commission. In their places we would receive green seamen, who would have to be trained on board. We kept shipboard schools in progress at all times for officers and men alike, to train them in their present duties and prepare them for advancement. Like the Confederate Naval Academy, where frequently the midshipmen would leave their studies to man the guns outside on the banks of the James and send a few shells toward enemy ships in the river, there was often an unscheduled recess in our own schools for quick practical demonstrations of gunnery and tactics.

The wide cinder sidewalks along the water-front streets were packed with soldiers in combat kit and the green uniforms of jungle warfare. They lounged against the warehouse walls, sprawled in the dust with their heads on a pack, sat on the curb with gun between their knees. There was no shade. The men were hot; faces streaked with sweat and yellow sand from the countryside barracks. There wasn't much talk. Talking required energy and there was none to spare. A man tipped up a canteen, swished the tepid water around in his mouth and spit it into the street. The officers were weighed with pistols, cameras, glasses, map cases, canteens, first-aid kits.

Most of them wore helmets with camouflage net drawn over the top. One captain had on a beautifully tailored shirt, smart breeches and the shiniest boots I've seen since the last Fort Myer horse show. His holsters, his camera case — all of his leather glistened in the sun. General's aide? I don't know. He climbed into the troop lighters with the others and ferried out to the transports. He made me feel seedy in my worn and faded khaki. I wondered how long he could remain immaculate in the mud and muck of Guadalcanal for which he was bound.

In a few minutes with Dave Roberts it was arranged for the G to receive the personnel we needed. The men were in camp about five miles from town. I thought it best to go out and make sure of getting them on board before we sailed early next morning.

I was having lunch with the Commanding Officer of the camp in a long mess tent with the sides rolled up when a strange little procession entered. The man in the lead was under five feet in height. The man behind him was a good two inches over six feet. There were half a dozen others, including a Negro cook, and in the rear was one of the fattest men I have ever seen. All were dressed in undershirts and dungaree pants; all carried life jackets — except the fat man, who had his, a brilliant red affair, strapped tightly about his middle. His head was covered with a blue bandanna handkerchief, knotted at the edges and worn like a beret. The little man in the lead, I noticed, had the handle of a .45 caliber pistol sticking out of his hip pocket. They were part of the crew of a merchant ship that had been torpedoed earlier in the morning close off shore. Their ship had not sunk. The navy towed it in. It was a fortunate business all around. As the fat man came past he stopped alongside our table. He looked a little wild eyed, and he was breathing heavily, which was understandable, dressed as he was, with the temperature in the upper nineties.

"Do you know what our cargo was," he demanded.

"Yes, I heard about it." I replied. "You were pretty lucky."

He glared down at us. The sweat dripped from beneath the bandanna and slid into the thick collar of his life jacket. "Lucky!" he snorted. "That's a hell of thing to call it. It was a goddam miracle." He walked away, muttering to himself.

The camp CO. looked amused. "What kind of cargo did they have?"

I told him.

"Jeepers. No wonder he thought you were sort of understating things. Depth charges and torpedo war heads! And the ship didn't blow up!"

On the way back to the G we passed the transports that we were to accompany in the morning. All the troops had been embarked, and now they were being drilled in how to disembark in a hurry. Heavy manila nets were strung along the side. The loudspeaker blared "First wave — embark." Over the bulwarks came the soldiers — dropping hand over hand down the nets into the landing boats that waited alongside. As the boats filled they shoved off, spun around the ship and let their passengers out at a gangway. The troops climbed slowly up the ladder, weighed down with rifle, helmet, ammunition, packs. When they arrived on deck it was time to go down the nets again. "Second wave embark. Get some speed in it." I don't envy the soldiers in this war.

I returned to discover that the G had found a little adventure of her own during my absence. Another destroyer, trying to come alongside under difficult conditions of wind and sea, and with a reef close under the stern, raked our starboard side for a distance of thirty feet, ripping off everything that was rippable, and some things that I thought were pretty solid. We had welders working all night and pulled ourselves together in time. Fortunately the shell plating was not holed.

We were getting underway at four-thirty. It was almost time for reveille. I got up and found inside the door the Birthday Edition of the Fantail Gazette — our occasional newspaper; the "Mouthpiece of the Mighty G." Today the G was two years old. On Valentine's Day, 1941, she first wore the commission pennant, when Lieutenant Commander Murray Stokes read his orders and accepted his ship from the Commandant of the Charleston Navy Yard. In the twenty-four months since the first watch was posted she had not remained stopped long enough for barnacles to gather along the keel. The Atlantic — from above the Arctic Circle to the broiling temperatures of the Horse Latitudes had been her home. She came to the Pacific in time to join the Shangri La expedition to Tokyo. Since then she had been a South Pacific unit and a most fortunate ship. She had an angel on the yardarm that looked after us in battle. One bright morning some of our crew were on board a tender and ran into a sailor who wanted destroyer duty. "Any ship but the G," he said. "And what the hell is wrong with the G?" demanded our people, getting ready to square off. "Nothing — nothing at all," answered the sailor, "but she's the only ship in the Task Force that hasn't caught a bomb or been badly shot up. She can't go on being that lucky."

We cleared port and took our station in the screen. This time there were several destroyers; a few large transports and a fleet oiler. Convoys to Guadalcanal were becoming an old story to the G. This would be our thirteenth visit to the Solomons; an average of two a month since we had gone in with the occupation forces. All previous voyages had brought excitement, diversion, generally action of some sort. Trip 13 promised to be quiet, for the enemy had been driven from the island and our forces were in possession through all the hundred miles of mountains and jungles from Kau Kau Bay to Cape Esperance. There would be submarine encounters, of course; a solitary Japanese patrol bomber, perhaps, but nothing in the way of real opposition. That was what we thought, but we were due to be fooled. Trip 13 was not a humdrum journey.

The first two days were without incident. There was a dim chance that we might be selected to go south with the transports to Australia or New Zealand but as usual our plans were subject to change without notice, so we kept our fingers crossed and hoped. It didn't matter a great deal where we were sent; we wanted to get some mail, for with the exception of a handful of air-mail letters there had been no news from home for four months. It seemed that our mail was resting in a small island that we had not visited for half a year, though why it was being held up we were unable to discover. For our purposes the handiest post office was the one on Guadalcanal. We had based there more than in any other spot. It was disturbing to everyone to think of all the letters from home, all the Christmas boxes and the packages from Thanksgiving, sitting in a warehouse within four hundred miles of our track. In the Boise we had been mailless from November to April, a period that included the attack on Pearl Harbor — at a time when most of us had families in and around Honolulu. To have no knowledge of whether they were alive, or injured, or in the islands or on the mainland was not consoling. After five months, when we pulled in to an Australian port, we wanted mail from home, American cigarettes, and the straight news of Pearl Harbor, in the order named.

Aboard the G we held school twice a day, exercised at Damage Control problems, and managed to get in some shooting for the 20-mm battery. In —— the commissary officer found some fresh carrots, which we had been trying to get for the lookouts and machine gun and director crews as an aid to night vision. The medical reports indicated that if we ate enough carrots we would have eyes like cats in the night. It was worth the trial.

It was cloudy, with patches of rain, during the afternoon of the 17th as we approached San Cristobal Island and the now familiar entrance to Indispensable Strait, but by sunset the weather had cleared, and at six in the evening Cristobal and Malaita were in full view, and to the eastward a large round moon hurried up the sky. With Guadalcanal less than twelve hours away it looked, still, as if Trip 13 would be a light workout under wraps.

After dinner I climbed on to the hard wooden seat abaft the port pelorus where I could keep an eye on the transports and enjoy the light breeze that our speed brought to the bridge. Under the full moon the surface visibility was easily three miles. The transports and tanker could be clearly seen, running their zigzag courses with precision along the quiet waters. We were watching them, and wondering the usual things — when will we get mail; will we be chosen to take this crowd south to New Zealand; when will this thing be over so we can go home — when it happened. The helmsman was winding the wheel over on the right leg of a zig; the O.O.D. had stepped to the pelorus to check our bearing on the Formation Guide; Hal Strong, on watch at machine gun control, was chatting with John Brundage — something about not needing carrots for vision on a night like this — when a flare burst silently over the center of the formation and bathed the transports in intense blue-white light.

The next few seconds were filled with the things that you do without thinking —

"Go to General Quarters!"

"I relieve you, sir. Left full rudder; all ahead flank."

"Tell the engine room to light off the other two boilers and be ready for maximum speed."

"Tell all stations — all hands on the topside are anti-aircraft lookouts. Stand by for air attack."

The usual reports came in — cut short by the urgent need to keep the circuits clear for battle orders.

"Main Battery ready — Depth Charges set on Safe."

Over the radio came the quiet voice of the Task Group Commander: "Emergency ships right forty-five degrees."

The transports swung to starboard toward the moon. The destroyers closed in and formed a protective arc. The first bright flare was astern, now, nearing the water, swinging slightly under its parachute. So far we had seen no planes, but we suspected we were well surrounded.

Another flare opened in the blackness overhead, and on the surface of the water little pin points of light flickered along both sides of our advance. Float lights; they were trying to box us in, to make an easy and clear target for the torpedo planes and bombers.

"Emergency ships left, forty-five degrees."

On the opposite side of the formation a destroyer opened fire with 20 mm. We watched the red tracers arch upward for a moment — then fire and flames, down so low that we thought it was a ship. A mighty bonfire on the surface of the sea. "They got one of the transports," someone said. Another voice: "No. I can see all of 'em. It must be a destroyer."

Suddenly our own 20's began to shoot. I followed the tracers — saw nothing at the end. "Machine gun control; what are you shooting at?"

"There" — someone pointed — "planes."

I looked through my glasses. Not planes, but the round balls of smoke from large-caliber AA projectiles. "Control — Cease Firing — you're shooting at AA bursts." It took a little time to stop them. At the guns, the crews saw a plane in every grey globule of explosion and they were taking no chances.

No further excitement for five or six minutes. The little float lights continued to start up on either side of our path. There was no hiding a formation on a night like this. Even without float lights and flares the moon showed us clearly to one another. It must have been an easy mark from the air. But where were the attackers? We watched the sky; followed the motions of the large ships as they turned to get outside of the lights.

"Engine room reports the other two boilers on the line; ready to make maximum speed."

"Mr. Linehan reports he can count at least seven planes."

The bonfire on the ocean flickered down. All of our ships were accounted for; none were damaged. The flames were Japanese — one torpedo plane.

A rocket popped over the exact center of the formation and exploded in a shower of green stars. Over voice radio: "Stand by. They'll be coming in now."

From Control: "Plane coming in low on the starboard beam."

Suddenly we could see him — tearing in from the direction of the moon — a two-motored torpedo plane that looked the size of the Empire State building. He would cross just ahead of us, a hundred feet above the surface. Once inside of the G he had an unrestricted view of the transports.

"Machine guns — pick him up — bearing nine five, relative — position angle two — commence firing!"

From our starboard side the guns commenced to crackle. Red arcs flashed out, ending at a single point. Maybe that first wild shooting at smoke puffs had been a good thing after all, to release the tension of the gunners. This was superb firing.

We went hard left to keep the guns bearing. The plane was so close that we could see the blue jets of flame from the exhaust of the engines. There was a red twinkle — a spreading flame — the fire raced across from wing tip to wing tip. It looked like a circus diver who sprays himself with gasoline and makes a human torch as he springs down to the tank. Our Mitsubishi hadn't far to go; he was still a silhouette of fire when he smashed into the sea.

From Task Group Commander to G: "Nice shooting."

Now that the business had started it continued with no let up. Every ship was firing. The heavier crack of 5-inch provided the sound effects for the crimson streams of 20-mm tracers. Under the noise came the calm orders from the flagship: "Left forty-five; emergency right, forty-five; emergency left, sixty."

I knew that the G was shooting, but, as in every battle, I did not consciously hear the sound of the guns. It was always like that — after I ordered "Commence Firing" the guns could, and frequently did, speak up with their muzzles only ten feet from my ears, but I never heard them. Things happen so quickly at battle speeds that the conning officer has every nerve concentrated on maneuvering the ship and watching for targets that are not under fire. The noise of his own ship's battery becomes a subdued murmur.

The little float lights bobbed about and icy blue flares kept us bathed in brightness. On the surface there were four fires now; and still no ship had been hit. "Emergency ships left, forty-five."

"Plane coming in — seven-oh, relative — position angle one."

I don't believe he saw the G until we opened fire. He was headed in for the transports, but he changed his mind and swerved toward us. He was very close — very low — very big, and moving fast. We saw the torpedo drop from beneath his fuselage, strike the surface — make a phosphorescent wake that lined up with the exact center of the G.

"Left, full rudder. Torpedo —"

We swung left across the track. The torpedo was now paralleling us, on an opposite course. It cleared the stern. On the port bow — two hundred yards from the ship — our second torpedo plane lost his left wing and fell into the sea.

We changed course to the right to take up our station and waited for reports to come in. The news was good. Our angel was still holding fast to his perch on the yardarm.

The G's leading signalman, Fulp, who could see better with naked eyes than most of us with binoculars, stepped up and reported, "There's something on the port quarter that looks like the conning tower of a sub." I put my glasses on it — a square, grey mass rising from the sea. We swung left to make a closer inspection. There was a strong smell of gasoline in the air. Now that we were almost alongside we could see that the "conning tower" was the rudder of a plane — all that remained of the G's second target, the one that had not burned. "Tell machine gun control to put a few in that tail section." Down on No. 2 20 mm the gun captain — a yeoman named Krause, put a beautiful short burst into the exact center of the target. It flared up and in the light of the flame we could see two figures struggling with a life raft — trying to get clear of the lake of gasoline before it, too, caught fire.

I reached for the phone and reported that we were coming in from the direction of the burning plane. Aboard the G we had one more target — another torpedo plane that came up from astern so quickly we were able to fire only a few shots before he passed. We nipped him, but didn't bring him down. The transports were waiting for him. He was another wingtip to wing-tip torch as he went into the sea.

During the next lull I reported that "there are a couple of those guys in the water by the burning plane, if anyone wants them picked up." For one of us to stop for rescue work at this point was not to be thought of, but possibly the Task Group Commander might want to pick up prisoners later on.

There was a moment of silence, then our destroyer Commodore spoke up in a laconic voice, "Did you toss those guys any emergency rations?" he inquired.

In the pilot house someone chuckled. "Negative," we replied, "no emergency rations."

The Task Force Commander decided there had been enough inter-destroyer by-play. "Clear the air, please," he ordered. The destroyers piped down.

One by one the float lights went out. There were no more flares. The Japanese had lost at least five of the attacking group, and had failed to make a single hit. As Lieutenant Brundage said, in the after-action report that is made by all officers: "The party was a complete success and everybody had a swell time — that is, except for those who tried to crash the gate."

When we knew for certain that the attack was over; when the ship had secured from General Quarters, and the formation was once again on the course for Guadalcanal, the officers came on the bridge for the usual informal post mortem of the fight. The gun crews had done a beautiful job — especially Hal Strong's machine gunners, who brought down two of the big attackers in a magnificent exhibition of shooting. We could forgive the wild firing at bursts. In fact, if that was the training they needed, we'd let them shoot at anything, if it served to develop the pin-point accuracy they had demonstrated. Our grizzled chief boatswain's mate listened to the talk for a few minutes, then came in with the remark that capped the evening. "Jeez," he said, "the boys is better night fighters than day fighters. It's them carrots they been eating that does it."

BASKET

Our first visit to this port came at the close of seventy days uninterrupted steaming. After an hour in port we reached the conclusion that we might as well have stayed at sea. In subsequent infrequent visits we came to know the place better, and when we had been eight months in the more sparsely settled areas of the South Pacific we viewed it as a part of the routine. We accepted it, but we never liked it. We managed to get a modicum of rest in its tricky harbor, but we never came to regard it with affection, though we were forced to admit that in the early morning at slack water when the sun painted the reflections of our ships in pink and pale blue on the smooth surface of the harbor, and the fringe of coral beach lay crisp and cool beneath the shadows of palm trees, there was a delightful atmosphere of "dolce far niente" and a hint of tropical paradise au Gauguin in the depths of the forest and along the banks of quiet little rivers sauntering past the plantations and villages that sprawl on either side of the channel.

For an hour or so at dawn and dusk Basket is as pleasant a tropical island as one could find in the pre-war travel books. For the remaining hours it is a nightmare. The harbor is deep; the current runs more swiftly than in New York's North River. With the exception of a few spots, where the anchor finds sand and clay, the bottom must be made of polished slate. You enter port in the deceptive quiet of the early morning or late afternoon. With a sigh of relief you secure the sea watches, put the engines on an hour's notice and go below for a bath. In the midst of singing and soaping under a warm shower you feel the ship give a suspicious tremor. Then a bang on the door and the disturbing announcement: "Sir, the officer of the deck reports we're dragging anchor." With a sailor's prayer that the engineers can crank the wheels before the current sets you on the reef you leap for the bridge and, after an eternity, while the stern creeps nearer and nearer to the white water that sizzles across the edge of the shoal, you get underway and shift berth. If you are a newcomer you might repeat this procedure two or three times before you consign Basket to perdition and resign yourself, as we all did, to keeping steam to the throttle; spinning the propellers against the strength of ebb and flood, and maintaining a full sea watch, thus having most of the discomforts of being at sea, without the refreshing coolness that your own speed gives you when underway.

In the evening you decide to celebrate being at anchor by having a movie on deck in the cool airs beneath the tropic stars. It is perfect. You rig the movie screen on the forecastle or fantail, you sit long over dinner in the wardroom (the same old canned dinner) then, when the messenger reports "Movies ready, sir," you light your ten-reel cigar and follow the hooded flashlight to your chair near the screen. Suddenly the stars disappear; a black cloud rolls out from the shore, and as Mickey Mouse and Donald Duck begin their nostalgic scampers the rain comes down in torrents. Sometimes you will sit through it under the scant protection of a rubber slicker but unless you are an indefatigable fan you give it up as a bad job and return to your cabin and the official reports that you should have been working on to begin with.

From a letter home: "Yesterday afternoon I met a nice old Frenchmen who owns a sprawling plantation that stretches along the shore about two hundred yards from where I am anchored. I asked if there were any horses and he invited me to ride with him this morning. So at 6:45 I went over in my little boat — met the patron, and for an hour and a half I forgot the ship and the war as we rode through pleasant paths and narrow trails that wound first through groves of coconut palms, then through acres of coffee bushes with red berries and waxy, dark green leaves. Beyond the coffee were more fields of cacao, from which chocolate is made. The usual papaia and breadfruit abound. In my fluent and graceful French I asked my host many questions. He has fourteen children, ranging in age and size from two and a half to thirty, 'Comme un escalier,' as I so neatly put it. He must have slackened off in the past year or so but he seemed pleased when I commented that 'Frenchmen are noted for their industry.' However, there was an expression of envy about his face when he admitted that his brother has twenty-two children. But there is little to do of an evening in these islands, and his form of diversion antedates the cinema. He told me that I could 'Galop' if I wished, but that because of his heart (certainly he must have strained something in all these years) his doctor had forbidden him the 'galop.' But I chose to walk my horse and chat with the patron, with occasional easy canters for a few yards.

I returned aboard with an enormous appetite, after arranging to ride again tomorrow if we are still here. Soon after I got back we started dragging anchor, and before I could get underway and move we had dragged six hundred yards and my stern was in speaking distance of the reef."

That was my first meeting with Monsieur Dessonville and his horse Madame Clemenceau. Madame C was a sad-eyed beast who had lived so long in the tropics that any change in her routine caused distress and alarm. Not having seen her before the morning that I accepted the patron's invitation to ride, I went ashore booted and spurred. I realized my mistake as soon as I climbed the rise above M. Dessonville's little dock and found myself in his barnyard. Wearing faded trousers, a much-laundered white shirt enveloping his well-developed estomac and a floppy straw hat pulled over his bald head, he leaned against a post under an open shed and chatted in island French with his horse. They saw me at the same time. They looked at one another, and Madame C fretted visibly under her well-worn saddle with the machete hanging from the knee pad. She leaned over and muttered something in her master's ear. He nodded in agreement and pointed at my spurs but I was already one ahead of him, for I had started to unstrap them the moment I sighted the weary frame of poor Madame Clemenceau.

Nonetheless we had an enjoyable and agreeable ride on each of the three mornings my ship remained at Basket. On the second day I took my Assistant Machine Gun Officer, a former V.M.I, boy and intercollegiate boxer. When we disembarked at the Dessonville landing he gave a sprightly leap, overshot the flimsy boardwalk dock and fell headlong into the river. He dried himself off as best he could, but his appearance amused our host who asked if it were an American habit to take a light workout along the plage before commencing a promener a cheval. The Fantail Gazette carried a note in the Social Column:

"This column is curious as to One-Round Eastham's early plunge at a recent port of call. His rig upon leaving the ship definitely indicated a bit of equine showmanship. We have it from an eye witness, however, that his first move upon reaching the landing was a simulated swan dive into the channel. The ex-leather pusher claims he couldn't resist the clear, sparkling waters. We think he was groggily staggering toward a neutral corner."

On another morning my companion was Lieutenant John Brundage whose long legs proved a trial to his horse, a reluctant animal called August Dupin. John rode him as he would a sled, braking with his foot when he rounded the sloping trail along the upper reaches of the plantation.

Those three mornings were delightful breaks in our routine. We could not ride far — the ship was on the usual hour's notice for getting underway and we had to remain within range of her whistle, but how refreshing it was to move through the green undergrowth and forget General Quarters and battles while we practiced our rusty French on M. Dessonville. When we left Basket we sent him a gift of flour and sugar, so possibly the younger steps in the escalier enjoyed a treat of cookies and candy, rare indeed in those war-suffering islands.

In the adjacent plantation was a family that owned the general store and a small inter-island coasting fleet of schooners. The shelves in the store were empty and the little trading boats were drawn up under coconut trees along the beach for there was no longer any traffic between the islands. We found that the children of this family were ill and sent the doctor of the G over to have a look at them. He took along some medicines for their colds and aches, and was rewarded with a gift of excellent limes and papaias and an invitation for the wardroom to come over and help sample some homemade wine. The doctor, who was also our Mess Treasurer, found it necessary on each subsequent visit to go ashore and buy fresh fruit for the Mess. Occasionally he returned with one or two limes — sometimes with a papaia, but always with a mild glow from the wine that somehow was forced upon him during his quest for fruit.

A few hours in Basket were sometimes like a Class Reunion or a surprise encounter with former shipmates. We decided that there was nothing like a war for renewing old friendships. One morning I was inspecting the enginerooms when a messenger came below to report that the Captain of the Duncan was on board. I went up and found Teddy Taylor, whom I had not seen for several years, and with him Bill Smedberg, whom I had last seen in Washington. A little later their Division Commander, Tom Ryan, recently Flag Secretary to the Commander in Chief, came over and we had an enjoyable get together. Teddy said: "We've just come from the Atlantic. You've seen plenty of action out here. What's it like?" He found the answer in a more realistic manner than I could tell him, a few evenings afterward, when he played a busy role in the night action off Savo. The Navy Department communique announced that the Duncan had been sunk but that the Captain and most of the officers and crew had been saved. Teddy and his men did a beautiful job in that melee that caught the enemy by surprise and that brought our destroyers on top of them and well within torpedo range before being discovered.

There were many familiar faces among the captains who came in for fuel, or who brought their ships alongside the G for an hour or two before carrying out orders to "Proceed on duty assigned." Bill Hank, of the Laffey, one of the wittiest men I have ever known, came over to see us. He was from my home town, and an old friend of Commodore Holcomb, who had his flag in the G. Bill could find humor in the most difficult and trying situations, and he was a born raconteur. Our weariness seemed to drop away when he was around. It was a heavy blow to all who knew him to learn that he went down with his ship in the vicious night action off Lunga Point, in mid-November.

Tom Fraser of the Walke, came in one afternoon. He sized up Basket more quickly than most of us. "This place looks like Alcatraz in technicolor," he signaled as the Walke steamed by on her way to a tanker. Tom came on board later in the day for an enjoyable hour of shop-talk. It was the last time I saw him. He led the destroyers in the second Savo night action and was lost when the Walke blew up in the closing phase of the battle, after helping to annihilate the enemy force.

Joe Worthington, of the Benham, we saw frequently. Upon our graduation from the Naval Academy, both Joe and I had gone to the old Texas, where his roommate in the ship was Hanson Baldwin, who later resigned from the Service to take up the newspaper work in which he has so eminently succeeded.

Ches Daniel and Wally Petersen, classmates and friends of many years, brought their destroyers into port several times when the G was there. I kept a little guest book in my cabin aboard the G. Wally wrote: "My fondest expectation is to write in this book again — forty years from now." I hope so too, Wally, and I hope I'm around to watch you write in it.

From time to time we fell in with other destroyers, many of whose skippers I had not seen for years as our peacetime duties took us to different fleets and widely separated shore billets. Eph McLean and Ed Wilkinson and Pop Seaward, Frank Gardner and Roy Hartweg and Bill Brown, Dick Stout and RoUo Wilson and Don Ramsey, Max Stormes and Gus Roane and Al Calvert, Hal Tiemroth, Bill Cole, Angus Sinclair, Dixie Carroll, Ed Young and O. F. Gregor; in those early months of the campaign all of us had destroyers and if there hadn't been that one hour's notice (frequently reduced to "Get underway immediately") hanging over our heads we might have had a reunion of the Class of 1924 ashore under any convenient group of coconut palms.

One afternoon in October we had just cleared the tanker and were headed for an anchorage after a routine trip up the line when Rear Admiral Scott's Task Force came in from their Savo Island victory. To my regret I cannot give their names, except to say that the cruiser bringing up the rear — down by the bow; water pouring from hoses in her scarred forward turrets, was my old ship, the Boise. I hastened aboard. Lieutenant Commander John Laffan stood at the top of the gangway ladder. "We gave 'em what for," he said. "Is the Skipper all right?" I asked. "Fine." John smiled. "Gee," he added, "he was wonderful."

"And the others?"

"We lost Chips and Garf Thomas and Evarts and about a hundred of the crew," he said.

"Chips" was the Chief Carpenter, Harold Thomas, one of the most outstanding officers of any grade that I have ever known, and the mainstay of the ship in Damage Control. In my fourteen months in the Boise our key Damage Control Assistants were Lieutenant Fred Dierman, Ensign Tom Morris, Chief Carpenter Thomas and Boatswain O'Neill. "Chips" and "Boats" were each in charge of a Repair Party; Fred Dierman was in Central Station with me, and Tom Morris was a roving trouble shooter — sometimes in Central, sometimes at a Repair Station, and doing a fine job wherever he was. Under Commander Tom Wolverton, her Damage Control Officer at the time of the engagement, these officers, and the men of the repair parties, had performed a task of gigantic magnitude, for the Boise was badly mauled in the later phases of the action. She had matters her own way in the opening rounds. "They didn't lay a glove on us for ten minutes," was Captain Moran's remark when I went to the bridge to offer my congratulations.

The two forward turrets were charred and black in the gun chambers and control booth. There were few survivors among the crews that had served these six guns and who had inflicted terrific punishment on the enemy before they came under the fire of Japanese 8-inch. Turret No. 3 was jammed in train. When this occurred and the guns could no longer fire, the turret crew — all Marines — converted themselves into a repair and fire-fighting party on the blazing forecastle.

The captain's cabin was gutted by fire. The outboard bulkhead was split with a shell hole large enough for a Jeep to drive through. The Admiral's cabin was a sieve — scarcely a square foot that was not ripped by fragments. On the second deck we followed the easily traceable path of an

8-inch projectile. It entered the ship on the starboard side, above the waterline; demolished the crew's library; dished the armored deck without penetrating it; bounced around in a living compartment; cut off the muzzles of the marines rifles but left the remnants of them standing in their rack; turned left and ploughed through the Marines' clothing locker; ripped through the gunnery office and the supply office, leaving a wreck of ledgers, forms, typewriters and furniture; turned ninety degrees to the right, left the ship via the port side, still above the waterline, and exploded harmlessly in the air.

I visited the Forward Repair Station, where Chief Carpenter Thomas and so many of his men lost their lives. The thin partitions between officers' rooms in this area were crushed like a paper bag by the concussive force of shells that exploded near by.

Wolverton and his men waved a weary greeting but they had no time to talk. They were still at the job of pumping out flooded compartments, stopping leaks, strengthening bulkheads and continuing the melancholy task of bringing bodies from the magazines far below. Captain Moran said: "The Damage Control Organization worked like a clock." The fact that the Boise still lived to fight again was tribute not only to Wolverton and his aides, but to the entire ship's company, for in the Boise Damage Control was something with which all hands were familiar. As I looked at what these men had done I hoped that our training in the G would bear as fine fruit if the occasion ever arose.

Captain Moran told me that the dead who were still in the ship would be buried next afternoon at the little cemetery on shore. I went over for the services, and landed at a small dock about three miles below the cemetery. An army truck came by and I hailed it and clambered up between the two Negro soldiers in front. One of them had enormous hands wrapped around a rifle. "What are you going to shoot?" I asked. "I'se gonna shoot anything that comes along," he answered, looking hopefully around us in the bush. "Have you seen any action yet?" "Nossuh," he said, "but I'se ready."

I asked him where he was from.

"I'se from Norfolk, Virginia," he said.

"What part of Norfolk?"

"From a place called Princess Anne Road," he replied, giving me a look.

"Whereabouts on Princess Anne — as far out as the waterworks?"

He rolled his eyes, "Gunnel, suh — how come you know about the waterworks?"

When I told him that I had lived in Princess Anne County, just outside of Norfolk, he was ready to drive me anywhere, and wait, if need be.

The roadside scenes were startlingly like Civil War photographs — a tent under a tree in a clearing, with one Negro soldier cutting the hair of another; a group bathing in a narrow river while the natives — as black as the soldiers, but pygmies, watched, entranced.

Jack Greenslade, on Admiral Fitch's Staff, asked me for dinner that evening. Admiral Scott was present, and he gave us a full account of the recent night action — one of the most overwhelming victories of the war. It was my last meeting with Admiral Scott, who did not live to see the completion of another vicious battle by night in which both he and Admiral Callaghan were lost when their combined Task Forces overwhelmed a greatly superior enemy fleet and broke the back of Japanese naval opposition against the Eastern Solomons.

One afternoon when we were anchored for a few hours close to the mouth of a small river we were able to let some of the crew go over for a swim. As the Fantail Gazette reported it: "The lads of the Mighty G were recently invited by the Marines to use their swanky swimming pool. This pool features fairly fresh water (no salinity indicators available, though a few soap hardness tests were run) and is subject to ultraviolet rays when the sun is shining. A lovely rustic bridge completes the rural scene. The 'Birthday Model' bathing suit, in natural colors, was in vogue. After swimming, many of the bare —— bathers enjoyed a drink of coconut milk, fresh and straight."

On one of our rare all-night stopovers, Frank Peters and I went ashore to accept Red Monaghan's invitation for a glass of beer. We worked up a good thirst and covered ourselves with red mud before we stumbled on Monaghan's abode, the typical canvas cottage, but distinctive in that it had screens on four sides and a substantial wooden floor. Red had a house guest — Foster Hailey, of the New York Times, who had just come down from Guadalcanal where he watched the terrific night action that took place a few thousand yards to seaward of his position on the beach at Guadalcanal. He witnessed the entire affray; watched the crippled remnants of the Japanese forces creep away in the early morning, and, after daylight, helped pull survivors out of the water. Several of our destroyers were lost while Hailey was on Guadalcanal and he expressed himself in a decided manner with regard to the sanity of men who would go to sea in the tin cans. In consequence I was surprised when, later in the afternoon —

it was perhaps after the third or fourth beer — he said "Skipper, if I can get permission from the Senior Officer Present, how about taking me for a ride in the G?"

I told him that the G would be delighted, and to hold himself on short notice. At four the next morning we got orders to get underway at daybreak for a passage to Guadalcanal. We sent word ashore, though I didn't expect that Hailey would be able to make it. But he must have worked fast, for just as we were at "short stay," with the anchor coming up fast, a motor launch came off from the beach with Hailey standing in the stern. He tossed up his typewriter and a kit bag, gave a pier-head leap and clambered over the side as we went ahead down channel. That began one of the pleasantest associations of an active year, for Foster Hailey, in a quiet unobtrusive way, adjusted himself to destroyer life and became a full-fledged member of our ship's company. He was with us for six weeks, when he left to join a destroyer group that was making a night attack in the Kula Gulf, in which the G was not scheduled to participate.

When we came in to port one afternoon to find that two ships regularly stationed there had built an Officers Club, of sorts, on the side of a hill in a coconut grove, and a recreation field complete with swimming floats and beer garden for the men, we knew that the war was drawing farther away from our little island point of call. In the certainty that we would be in port overnight we sent half the crew to try the new beach resort, and a delegation from the wardroom to investigate and report on the attractions of the Officers Club. One of our wardroom calling committee was a young officer who at Princeton went under the nickname of Peanut, as he was neither very tall nor very broad. On the way ashore he developed an attack of hiccups that seemed immune to the usual remedies. At the club he followed all the suggestions of his unsympathetic shipmates, but the hiccups grew in intensity and volume, and Peanut was very miserable. A tall, broad-shouldered Second Lieutenant of Marines watched for a while, then leaned across and whispered to Lieutenant Linehan, the senior member of our group: "I think I can stop his hiccups, sir, if I have your permission." Linehan nodded approval.

The hiccup victim had not witnessed the conversation. The first he knew was when a heavy hand clutched his shoulder and lifted him to his feet. He squirmed around and found himself gazing at a strange giant of a Marine who stuck his chin close to Peanut's startled eyes and growled: "I've got you now, and I'm going to give you the blankety blankest beating you ever had in your life" — all the time shaking him with violence.

The Marine dropped him back in his chair as suddenly as he had picked him up; turned to Lieutenant Linehan, saluted, and said: "I believe he'll be all right now, sir."

When Peanut collected his breath and his shattered nerves he managed to gasp: "What the hell has that guy got against me?" But his hiccups were gone.

ATTACK — REPEAT — ATTACK

The Japanese received their first great defeat in the Battle of Midway; they received their second in the night actions off Guadalcanal in mid-November, 1942. The Midway battle was a victory for our carrier-borne and island-based aircraft. In the Solomons engagements air power played a part, particularly in the mopping up, but surface craft carried the fight when the fleet of Japan steamed boldly into the narrow triangle bounded by Lunga, Savo and Tulagi, and were thrown back in battered fragments by our battleships, cruisers and destroyers.

Between the 7th of August, when we first landed on Guadalcanal, and the Middle of November, there were four major engagements. The Battle of the Eastern Solomons, in late August, and the Battle of Santa Cruz Islands, in late October, were fights between carrier-borne planes, with the surface forces widely separated, and the aircraft of each side endeavoring to strike the opponent's carriers. The other two actions were at night, between forces comprising cruisers and destroyers. The first one, on the night of August 8th, was an American defeat in that we lost more ships than the enemy; a victory in that we prevented the Japanese from attacking their principal objective — our transports. The second, in mid-October, caught the Japanese by surprise when Rear Admiral Scott's Task Force found the enemy west of Cape Esperance and sank the greater portion of his cruisers and destroyers. On our side we lost the destroyer Duncan, and two of our cruisers sustained damage.

These were the four principal meetings with the enemy. We met him daily and nightly in smaller units. The Tokyo Express was running on a timetable schedule from late August throughout the early fall. The damage inflicted by these hit-and-run attacks was not great, but they were made with persistence and vigor and successfully kept our marines on shore from getting enough rest. There was occasional damage to Henderson Field and to parked planes, by the night attacks and by the daily serial bombing, but while this form of attack was a nuisance and at times a menace, the Japanese had avoided any major effort to regain their lost positions. We expected such an effort and several times we took station to oppose it, but conditions at the time did not permit us to commence a sea offensive for we were hanging on to Guadalcanal by our eyebrows and the primary task of the fleet was to bring in reinforcements of men and material in order that our newly won positions could be consolidated. Then, and not until then, could we start another push.

Meantime we had lost the Wasp and the Hornet and our carrier strength was thereby considerably weakened. It was fortunate that our naval aviators had been successful in sinking even more enemy carriers. After the Santa Cruz Battle no Japanese carriers approached to within striking distance of the Eastern Solomons. Both sides had suffered losses; the enemy in far greater proportion than ourselves. Unless he intended to relinquish Guadalcanal it was apparent that there would be at least one all-out attempt to push us from the island. We prepared for it; rushing equipment to our marines; waging continuous war against submarines and aircraft; trying to avoid loss by the attrition attacks of the Japanese while keeping our fleet units in a covering position from which they could quickly meet the foe. By early November we were fairly strongly established. General Vandergrift's Marines, and the army units that had recently been landed, were pushing the Japanese army along the entire perimeter of attack. Our bombers worked regularly to the westward, softening up the enemy bases in the Central Solomons. The push was on in New Guinea. Japan was on the defensive throughout the entire archipelago, but her strength was still numerically superior and her doctrine of "No Surrender" still applied. All along the line events were moving rapidly toward a showdown.

On the night of November 12-13 strong American Task Force was in the Guadalcanal Area. It was commanded by Rear Admiral Richmond K. Turner, who was the Commander, Amphibious Force, South Pacific. The combatant strength of cruisers and destroyers was led by Rear Admiral Callaghan, in the San Francisco, and seconded by Rear Admiral Norman Scott, in the light cruiser Atlanta. This was the force that met the enemy off Lunga Point and administered one of the most crushing defeats in the history of naval warfare.

The Japanese fleet consisted of battleships, heavy and light cruisers, destroyers, and an estimated sixteen large, heavily loaded transports. Off Lunga Point, in the darkness, the two fleets met. The Japanese were in a double column. The American ships drove down between them, shooting and firing torpedoes on either side. The distance between the opposing lines of battle was absurdly small; the range in which frigate actions were fought; the ships so close that the fall of shot coincided with the flash of salvoes. Actual collision was narrowly averted, and the confusion was so great in this hand to hand melee that when our ships drew clear the two Japanese columns continued to fire on each other.

It was to be expected that destroyers would suffer quickly in such close combat where they were pitted against cruisers and battleships at machine-gun range. The Laffey fired her torpedoes and watched them hit home before she began to suffer damage. She was struck heavily and hauled out of column, burning fiercely. It was obvious that nothing could save her. Captain Hank gave the order to abandon ship. They left her over the forecastle, the only portion of the ship that was not an inferno. When everyone was in the rafts the Captain leaned over the life line and told them to get clear. "I'm going to have another look around to see if we've missed anyone," he said. In the light of the flames the men in the rafts saw him wave his hand and walk aft. He had taken only a few steps when there was a gigantic explosion and the ship slid beneath the waves, taking her Captain with her.

Both Admiral Callaghan and Admiral Scott lost their lives when the enemy concentrated his fire on the bridges and upper-works of our ships. The losses among our destroyers were heavy, that night, but they struck their blows before they sank and, with the cruisers, scattered the Japanese fleet in a turmoil of confusion.

One of our destroyers received damage to her engineering plant of so extensive a nature that she could not move. Otherwise she was reasonably intact; all guns operative; no danger of sinking. When dawn came she found herself alone, to the southwest of the approaches to Tulagi. As it grew lighter she saw to the west, beyond Sand Fly Passage, a large ship which she soon identified as a Japanese battleship. It, too, was motionless, because of damage received in action. The distance between the ships was about 20,000 yards — far out of range for destroyer guns, but an easy shooting distance for the 14-inch battery of the battleship. There was nothing the destroyer could do — but wait — and try to get word to Guadalcanal for our bombers to come out and make the kill.

They watched the battleship through their glasses. They saw the turrets train out, the guns elevate. There was a flash from the muzzles, and aboard the destroyer they started their stop-watches. At least they could check the time of flight of the projectiles, so they would know when their ship was going to be hit. The hands of the watches crept slowly around the dial.

Time seems to hang, motionless, when you are waiting for twelve tons of armor-piercing shell to reach the end of their parabola over ten miles of water. They hit, finally, five hundred yards short of the target, and bounced over the destroyer in ricochet, with the noise of thunder. They waited for the next one. It came. It was over. They had been bracketed — one salvo short; one salvo over. The third one would hit. Through the glasses they saw the guns come down to loading position; elevate; fire. The range was perfect, but the deflection had crept off. The salvo landed in line with the ship, but slightly ahead. On the bridge of the destroyer they looked at one another a little shakily. They had been given a short respite. It would be the fourth salvo that got them. Someone called out: "Planes coming over from Guadalcanal!"

The final installment of the Perils of Pauline had nothing on the last-minute rescue of the destroyer. There was no fourth salvo. There was not, and would never be, another salvo fired from that Japanese battleship. The bombers went into action. Aboard the destroyer they had the supreme pleasure of watching their late antagonist blow up and sink.

Four days earlier the G had entered the harbor of a southern port, and on the list of ships present that the signalmen made up as soon as we moored, I saw the name of the light cruiser Juneau. Her navigator was Lieutenant Commander J. Stuart Blue, my Naval Academy roommate, whom I had not seen since before the war, when our two families lived for a while in the delightful, rambling house that the Dillingham family owns, on the edge of Pearl Harbor.

I sent a signal asking Stuart to come aboard the G for dinner. In a few minutes the bridge phoned to report the Juneau underway and to tell me that Stuart had answered, "Delighted, next time in port."

The Juneau did not return to port. She fought in the night action of the 12th-13th; she was damaged, but not too badly; she left the Solomons with her task force, and was lost on the way south. Stuart Blue was not among the survivors. His death ended an association that began in the fall of 1919 when I left home to attend Bobby Werntz's school, at Annapolis, and prepare for the Naval Academy Entrance Examinations. I was fifteen, and already a little homesick when I arrived in Annapolis and went to live with the Misses Walton, at 10 Francis Street, where my mother and father had arranged for me to stay. Miss Katherine Walton, plump, pleasant and vivacious, and her older sister, Agnes, equally kindly if slightly more remote, did their best to make me feel at home in the friendly atmosphere and comfortable surroundings of their house. "There will be another young man with us tomorrow," Miss Kitty told me. "His name is Stuart Blue, and he is the son of Admiral Victor Blue." Stuart arrived and we were friends at once. Indeed, everyone that Stuart met was his friend, for he was one of the most natural persons I have ever known.

He had spent several years at a military school and was used to being away from home. As soon as he had unpacked his bags in the little room adjoining my own, we went downstairs to report that we could like to take a walk around the town. Miss Agnes cautioned us against going to a certain drug store. Stuart and I nodded obediently, but we were no sooner out the door than he said, "Let's take a look at that place." We did, and while it may have been a den of evil, we never found anything wrong with it, except that the chocolate sauce for the ice cream — cooked up in large cauldrons in a back room — would by no means be passed by a sanitary inspector today.

Another boy, Harry Chariot, came to occupy the remaining room at Miss Walton's. The three of us were inseparable. We were sincere in our desire to enter the navy. We studied like dogs and spent little time in recreation — getting most of our exercise in running through the streets to the fires that seemed an almost nightly occurrence in Annapolis at that time.

We passed the entrance examinations the following April, and entered the Naval Academy in June. Joe Dahlgren, who broke all of the Academy strength test records, and Donald Olsen, from Seattle, were the other members of a quartette that worked and studied and played together during our Candidate year. At the Academy we were joined by Guy de Buisseret, a young Belgian boy whose government had sent him to receive a naval education in America, and Rosy Harrison, a tall, handsome young man from Massachusetts, who had entered the Marines before deciding to try for the Academy. Those were the seven of us who started plebe year together.

We survived the academic year and went on our first midshipmen's cruise the following summer — to Norway, Portugal and Gibraltar. Guy de Buisseret became ill. He refused to turn in; he stood his watches, and he spent forty days passing coal, as we all did, when he should have been in a hospital bed. He became worse when we got home. An operation failed to save him, and he died, early youngster year. At about the same time Harry Chariot resigned from the Navy and Don Olsen discovered that he had rather serious lung trouble. He was sent to a naval hospital in Colorado.

The remaining four of our original seven completed the course and were graduated. Rosy Harrison was one of the first members of our class to go into aviation. He was killed in 1926 when his training plane crashed near Pensacola. Joe Dahlgren and Stuart and I went along in the peacetime routine. We had duty in battleships and cruisers and destroyers. After seven years we went ashore, where Stuart became an aide at the White House, and later had command of the President's yacht. A year before the war Joe was retired for physical disability. That left Stuart and me, and now the Juneau was lost and Stuart was not among the survivors. It was difficult to realize that a friendship — almost a kinship — of twenty-three years, was at an end. One of the first of our destroyers to be sunk in the Solomons had been named for Stuart's father. There will — I hope — be another U-S.S. Blue in the service before long, as a reminder of an outstanding officer and gentleman.

The second phase of the mid-November battles took place on the night of the 14th-15th when Admiral Lee's battleships, whose presence was unknown to the enemy, obeyed Admiral Halsey's injunction to "go in there and given them a few 16-inch surprises." This they did so thoroughly, in the Second Battle of Savo, that the Japanese literally did not know what struck them, as salvoes came roaring out of the night and sent their ships plunging to the bottom.

Our destroyers were in the van, leading the battleships, in that action, and again they suffered because again certain phases of the battle were fought at almost pistol range. They rounded Savo, left it on the starboard hand, continued for a while towards Lunga, then changed course to the west. When Savo was about abeam, our destroyers, silhouetted by the moon, were fired on by ships close in to the island. They returned the fire immediately, but it was soon obvious that they were being engaged by a force that not only was more numerous, but consisted of larger ships than destroyers.

The Preston, commanded by Max Stormes, was the third ship in column. Months later one of her surviving officers, Lieutenant McKee, who was in the Convalescent Hospital with me, told me some incidents that happened aboard his ship during those furious minutes.

On the bridge of the Preston a signalman noticed that someone had overturned the signal gang's coffee pot. He was growling about it when two high columns of water rose up close aboard to starboard. "What's that?" he asked. "Those are Jap salvoes, falling just a little short,"

Lieutenant McKee told him. The signalman gasped. "Well, why the hell am I worrying about a coffee pot?" he demanded.

A moment later the Preston was hit. The salvo struck in the midst of the vegetable lockers, and showered the bridge with potatoes and onions. In a few seconds there was a tremendous explosion aft, on the starboard side and the ship rolled over on her side. She sank by the stern, and in less than two minutes she was out of sight.

Lieutenant McKee took a step down the bridge ladder and found himself up to his armpits in water. He struck out to get clear of the wreck and, after taking a few strokes, his hand touched a fragment of a life raft. Most of it had been shot away. There was no grating; no emergency rations or water, but the part that was left was sufficient to hold his weight.

All around him, in the water, he could hear men calling and trying to direct their shipmates to rafts that they had discovered. The Japanese salvoes continued to fall among and around them, but these did not worry them so much as the thought of our battleships that were coming along in the path of the destroyers. There was a rush of water as they ploughed past, and as they roared by, already engaging the enemy, they dropped additional rafts to the men in the water.

The battle drew away from the men in the rafts. To the north, toward Florida Island, they saw a large Japanese warship, on fire. Every few minutes it would flare up in another explosion. Finally, at about four in the morning, there was a gigantic detonation as the magazines blew up — then silence. There were no survivors from that particular ship.

Meanwhile, our battleships were having a field day. It was a complete victory for Captain Gatch's "Old Nameless" and her companion; it was a shocking surprise to the enemy.

In the early morning several planes flew close over the heads of the destroyer survivors and wobbled their wings to let them know they had been seen. For several hours there was no time for a rescue, as all of our planes and destroyers were concentrating on the four Japanese transports that had slipped in during the night — all that remained from the original sixteen — and were trying to land their troops after beaching themselves on the Japanese section of the coast. When all four of them were burning beyond control, some of our small craft started towards Savo to pick up survivors. Meanwhile several natives had paddled out in canoes from the island and had taken the rafts in tow. When they sighted our small boats they asked what they were. As Lieutenant McKee reported it: "Some wise guy in the raft said, 'They're Japs.'" The natives dropped the tow and paddled hell-for-leather toward the island."

The survivors were landed at Tulagi, across the bay from the four columns of smoke that marked the burning transports. We did not know it at the time, but the last major effort to retake the Eastern Solomons was over. There would be more fighting — months of it, before the enemy troops were driven from Guadalcanal; before we could commence our push to the west, but the Japanese had their backs to the wall. There would be no pause in the American Offensive.

ON DUTY ASSIGNED

Even though we were in the front lines of the South Pacific War there were many periods when we roamed the sea on various missions without having occasion to fire a shot. Except for three brief visits to New Zealand we were always in the forward combat area. We could never drop our guard; we were apt to have action without warning; but still and all there were times when we subscribed to the theory that warfare is ninety percent boredom and ten percent bloodshed.

This did not mean idle moments at sea, or opportunities to stretch out in a deck chair and enjoy a book. Drills, school, surprise firing for the gun crews, and watches — always watches — filled our days. There is a story that is told of six naval officers of assorted nationalities who were cast up on an island. The two British officers organized a club; the two French officers discovered a narrow trail and followed it in search of feminine companionship; the two Americans began immediately to stand watch-and-watch.

On the rare occasions when the G was steaming independently, with no responsibility toward a convoy or task force, we were able to catch up in our homework, so to speak, and use the days for instructing our personnel. The following Plan of the Day is typical of a time when we were alone.

Plan of the Day

Sunday, March 14, 1943

0540: Call duty Masters at Arms, mess cooks and mess attendants.

0550: Call Division Petty Officers.

0600: Reveille.

0645: Breakfast for the oncoming watch.

0700: Breakfast.

0800: Muster on stations. Turn to.

0815: Sick call

0845: All hands making out new allotments report to ship's office.

0900: Division officers inspect division spaces.

1000: Damage Control instruction for repair parties on boat deck, Lt. (jg) Garrett.

1000: All torpedo strikers assemble on After Conn for instruction, Lieut. Strong.

1030: Gunnery lecture in wardroom for all officers, Lieut. Linehan.

1045: Inspection of mess cooks by Medical Officer.

1145: Early dinner for the oncoming watch.

1130: Inspection of mess attendants by Medical Officer.

1145: Dinner.

1300: Communication lecture in wardroom for all officers, Ens. MacRae.

Signal school on bridge — Fulp, Signalman, 1st class.

Sound school — Howell, Soundman, 3rd class.

Radio school — Miller, Radioman, 1st class.

1430: General Quarters for drill. Hold Damage Control problem and steering casualty drill, followed by steering casualty drill with ship in Condition 11.

1615: Early supper for the oncoming watch.

1645: Supper.

1800: Evening inspection of lower decks and living spaces by Lieut. Etheridge.

1930: Night General Quarters with surprise firing on flare target.

When we were in company with a convoy or task force we could carry out certain forms of firing, but it was only when we were alone and completely free of restrictions that we could use our battle experience to best advantage and simulate damage to such an extent that, at the close of the problem, the ship was being controlled from auxiliary stations and the guns fired by hand — all principal circuits and electric leads being assumed out of action or severed. Belowdecks the repair parties fought fierce imaginary fires and hurried to erect wooden shores against a bulkhead that was about to collapse — according to our problem. Throughout the ship, officers and men opened envelopes at the "Problem Time" written on the outside, and discovered that they were wounded or dead; that a shell had just exploded in the vicinity; that a torpedo was sighted close on the beam; that a bomb had struck the fantail, or that any other casualty, from our own or another ship's experience, or from the fertile imaginations of the problem-makers, had occurred. In this manner we kept the team in condition for the Big Game. In this way, too, we discovered various weaknesses in our system, and attempted to devise remedies. By emphasizing the fact that no one has a monopoly on good ideas we encouraged every man in the ship to step forward with suggestions as to how we would better prepare ourselves for combat; how we could shoot more accurately; how we could insure that our ship would remain afloat though badly damaged. In peacetime the importance of Damage Control is sometimes difficult to instill, for casualties can only be simulated. But in war, when men have seen what can be done by smart repair parties, it becomes a fascinating game and one that pays big dividends when the enemy is sighted. By "killing off" the seniors we gave junior officers and young seamen and firemen an opportunity to handle the ship and the guns and engines. This proved an efficacious antidote to thoughtless criticism and gave us a yardstick for measuring the comparative talent of the younger men.

Early in the spring we found ourselves again ordered to New Zealand, after first picking up a large passenger-liner transport near Australia. We arrived at Wellington at nine in the morning, fueled and sailed at four in the afternoon. The Netherlands Consul gave a luncheon for the captain of the liner and for two senior officers of the Royal Air Force who were coming to the United States. Conversation turned to flying, and the Dutch captain asked if the Air Commodores had ever flown an ocean. They had, several times. The Dutchman reached in his pocket and pulled out a dollar bill covered with Signatures. "Here's my Short Snorter ticket," he said, with a meaning look at the British airmen. He caught them both; neither had with him the certificate of membership that Short Snorters must carry at all times. They paid their fine — one dollar apiece.

Two days later when the G was zigging across ahead of the transport in an exceptionally stiff sea, taking green ones over the bridge and showers of salt spray down the stacks, we looked back at the big liner and wondered how her RAF passengers were making out. We sent a signal to the Air Commodore: "It is easy to be a short snorter. To qualify as a rough rider you must cross the ocean in a destroyer. The entrance fee is five dollars," to which we received the reply: "Would cheerfully pay five dollars never to have to ride a destroyer in weather like this. Commiserations."

On the northern end of our caravans to Guadalcanal we saw the little New Zealand corvettes that had come out with us from the coast, months before. One afternoon when the G and another destroyer had boiled up to Guadalcanal to join a surface striking force we entered Tulagi for fuel. On the other side of the tanker was the corvette commanded by Lieutenant Commander (Smoky Joe) Phipps. My fellow skipper and I accepted an invitation to go on board the corvette while our ships were receiving oil.

With Phipps, under the quarterdeck awning, was a big, jovial-looking commander in the New Zealand navy, who had stripped down to a sensible uniform of khaki shirt and shorts, and pith helmet. He hadn't bothered with shoes or socks on this blistering afternoon. His name was Brittson, and both he and Phipps had recently gained a measure of fame when they discovered a large Japanese submarine on the surface, near Guadalcanal. Alternately firing their guns, then backing off, coming ahead at full speed and ramming, they sank the Jap, who was bigger than the two corvettes put together. Brittson received our Distinguished Service Medal, and Phipps the Navy Cross, for this encounter. After the sinking, Smoky Joe picked up a wounded Japanese officer from the water. "He wanted a knife or a gun or something for a little hara-kiri," Phipps said, "but when we refused him, and told him that he had fought bravely, he quieted down and became quite a good chap."

After a few minutes a native dugout canoe, paddled by two New Zealand sailors, came alongside. "My gig," Brittson announced. He said good-bye, lowered himself carefully into the middle of the shaky little craft and paddled off across the quiet harbor to his own ship.

Another time we entered Tulagi harbor with a transport. Japanese planes were active, that day. We anchored; there was a "Condition Red"; we got underway and circled our transport in the open sea beyond Tulagi; the planes concentrated on the air field; we returned and anchored and resumed unloading; the voice radio blared "Condition Red! Condition Red!" and out we'd go again. That sequence continued for two days and nights. We had been sleepless for forty-eight hours, and finally, when we came in after about the twentieth alarm, our men on the forecastle forgot for a moment to count the shackles as our anchor chain ran out through the hawse hole. As the Fantail Gazette put it: "It's sixty they cried, when ninety they spied — and the bitter end done the rest." So we lost our port anchor and chain, and were fortunate not to lose any lives, when the bitter end roared up from the chain locker and slashed across the deck among our weary seamen, before plunging to the bottom of Tulagi Harbor.

There were surprisingly few accidents and mishaps among the Task Forces of the South Pacific, considering the exhausting routine of those first few months in our campaign when we cruised and fought and convoyed and patrolled with no letup and no rest. Even among the destroyers, whose duties took them alongside large ships in blackest night, and through narrow passages in poorly charted reefs in any kind of weather, there were only a few crumpled bows and buckled plates. And it was so easy for a helmsman whose body cried for rest to put the wheel the wrong way, and to have the mistake unobserved by a tired young officer of the deck during the short seconds that are required for two fast ships to cross the narrow waters separating them.

One collision occurred in the night following a heavy engagement when the ships of the Task Force had been cruising for three months without pausing. During the battle a destroyer was sunk, but with small loss of life. Her survivors were picked up by another destroyer and transferred to a battleship. The captain of the sunken ship was given a room and he stretched out in the bunk to rest. He was just beginning to doze off when there was a terrific crash. He grabbed his life Jacket and started to go on deck. As he passed through the wardroom there was another crash, followed by a grinding, scraping noise and a startling series of thumps. When things quieted down the somewhat unnerved survivor discovered that a destroyer had struck the battleship a few feet from the room that he was occupying, and that the clanking sound was caused by her anchor chain, which paid out along the deck of the battleship when the fluke caught and held in the wardroom door. The forward storeroom of the destroyer had been holed and in some manner her supply of toilet paper had gotten adrift. Daylight revealed it — hundreds of rolls looped in graceful garlands — waving and curling in fluttering streamers on the quarterdeck of the battleship.

Not only were collisions and accidents very rare, but in waters where the movements of our own units could not always be foretold, and where surprise meetings with the enemy were constant possibilities, there were no night encounters between our own ships that led to anything more serious than going to general quarters and training out the battery. It is true that we were trained to ensure prompt recognition and identification, but training is for naught if an officer makes up his mind that there are no friends in the vicinity, and that the ship he has sighted is an enemy. In the early months of the Guadalcanal campaign, when both we and the Japanese were reinforcing our respective armies on shore there were many unexpected meetings. We know that on at least one occasion the enemy fired on each other. It is not so silly as it may sound to a civilian to express satisfaction that we avoided similar disaster.

In one of the great night battles off Lunga an American cruiser was struck by a torpedo near the stern, jamming her rudder hard right, so that she was incapable of moving it. Like the Warspite in the Battle of Jutland, she commenced to travel in circles, firing at the enemy when her guns bore, hoping that she would avoid collision as she swung round and round amidst the melee of gun flashes and exploding ships. Gradually the action drew to the westward and the cruiser found herself alone, undamaged except for the hole in the stem and the jammed rudder that forced her to circle, for she could not stop her engines without running the risk of becoming a fine target for a submarine.

Finally all was quiet. The repair parties were working feverishly to free the rudder, when suddenly the captain was startled to hear one of our PT boats call another and announce: "There's a big one. He looks like a Jap. Let's get him!"

He jumped for his phone and said: "This is the Blank. Do not attack!"

There was moment of silence, then one of the PT skippers called the other and said, in incisive tones: "That's a bunch of malarkey. He's a Jap. Let him have it!"

The cruiser captain could hear the roar of the engines as the unseen mosquito boats dashed in to fire torpedoes. He spoke to them again, in exaggerated calmness: "This is the American cruiser Blank. This is Captain speaking. There is a tug standing out from Tulagi to assist us. The name of her captain is ——. We are not — repeat — not — a Jap."

The PT skipper was convinced. He acknowledged in tones that indicated disappointment at a lost opportunity, and, with the other boat, swung off to look for a bona fide enemy.

In tense moments of this kind the radio phone is a captain's joy. Among the aviators it is an invaluable means of communication which is sometimes employed to such an extent that at least a portion of Tennyson's prediction of aerial combat and commerce is borne out, for most certainly we "Heard the heavens fill with shouting" as these "Pilots of the purple twilight" went about their "grappling in the central blue." In our many caravans to Guadalcanal we came to know the voices of the two men who operated the voice transmitter at Henderson Field. When they were not announcing "Condition Red," or directing aircraft to investigate suspicious vessels or movements on shore, they were helping the aviators to check the tuning of their radios. A plane would call "Candy Control; Candy Control; how do you receive me; go ahead." In the forenoon a patient, slightly bored voice would answer. In the afternoon and evening the operator at Henderson Field must have been a man who was a tobacco auctioneer in civil life. In a high-pitched singsong he would rattle off: "Thisiscandycontrol — thisiscandycontrol — goahead — goahead — callingplanethreeonefivefromcandycontrol — comein — comein." When this bit of yodeling was completed someone on the bridge of the G, reminded of the commercial radio program at home, would usually add: "Sold to American."

The worldwide method, both civil and military, of helping an aviator to check the frequency of his radio, is to count slowly to ten or twenty. "Candy Control; Candy Control; gimme a count; gimme a count; go ahead." Whereupon the patient voice or the double talk gibberish of the tobacco auctioneer would comply.

The little New Zealand corvettes, patrolling day after day along the coast of Guadalcanal, grew weary of the constant counting, and invented an antidote that brought us much amusement. Eschewing the abrupt, staccato method of using voice radio, they leaned over backward in employing a formal politeness. During a period of inactivity along the airways one corvette would call another: "Would you please be so kind as to give me a veddy short count." "With much pleasure," the other would reply. "Please stand by." Then, instead of counting rapidly to twenty, he would say "Uh-wun. How do you receive me? Go ahead." With great punctilio the other corvette captain would answer: "Thank you veddy much. I hear you quite well indeed." We used to look forward to the "veddy short counts" of our New Zealand friends as bright spots in the day's operations.

On the half a dozen occasions when we received mail while proceeding on duty assigned during the first five months of the Solomons Campaign there were sometimes large packages addressed to the Captain, Officers and crew of the G. Before leaving the mainland of the United States I had written to a number of civilian friends, and wives of naval officers, all of whom were busily knitting and wrapping various Bundles for some organization or another, and suggested that they bring their efforts a little closer to home by organizing "Bundles for G." They responded with enthusiasm. We had "Chapters" in Pasadena (Mr. and Mrs. Gage Irving), Abilene, Kansas (Mr. and Mrs. Alden Hart), Alexandria, Va. (Comdr. and Mrs. J. M. P. Wright), Baltimore (my wife, and Mrs. J. H. Lee Fisher), and other small groups in the various cities and towns where the wives of the G's officers were living. By great good fortune their bundles arrived at times when the contents were badly needed. Just before we recovered the survivors of the Meredith and Verity we received a large box from the

Alexandria Chapter with dozens of games, puzzles, books and sweaters. They were life savers for the men who were forced to remain with us for ten days before we could give them the hospitalization and quiet that their exhausted condition demanded.

Again, when we had gone for almost three months without mail; when our storerooms were bare and all of us craved something sweet to gnaw on, we went up to a tanker for fueling at sea, and they passed over a box from Pasadena which contained twenty-five pounds of candy. We sent one box to the wardroom, another to the chief petty officers quarters, and put the remainder on the cafeteria table in the messing compartment, for the crew to have as dessert. Anything, no matter how trivial, that breaks the routine and gives the crew something new to talk about is a stimulus to morale. In the wooden ships of the Old Navy the high spot in the day's routine was just before the noon meal, when grog was served. We have no grog, of course; we could not use our shipboard radios or phonographs; our letters were read and reread and carried about in dungaree pockets until they were undecipherable. When the crew came off watch they wanted to relax with something that would take their minds from the interminable grind of keeping the sea. "Bundles for G" was what we needed.

In every ship of the navy there is a library, maintained by the Bureau of Personnel. Its contents are well selected and kept up to date by frequent replacements. The crew of the G read everything we had. They started with fiction and western stories and thrillers. When they reached the end of these they began on heavier volumes. It was by no means unusual to see an off-watch group reading, and enjoying, Shakespeare, Dickens, Conrad, Dumas, Scott, and the other standard sets that our library contained. It was a rather startling demonstration of cultural progress in the midst of war. The Book of the Month Club sent us copies of their issues regularly. and they were excellent. Our Abilene Chapter, Bundles for G, specialized in books of all kinds. They went from hand to hand, pocket to pocket, engineers, deck force, wardroom, C.P.O.'s. The Bible, in its many versions, was always in use. Mail, news from home, books — these are the things that our sailors wanted.

Not only did we receive fuel and food and mail from tankers and large ships, we also received our personnel in that fashion. One afternoon our carrier signaled: "Come alongside and receive passenger." We left our station and closed her, wondering what sort of passenger they might have, debating the pleasant possibility of receiving a high-ranking officer who wanted to be taken to one or another of our bases. We put our bow under the quarter of the huge carrier; she swung out a short boom and lowered a canvas bag to our forecastle. A red-headed, freckle-faced youngster emerged. "Ensign Woodward, reporting for duty, sir," he said. He had been several months on his way to the G, and had witnessed some of the great battles of the war from the ships in which he was taking passage. After receiving Woody in this fashion we speculated on other ways of having Ensigns report. Possibly the next one would come alongside in a submarine, or leap out of the sea from a large green bottle, like a child's pop-up.

Another time we closed a large ship and received "a hundred and fifty bags of men," plus machine guns, ammunition, airplane spare parts and propellers. The G was a top-heavy destroyer when that load was aboard, and we were taxed to find room for the material and sleeping space for the men. We were ordered to take them to a small island base that we had not previously visited. We entered the port, rounded a wooded point and found at anchor my old ship, the Boise. It was a happy meeting in more ways than one, for we still had been unable to stop long enough to put a proper patch over a bomb hole in our side, and in the ordnance storeroom we continued to bail each hour to keep the compartment free of water that entered though our cracked plating. We sent a signal: "May we have the use of the Bombay machine and some of those good Boise welders to repair hole in side and ripped seam in shell plating."

In a few minutes a motor launch came alongside with all the welding equipment needed to repair a sinking battleship, plus several welders, headed by Ensign Tom Morris and Chief Carpenter Harold Thomas. They took care of our damage in short order, and made a few more repairs for good measure. I was able to go on board and pay a quick visit to Captain Moran, and say hello to old shipmates. Now that they were back in the area they wanted action. They got it — plenty of it — a few nights later.

Although we were usually tired and more or less worn down from the perpetual grind of shipboard life, we missed not being able to take regular exercise. In a large ship there is room for deck tennis, medicine ball, boxing and wrestling, all of which help to cleanse the system of physical lassitude and mental mists. Aboard a destroyer there is no space for games. Occasionally, with a smooth sea, there might be sparring matches on the fantail, but that was about all we could do, except engage in marksmanship, using a pistol, rifle or tommy gun. Patrolling off

Guadalcanal one afternoon we were firing tommy guns from the bridge at coconuts, bits of driftwood — any target available. We passed a half-submerged log on which several dignified-looking birds were perched. The machine-gun officer asked permission to put a few rounds near them. This form of surprise firing, timed to the split second, not only relieved the tedium of watches, but developed an amazing accuracy among the machine gunners, who became seafaring Daniel Boones, able to part the hair of a coconut at five hundred yards. We told him to go ahead, and the port battery laid their shots within inches of the log, showering its passengers with spray, but giving them no wounds except to their injured feelings. The Fantail Gazette commented: "It was noted yesterday the manner in which the port 20-mm battery attacked an utterly defenseless bird haven. With fiendish glee and wild abandon they routed some seven feathered friends of the Solomons swish-bird variety, they spattered the seagoing perch with hot missiles of death, and Needlenose Lyons admits he screamed with sheer delight when one of the fleeing fowls faltered and seemed about to crash into the water. We suggest that the local Audubon Society investigate the incident and bring the vandals to their due and just deserts."

The little personal griefs were always with us, adding their weight to our worries, doubly poignant because we were so far away from wives and families. One mid-watch an officer of the G received word that his baby had been born, dead, and his wife was grievously ill. Although there was nothing he could do, we would have understood if he had phoned down to request permission for an early relief, so that he might go to his room and be alone. But he remained in Control until his regular relief appeared at a quarter of four, made his routine reports, and then, his duty completed for the time being, he went below.

A young seaman from the Tennessee mountains came to my door one day with a letter from home which told him that his father was not expected to five. I knew that his mother was an invalid, bedridden and helpless. With tears in his eyes, the boy asked if he could go home. It was, of course, impossible, but we were able to make him a loan from our Welfare Fund to send to his mother, and we arranged for our Navy Relief Society to help as best they could. Fortunately his father recovered. The money that the son sent home was enough to take care of his hospital expenses.

As our absence from home approached the half-year mark we discovered that we had many expectant fathers on board, none of whom could be present for the launching of their new craft. Then, as the babies appeared, each mail brought photographs of new junior members of the G; rollicking young ladies and gentlemen whose pictures were tucked in the pockets of their proud papas' dungarees, and shown to their shipmates with the air of "see what I did." It was amusing, and pathetic, to hear a pair of new fathers comparing notes on the care, feeding and appearance of their first born; babies whose mothers, on the other side of the world, were beginning to learn the complexity of the problems that they must cope with, alone.

LUCKY BAG

The most surprising thing about a war is how quickly you forget. It has been less than four months since I stood on the forecastle of the G and heard Lieutenant Commander Hansen say, "I relieve you, sir." It has been slightly more than five months since the G and I were in a strenuous engagement. Yet, in spite of the fact that both of the ships in which I have served since December 7, 1941, have been in the front line of our war at sea I cannot escape a sensation, now, of remoteness to battle. Somehow it all seems long ago; the week on week of steaming, the absence of rest, the "Condition Red" and the air attacks, the conviction that we had lived a lifetime in the midst of war.

And if I have that feeling of remoteness, of fighting a war vicariously, after only a few weeks' absence from action, then it becomes easier to understand many aspects of the attitude at home which I found so perplexing during the first few days after my plane landed at Treasure Island. The contrast is so great, the mental shock so violent, that the man coming home from war feels he is a stranger in some new and completely unfamiliar world.

Lord Fisher, who did much to revitalize Britain's navy once wrote a little verse that went somewhat as follows:

"The country threatened and the foeman nigh,
'God and our Navy' is the Nation's cry.
The victory won and the wrongs righted,
God is forgotten and the navy slighted."

I thought of this often in the late twenties and early nineteen thirties when we were so woefully short of ships and when our naval purse was so empty that any destroyer captain who employed a speed in excess of fifteen knots was required to write a letter of explanation. "Big Navy man" was a term of opprobrium in that time of national feasting when our diminishing fleet was considered a drain on the public treasury, and when our senior officers were viewed as alarmists if they suggested that perhaps, at some future date, we should once again find ourselves engaged in war.

This attitude is a usual aftermath of war; it has always been so, but must we again be subjected to such a phase? To the warriors of the future we owe more than merely a prayer for those in peril on the sea. Because there will, of course, be warriors of the future, for old hatreds, like old fashions, are so quickly outmoded. Bitterness gives way to forgetfulness — unless you are a loser. And therein lies the danger for the victor.

Meanwhile we have a serious fire to put out in the Far East; to put out so thoroughly that we hope there will be no smouldering embers to set off another blaze that will rise up to plague us in the future.

It's going to take a lot to make up for those early months of 1942. I don't know the Japanese equivalent of "Condition Red," but I would like to be there when they shout it over the radios of Tokyo; when our flyers go in to pound that troublesome Empire and our ships seek out the remnants of the Nipponese fleet. I would like to be once more with the destroyers — those little grey ships that strike hard and fast at any enemy they can find — over, or under, or on the surface of the sea. Gun for gun, ton for ton, they are the fightingest thing afloat.

Made in the USA
Columbia, SC
10 February 2019